music
teaching
and
learning

Longman
New York & London

Music Teaching and Learning

Longman Inc., 19 West 44th Street, New York, N.Y. 10036
Associated companies, branches, and representatives
throughout the world.

Developmental Editor: Gordon T.R. Anderson
Editorial and Design Supervisors: Diane Perlmuth and Joan Matthews
Interior Design: Diana Hrisinko
Manufacturing and Production Supervisor: Anne Musso

Excerpts from the following have been reprinted with permission, as noted:

From *The Psychology of Musical Ability*, by Rosamund Shuter. Reprinted
by permission of Methuen and Co. Ltd., London.

From *Concerns Based Consulting Workshop*, by G. E. Hall, Shirley M.
Hord, and S. F. Loucks. Reprinted by permission of Research and
Development Center for Teacher Education, University of Texas at
Austin.

From *Taxonomy of Educational Objectives*, Handbook 1, COGNITIVE
DOMAIN, by Benjamin S. Bloom. Copyright © 1956 by Longman Inc.
Reprinted by permission of the publisher.

From *Taxonomy of Educational Objectives*, Handbook 2, AFFECTIVE
DOMAIN, by David R. Krathwohl, Benjamin S. Bloom, and Bertram B.
Masia. Copyright © 1964 by Longman Inc. Reprinted by permission of
the publisher.

From *Teaching Music in Today's Secondary Schools*, Second Edition, by
Malcolm E. Bessom, Alphonse M. Tatarunis, and Samuel L. Forcucci.
Copyright © 1980, 1974, by Holt, Rinehart and Winston. Reprinted by
permission of Holt, Rinehart and Winston.

"Checklist for Self-Evaluation" in *Basic Concepts of Teaching*, Concise
Edition by Asahel D. Woodruff (Chandler Publishing Company).
Copyright © 1961 by Harper & Row, Publishers, Inc. Reprinted by
permission of the publisher.

Library of Congress Cataloging in Publication Data

Peters, G. David.
  Music teaching and learning.

  (Longman music series)
  Bibliography: p.
  Includes index.
    1. Music—Instruction and study—United States.
I. Miller, Robert F.   II. Title.   III. Series
MT1.P46   780'.7'2973   81-3754
ISBN 0-582-28142-3   AACR2

Manufactured in the United States of America

9 8 7 6 5 4 3 2 1

contents

preface

This book introduces the major components of the music curriculum as they have evolved in the American educational system. It focuses on musical meaning, the learning process, valuing of music, the exemplar approach, skills development, musical understanding, observation, evaluation, and curriculum review. These topics can help the student explore the facets of the music curriculum as applied to the traditional instrumental, vocal-choral, and general music curricula; in addition, there are new approaches to curriculum aimed at resolving pressures on the educational system.

This is a basic text, meant to introduce students in teacher education programs enrolled in overview courses with titles similar to Introduction to Music Education. Also, it is a basic text to introduce students in teacher education programs to school music curricula and to the decisions that must be made in developing a workable music program. The book can be used as a primary text for overview courses in Principles and Techniques of Teaching Music or as a supplementary text for various methods courses in instrumental, choral, or general music. Portions of the text can be helpful to the study of the acquisition of musical meaning as it applies to the schooling process. Other sections of the book focus on the learning of music skills and the motivation of students in the learning process.

We wrote this book for students in music education, although students in other fields may have some need of the information as it applies to music instruction. Students in elementary education, special education, recreation, and other music methods courses can apply the information to music in their own fields. We aimed our writing at the undergraduate student in music and education, although graduate students may find several chapters in the taxonomy sections of interest at their level of study.

We hope to heighten student perception of problems and solutions as they are applied to recurring curriculum decisions. The text will aid students in assessing the field of music education and their own qualifications as prospective teachers in the arts. The book relates the purpose of music instruction to the goals of general education and presents a comprehensive music program within the general education context.

music
teaching
and
learning

part
one

1/*introduction and purpose*

From the time of the early Greeks, Western societies have found music to be an essential component of humankind's assertion of its humanity. Manifestations of music and art are parts of the constellation of qualities that provide our identity as human, that remarkable realization that we are more than animal and that our consciousness gives rise to needs and satisfactions beyond those of other living creatures. The fulfillment of those needs and the cultivation of those satisfactions have given rise to philosophy, the visual and performing arts, literature, and music. These "humanities" serve to affirm belief in our own worth, document human existence through history, define the territorial limits of cultures, and allow for a creativity beyond the mundane necessity of physical comfort. They are the highest products of the human intellect; indeed, in any age or historical epoch, it is to these works that we must look to find the crowning achievements of the period.

It is only natural that the study of the humanities has become central to education. Throughout the history of our civilization, human beings have attempted to show their children the pathway to the "good life," the finest and truest evidences of humanity's importance to and uniqueness in the universe.

Music provides a large measure of that evidence. If for no other reason than this, music has won a well-deserved place in the education of the young. To most readers of this book that importance is well established, for the majority of the readership is either committed to music and children or considering such a commitment. While we sense that the potential importance of music to youth is great, giving expression to the reasons for the importance of that role, and deriving a basis for making decisions as to the best framework for teaching young people, may not be so clear.

The purpose of this discussion is not to demonstrate "how" music should be taught. The specifics of methods and materials are left to other books and for direct experience with the observation and study of teachers and children. Our purpose is, rather, to establish a set of principles with which decisions can be made concerning the effective use of music in the curriculum. This text investigates the processes by which children learn, develops a model for deciding which music should be used in the schools, outlines how teachers can best prepare themselves for the challenges of a teaching career, and establishes a way for teachers to examine and evaluate their work.

Of late, a "cookbook" approach to music education has arisen. A glance at any university summer catalogue will afford the teacher innumerable workshops and short courses in the methodology of teaching. Workshops that imply that two cups of this and a dash of that cause success in musical learning do no service to our profession. To the contrary, we have recently looked so hard at "how" that we have nearly lost sight of "what" and "why." Many undergraduate curricula require a student to take "methods" courses before any real foundation is laid as to the task at hand.

We may be losing our identity as a profession to that of a technical trade and, if so, this loss is regrettable. The path to professional competence is the establishment of criteria for decision making, a set of standards that will allow the teacher in the profession to approach the ever-new teaching situations with the confidence born of rational thinking.

Education versus Schooling

Education is not entirely, or even primarily, the responsibility of the schools. A major function of society is the education of the young in order to equip them to cope with and become functioning members of the society. This process begins at birth with the greatest portion of the task accomplished by the child's parents. The amount of education a child receives before entering school is immeasurable. The preschool child has learned to eat, to walk, to take rudimentary care of himself, and to use language. This last task alone is a monument to the unique position of humans among the animals. Never again will a child be called upon to accomplish anything so complicated as the acquisition and use of language. That such a task can be taught naturally and without systematic training is testimony enough to the enormous power of societal education.

This education by parents continues throughout childhood; at times it assumes a sort of formality as a parent teaches a child to bake bread or repair a bicycle tire. The majority of the education is not at all formal but the natural outgrowth of modeling born through a mimicking of parental attitudes and actions. A child who sees a parent reading easily comes to the conclusion that reading is simply one of those things that people do. Reading is perceived as a natural part of life, and so the child develops a perceived "need" to read.

The power of education by modeling is tremendous. The parent is a source of and a symbol for strength, protection, and power. The child wants to be like the parent and thus displays behaviors that are like those which the parent exhibits. Evidence of mimicry of adult behaviors has been found in infants only a few hours old.

In addition to the education received from parents, children learn from their peers. Complex value systems are learned along with a myriad of facts. This influence is easily identified in children and accounts for some of the bizarre behavior seen from time to time as children succumb to "peer pressure." Attitudes are shaped and knowledge is imparted from associating with other children.

Society has established other means of education as well. Children gain knowledge as members of church and religious organizations, sports teams, scout troops, and all the other structured groups in which our children may participate. Some of the education purveyed by these activities is of a high order. For example, aside from the concreteness of the likes of pitching, catching, and the mysteries of the "infield fly" rule, team sports instill abstract understandings about responsibility, competitive attitude, fair play, and sportsmanship.

And there is more to education. Over the past thirty years, television has assumed an increasingly large share of the education of the young. Aside from the result of "educational" or "public service" programming, we have recently been made aware of the educational effects of television violence, of the sheer weight of authority carried by fictional television personalities, and of the potential for both harm and good that exists with this powerful medium. We see that television fiction may be confused with real-world situations; children's actions at times are based only on a televised concept of the world.

Even from this brief and incomplete listing of educational sources, it is evident that schooling is only a minor portion of a child's education. The potentially small influence that schools have on their charges is made more easily understandable by the realization that apart from bus rides, class changes, lunch, and study periods, the American high school student spends less than five of his sixteen or so waking hours in formal instruction, and those five hours occur on fewer than half the days of the year.

Yet schools are asked to carry more and more of the weight of social progress. School personnel are asked to ensure the health of their charges through regular monitoring; they are asked to feed those who are hungry, and somehow provide attitudes and skills that will raise children from poverty. Teachers are asked to prepare students to live in a world in which information and technology are expanding at an accelerating rate. All this and more has been added to the traditional curriculum offerings, and still with only five hours' scheduling per day. Schools are asked to do what the rest of society finds itself unable to do. That even portions of these assigned tasks are accomplished is not the result of a miracle but the results of the proper application of the evolved role of the school as an institution.

What is the proper role of schooling? How do schools differ in their missions and influences from the other segments of the educational system? What is it that sets schools apart? Clues to the answers to these questions are best discovered in an examination of the characteristics of the educational *process* in both society and school.

Notice how a parent teaches a child to use language. If the child says, "Billy don't have to go to bed at eight," the parent, likely as not, will reply, "Billy *doesn't* have to go to bed at eight." The point to be made is one of proper usage of the English language; the method employed is that of "correcting" the error by providing a model or example. The parent waits until an example of incorrect usage is heard and then "fixes" it. The timing is not planned, for the correction occurs only after the error has been committed; it is, rather, opportunistic. Might schools accomplish all that is charged to them if they employed only such methods? No. Schools would approach the problem in a different manner.

Ideally, the school could anticipate the occurrence of common errors and provide the child with a set of rules *the child* might apply himself to prevent the errors in the first place. A prime example of this blockading of potential errors is the teaching of grammar, the science of making decisions about language. Rather than wait for each student to make all the potential errors inherent in the English language and then correct them one at a time, a school's teaching of the rules of grammar enables *the student* to decide on his own, without external assistance, which expression is correct and then act accordingly. Grammar serves to make the child *independent* of the English teacher.

The difference between the correction of errors of usage and the application of the rules of grammar is at the heart of the distinction between education and schooling. Education, in the broad sense, is often based on modeling and mimicry; such methods may be powerful, but they are at best inefficient. What direct involvement the society exhibits in this educational process is most often *ex post facto* and opportunistic, whereas the involvement of schooling is at least deliberate, and in the best of cases planned, so that students know how to make decisions when the decisions must be made. The inefficiencies of trial and error are thus avoided or at least reduced.

If a single concept sets schooling apart from education in general, it is the notion that schools are *systematic*. They serve to anticipate the difficulties of life and to equip children to make decisions on their own (by the application of rules and principles), which will lead to the best solutions to the problems. A primary function of schools is to allow people to operate independently.

Music Schooling as Part of Music Education

If the general function of schools is to provide students with the capability for independent action that heightens the general quality of life, then the general function of music in the schools can be no less. The goal of school music programs must be to equip students with the power to make rational choices about music. Earlier in this discussion we asserted that human beings exhibit needs (and the satisfaction of those needs) that are beyond those of other animals, that are distinctly "human." Music is both a device for the discovery and expression of those needs and a means of satisfying them. The old cliché that "music is one of the finer things of life" is not without foundation.

The discovery and satisfaction of musical needs is one of the finer things of life and one of life's pleasures. The satisfaction of a need is a pleasurable experience whether that need is one of the classical animal needs of hunger, thirst, procreation or territory or one of the purely human needs of love, security, or self-expression. One purpose of education is most certainly the introduction to and inculcation of human needs. The deliberate creation of an awareness of human needs, and the equipping of the individual with the capabilities for satisfying those needs, is an educational process. Every human being has needs, and they can be discovered, honed, and refined through proper education with the result that the satisfactions and pleasures derived from them can be heightened. On the simplest level, take the basic need for food and drink and contrast it with the "acquired tastes" (wants) for olives and martinis. That the "want" for the latter is a man-made one makes the satisfaction of that need no less a pleasure.

The lack of accomplishment in musical "schooling" should be of great concern to our profession. Unlike many of their peers in other disciplines, most music teachers are still operating at the level of "usage" and have not yet begun to teach "grammar" or independent decision making to their students. Typically, teachers in the studio teach *as they were taught*. The student plays a passage, and the teacher points out the technical errors. As the student masters the technical portions of the performance task, the teacher demonstrates the "musical" portions. The student imitates. In some European conservatories, such imitative learning has taken on a formalistic, almost ritual tone, with the students in a studio class seated in a circle or a line, each playing the assigned piece or orchestral excerpt after the artist teacher has demonstrated through performance. Success is achieved by exact imitation. Each successive attempt by a student gets closer to the teacher's example until it is deemed "close enough," and the next student in the line is given an opportunity. Decision making is taken out of the hands of the student and placed squarely in those of the master. The experience of most American students is similar.

The lack of training in systematic music decision making can be seen in a number of large performance ensembles in American high schools. Perhaps we should call these situations poor examples of the concept of "schooling," even though the performance by many of these ensembles is of high quality.

The situation in such settings is directly related to the effective operation of a professional music ensemble. Most of the time the rehearsal consists of a "correction" of errors by the conductor (teacher). There is little time or place for interpretive elements on the part of individual musicians; these, too, are left to the conductor. The difference in the educational setting is that the student does not have the opportunity to make musical decisions; the professional musician has developed these skills. This is as it *must* be with a large performing organization if it is to operate smoothly and in an artistically unified manner. In the attainment of the goal of performance, there is little wrong with this model; in the attainment of the goal of *schooling*, however, there are limited results in training. Students in such programs are not being equipped to make their own choices and musical decisions.

Little doubt remains that an ensemble whose members have been taught to make musical judgments, rather than have those judgments dictated, will perform at a higher level and with less expenditure of time and energy on the part of the conductor. To develop these experiences, the music teacher must consider the amount of time students are engaged in performance groups and divide the total time spent in music between the "rehearsal-performance" and the "schooling decision-making" experiences that are so valuable for individual development.

The organization of our traditional school music programs dictates the existence of large performing bodies in which all decisions emanate downward from the conductor. Such a structure may well doom the majority of public school music programs to ultimate failure if this is the only musical experience the students can find. Note the proportion of high school students who "graduate" from an instrumental program after as many as eight years of education (schooling), only to put the instrument on the shelf, never to be played again. In large part, the reason for this result can be traced to a feeling of insecurity in making musical decisions. Many students entering college in nonmusic areas discontinue their involvement with music performance groups because they feel that they aren't good enough to *compete*. The idea that music performance can be personally satisfying has not been conveyed during the eight-year experience with music teachers.

Several solutions to this common problem will be suggested as it relates to the building of a music curriculum. It is important, at this point, to stress the clear difference between the education aspects of music and the systematic approach that should prevail in music "schooling." A healthy, highly viable music program in the schools should encourage students to try to find musical solutions *on their own* and should allow them to experience playing for sheer pleasure, apart from performance pressure, thus serving to ameliorate the negative attitude many have toward music in later life. The importance of the music teacher *as a teacher* should be increased in a clearly defined role. The teacher should become a resource, using musical experience and pedagogical expertise to accomplish the goal of musical independence.

Far from threatening the existence of the large group performance programs that have served as showpieces for music education for years, the strengthened emphasis on individual musical skill and small ensemble participation can enhance the remainder of the program. Bringing to bear the motivational techniques that have served to increase participation in the large ensemble experience on the newer, more individual approach to schooling will increase musical independence.

Values and Teaching

An old saying in the folklore of education goes, "As the twig is bent, so grows the tree." Generally mentioned in discussing the teaching of moral, ethical, or other values, this metaphor is not without some measure of truth. The reason that it rings so true is that virtually *all* such values are products of the educational process, learned from parents, from peers, from society, from schooling, or from teachers. The preceding distinction between schooling and teachers is deliberate, for teachers and other personnel are apart from the remainder of society; they provide not only for the systematic learning of students by schooling them but also serve as models for the more general education by example provided by society as a whole—a potent combination. When the two components of teacher-instilled learning complement each other, when they are directed toward the same clear and well-defined ends, then knowledge, attitudes, and values can be transmitted to the young quickly and with lasting effect. The converse of this statement is equally true, and it points out the impracticality of educational hypocrisy.

Of the various kinds of learning that teachers impart to their pupils, values are the most powerful, for values are the roots of attitude, and attitude dictates action. Decisions as to the nature of values that teachers and schools are to present are thus of great importance. All the facts ground into students' minds, all the hard-fought-for understandings, and all the carefully developed concepts fostered in our schools are without purpose if values and attitudes are not developed to apply the knowledge to the real-world existence of people. Reinforcing the axiom that it is good to hold values and believe in them deeply is the responsibility of all teachers, no matter what subject they teach.

The quandary about which values to demonstrate is one of the most pressing problems confronting the young music teacher. Because of the great potential impact of values, the teacher must sort out his or her beliefs, judgments, and value systems before beginning to teach. In spite of the structure of school-wide objectives statements, in spite of the existence of state- and system-dictated "curriculum guides," and in spite of the pleadings and admonitions of music education professors, the personal decisions and actions of individual teachers are the ultimate arbiters in the schooling of children. Teachers' attitudes are catalysts for the foundations of values in their pupils.

The prospect of "teaching" values, both incidentally by example and systematically by deliberate process, is frightening to most young teachers. Some teachers assert that they have no "right" to alter anyone's value system. This notion is both false and dangerous.

Valuing is important to people, for valuing is another characteristic that is peculiarly human. The teacher who denies the importance of values denies humanity. Virtually every action implies an assertion of the human will and the affirmation of some value set. Either we are asserting the worth of some idea or action by adopting it or we are disavowing the worth of the idea or action by failing to adopt it. The teacher who refuses to teach values, by whatever method, is transmitting to students the idea that values are of no importance—advocacy of a form of anarchy.

A person who holds that an idea or action or experience is of great importance will usually feel compelled to present that value judgment for adoption by others. This attitude causes missionaries to suffer discomfort, hardship, and even martyrdom. The price of a teaching career is not nearly so high, but it does exact its toll. Even the most cursory examination of American teachers reveals that idealism, rather than monetary reward, keeps the profession afloat. Everyone entering the profession realizes from the start that teachers do not get rich from teaching. Yet they go to great expense and lengths of sacrifice to prepare themselves for the profession. Why? In these men and women musical values may be so strong and the drive to transmit these values so compelling that teaching becomes an imperative.

Most participants in music teaching can remember at least one teacher whose influence provided the inspiration, challenge, or example that led them to adopt music as an important portion of their value system. While motivations for persons considering a music teaching career vary, and will be examined in more depth later, a frequently given reason for the consideration of this commitment is the desire to emulate that individual. Music has proven to possess such a high level of personal value, and has become such an encompassing determinant of the participants' existence as humans, that it has dictated for them a major life choice.

Passion in and for Music Teaching

Music and music teaching are in the unfortunate position of being under attack as unnecessary portions of the school curriculum. For many, music and other arts programs are "frills," features of American education that are dismissable in times of monetary crises. Indeed, in a survey[1] of its membership concerning the goals of American education, a national leadership fraternity of educators placed the arts in a weak position. Of the eighteen goals listed in the survey, the only two that realistically supported music in the schools ("Makes constructive use of leisure time" and "Recognizes and appreciates beauty in the world") ranked seventeenth and eighteenth. That other objectives that might better express the true nature of the arts did not appear in the list is damning enough. That the two that did appear were at the bottom of the ranking poses real questions that must be addressed by potential music teachers.

Are music and arts programs actually of such low value? Or might it be possible that those participating in this ranking merely made a mis-

[1] "A Survey of National Objectives," *Phi Delta Kappan*, Dec. 1972.

take? Perhaps they do not know the potential value of arts education programs. Perhaps the leadership of American education does not include members of arts education programs.

Both reasons may well be true, and the correction of these deficiencies would seem to be first-priority tasks for members of our profession. In the past, too much of music teachers' efforts has been directed inward; faced with the pressures of performance and a drive to succeed in their narrow field, music teachers have not successfully placed themselves in positions in which they might shape educational policy. At the most basic level, the school level, music teachers sit silently in faculty meetings (if they attend at all), hoping that they will not be "volunteered" to serve on committees that set up school-wide and system-wide goals and objectives. Even if they are "unfortunate" enough to be chosen, music teachers often fail to exert real influence, not having prepared themselves to make an effective case. Many teachers assume that the responsibility for defining a place for music in the school curriculum rests with the "music supervisor," not realizing that these persons rarely carry the political weight potentially available from legions of principals, teachers, and parents armed with understanding from local music teachers.

With the emergence of "basic education" programs in schools across the country, many music programs have been threatened, and many will succumb. Music teachers must be equipped to provide substantive, rational arguments for the place of music in the curriculum if there is to be *any* music in the curriculum. As long as the power brokers of American education remain unconvinced, the threats of music program termination will continue. In addressing American businessmen's reactions to government regulation, Thomas Murphy, Chairman of the Board of General Motors, observed that it is the responsibility of business to place itself in a position in which it can help shape government policy rather than merely react to it. He argued that the available expertise in business professions might be useful to government agencies and that, rather than animosity, a spirit of shared responsibility might result from increased participation by the private sector.[2]

The same is the case for music teachers when confronting policy decisions handed down by others in the educational establishment. If music teachers fail to become active participants in the formulation of educational policy, then they shall most certainly become victims of it. It is important that we shed the stance, as Murphy says, "of a minister preaching to the choir and not to the sinners."[3] Music teachers must stop talking only to each other and start talking to the rest of the world. This discussion

[2]Thomas Aquinas Murphy, in a speech to the National Press Club, Washington, D.C., 20 July, 1978.

[3]Ibid.

can be accomplished at local and system levels by the teachers themselves, and at state and national levels by inspired activist influence on the part of music teachers' professional organizations. Instead of directing conventions and publications aimed only at other music teachers, teachers' groups might better spend their time, money, and expertise in making clearer the essential role music can play in the education of children and adults.

Perhaps the best summation of the necessary qualities teachers must possess has been given voice by Charles Leonhard, who throughout his career has called for "passion" in the teaching of music. Not just passionate attachment to music, and not just passionate caring for children, but also passionate commitment to ourselves and to our worth as a profession. Part of that commitment is the attainment of a deep understanding of the worth of music, the role of music in the curriculum, the inclination and ability to apply that understanding in education practice and the voicing of that understanding in educational policy.

The Worth of School Music Programs

The value of school music programs is roughly divisible into two large groupings: *extrinsic values*, which are products primarily of the structures within which we teach and use music; and *intrinsic values*, which are the result of the value of the music itself, as an art form. Of these two, by far the more accessible, and therefore more often cited as the rationale for music in schools, are extrinsic values, those that surround the *program* rather than those that surround the *music*.

Some extrinsic values cited as resulting from school music sources include those values that accrue to students through study *about* music rather than study *of* music. Such programs as civilization courses that examine music as a part of history and geography courses that examine music to exemplify the religious life of a particular culture, for instance, clearly fit into this category. So also do those "general music" programs that devote the bulk of their time to talk about composers, or theory classes that spend time on harmony as a manipulative device rather than a part of the overall character of music. In these studies, music is an excuse, not a subject. Benefits that students derive from such study are no different from those they might derive from any academic discipline: a general fluency in reasoning or a general sense of the unfolding of the human condition through history.

Other values stem from the study of other disciplines *with* music, such as the increasingly popular Arts in General Education (AGE) movement. This movement involves music specialists in all phases of the curriculum, with music's role relegated to that of a learning device or a motivation for nonmusical learning. In discussions of such programs one hears that music can be employed to teach reading or mathematics. Such activities as the singing of Theodore Roosevelt's campaign songs in a history class or the use of cowboy songs in a unit about frontier life fall under this classification. The values cited in AGE programs are not the values inherent in music but the values of whatever the prime subject matter happens to be.

A third group of extrinsic values may be characterized as "instrumental" values in that they use music and musical study as instruments for the accomplishments of other ends. Often cited instrumental values of participation in choirs, for example, include the attainment of self-discipline, confidence, goal directedness, the ability to cooperate with others, and myriad other general benefits of group activity. Marching bands are often justified on instrumental bases.

The fourth group of extrinsic values found in music programs stems from the use of school music as a focus for and expression of the identity of the school or community. Particularly in programs that involve the community directly in the operation of school performance groups through parent and "booster" organizations, one often finds a close relationship between the aims and purposes of the society or community that the school serves and the school's aims and purposes as demonstrated by the performance group. In some ways, then, American school music serves some of the same functions as another expression of culture's unity with the school programs: high school athletics. Although some mental and physical benefits doubtless are derived by the players, in most communities, football, for instance, serves the community in a far more important way. The real value of football (and of the more popular school music organizations, such as competing marching bands and school musical comedy productions) may lie in the assertion of cultural identity they provide to the American community. The situation is much like that of the hot dog, a third-rate sausage that is nonetheless an important cultural symbol, valued far beyond its intrinsic worth.

That all these and a thousand other nonmusical benefits might accrue to students engaged in study that is in some way related to music is hard to deny. In fact, many music programs have flourished with such rationales as their original motivations.

A potential problem exists in relying on extrinsic values as the sole ones on which to base school music efforts. If music programs and soccer programs serve the same ends, and soccer balls cost twenty dollars while saxophones cost several hundreds of dollars, does not logic insist that the less costly of the two should prevail?

There is a theory in sociology that if two institutions in a given culture serve the same function, in time one of those institutions will disappear.

Such is the danger in all music programs based solely on extrinsic values. They serve the society that condones them with no unique function. They are subject to removal from the school with no real loss. Some other discipline or activity with which they share the same function will simply take up the slack.

By far the more compelling set of reasons for music in schools lies in the values that may be derived through the study of music that can be gained no other way. These are tied to the intrinsic values of music as an art. The study of the nature and value of art has been dubbed "aesthetics," and is one of the major divisions of philosophy. The best use of music in the schools and the best reasons for the inclusion of music in the curriculum stem from music as part of what has been known as "aesthetic education." In order to present an approach to music as aesthetic education, some background must be laid as to theories of how music functions as art, and of the importance of art to man.

Questions for Discussion

1. Explain the difference between intrinsic and extrinsic value as it is attached to music in society and music in the schools.
2. Is it possible for teachers to function effectively as music teachers without revealing their personal values concerning music of various styles and types? What values presented by your teachers did you adopt or reject?
3. Describe the difference between a value and a need. Are the two concepts related in any manner when discussing music education?
4. What primary difference is described between education and schooling? Can schooling exist without education? Or education without schooling?
5. List three ways in which music education functions outside the formal bounds of the public schools. Are your selected ways as effective or more effective than the music schooling you received?

Recommended Readings

Bruner, Jerome S. *The Process of Education*. New York: Vintage Books, 1963.
Leonhard, Charles, and House, Robert. *Foundations and Principles of Music Education*. New York: McGraw-Hill, 1972.
Meyer, Leonard B. *Emotion and Meaning in Music*. Chicago: University of Chicago Press, 1956.

part
two

2/the situation in music education

Music schooling has been defined as the systematic teaching and learning of music in schools. We have discussed the various diversions from this concept, those of education for adults, recreational education programs, and self-improvement courses of study outside the "schooling" environment. The "certified teacher" is prepared to teach in the "public" schools to interact with children, to engage in the instruction of younger students, and to "impart knowledge" as outlined in a curriculum adopted by the school board, the principal, or a group of educators. The success of the curriculum depends upon the receptivity of students to the material and the teacher and the acceptance by parents of the program of instruction.

Good curricula are abandoned at times because of parental pressures resulting from financial considerations. Programs have been reduced in scope and dropped from the public schools based upon the perceived value of the subject within the school curriculum. In this chapter, music programs must be considered carefully as we assess the state of music education—as a profession, as an occupation, and as an intellectual endeavor. The programs that exist today in the schools are a direct result of the hard work of committed, dedicated teachers. The development of music curriculum starts with the teachers' desire to bring music instruction to the students.

Scope of Instruction

Although most students enrolled in university classes as music majors have had some encounter with public school programs, many prospective music teachers have not given sufficient thought to the state of music instruction in the schools.

Before attempting to "save the world" of music education with new and innovative plans, the professional teacher must be able to discuss the state of music education, not just in one town, but in a broader sense. It seems that the evaluation of the "current state of" anything reveals two divided camps of evaluators: those cynics who decry the gross shortcomings of education; and those "pollyannas" who, noting the large numbers of students involved in the music program, proclaim that "all is well." This big-is-better model continues to plague the evaluation of curriculum, for it seems logical that a program of 250 students is better (more relevant, if you will) than a program of 115 students.

According to the American Music Conference, 93 percent of the country's elementary schools offer some music instruction. The quality of those programs, however, is unknown. If there are numerous programs in the country, some of them must be of high quality. Such was the underlying notion behind the Manhattanville Music Curriculum Project, which was initiated in 1965.[1] The research conducted in this project revealed a wide variation in music programs across the country. Those programs of high quality were reviewed and synthesized into a new curriculum model for educators.

School music instruction can be measured qualitatively and quantitatively. Assessing the quality of programs demands some minimum standards that all educators would agree are essential in a given field such as music. At the upper end of the spectrum are the aspirations or goals for which the profession continually strives. Few programs attain these goals, and even fewer maintain their programs at this level for long periods of time.

Another issue must be considered in describing education and schooling: How far can a student progress through a curriculum and continue to learn? For many students, and many school systems, a two-year foreign language curriculum at the high school level is deemed sufficient. A more

---

[1] Ronald B. Thomas, MMCP (Manhattanville Music Curriculum Project), U.S. Office of Education, 1965.

sophisticated curriculum in other schools might offer a third year of instruction, and a few superior language programs offer a fourth year of instruction to meet perceived student needs in the community. The foreign language programs offer levels of increasingly sophisticated instruction. The third-year course presupposes mastery over the material in the second-year course. Music programs often cover many more years of student time than this, but does the fifth year of general music presuppose mastery over the fourth year? Does a high school senior in a band program receive markedly different instruction from the sophomore sitting in the next chair in the same ensemble? Usually not.

If we define *curriculum* as a "full body of courses" or, better, as a scope and sequence of instruction that result in orderly progressive learning, many music programs are devoid of a curriculum. This situation is compounded when one considers the broader curriculum or course of study in the arts in general. Countless years have been spent by teachers and curriculum specialists in designing "comprehensive" programs of study in the arts. The efforts have been duplicated in almost all cases in each school system that claims an arts program. Tailoring the program to the community causes these repetitive efforts, for the arts program developed for Detroit does not hold the same value for Laramie, Wyoming. The underlying concepts may be the same, but materials, activities, and instructional techniques are different. For this reason, two viewpoints must be taken in reviewing the status of music education, one in the schools and a second in the community.

Concepts and Approaches in Music Education

The concepts that hold value in music education can be defined and generally agreed to, but innumerable arguments are raised about how best to teach or convey these concepts. The concepts, then, are the basis for the objectives of the programs in music education in the schools. To achieve these objectives, teachers implement many different approaches, methods, and materials.

In defining the objectives for the music program, teachers generally agree with the broad aims of the educational system. The function of such objectives, as Leonhard states, is to:

1. Assure positive reaction of musical instruction to the broader aims of the school.
2. Form the basis for planning educative experiences.
3. Control the daily adjustment of methods and materials.
4. Provide criteria for evaluation of instruction.[2]

The program objectives most often listed in teachers' manuals and guidelines reflect the writings of Leonhard, Meyer, Mursell, and Bruner. Myers defines program content that should be planned to develop in children:

1. The ability to use music as a means to self-expression and communication.
2. An understanding of the musical expression of others.
3. An awareness of as much of the science of music as will aid in giving meaning to music as an art.[3]

An example of goals suggested for junior high school general music are listed by Metz.

Cognitive Area:
1. Knowledge of and experience with music's basic elements—melody, harmony, rhythm, texture, timbre, dynamics, and form —alone and in combinations.
2. Ability (*a*) to listen attentively and carefully, and (*b*) to identify formal aspects, from motif/phrase to differentiating larger whole parts.
3. Knowledge of leading composers, specific works, and styles from the seventeenth century to the present.
4. Ability to identify the terms and signs used in both traditional and avant-garde notation.
5. Knowledge by sight and by ear of the various tone-producing instruments (orchestral, vocal, and electronic). Recognition by ear is central; visual recognition, though helpful, is less important.

Motor Area:
1. Singing (both by rote and by note) simple melodies and ostinati with accuracy in pitch and duration.
2. Playing keyboard, fretted, and classroom instruments.
3. Listening to students' own work and to recorded/live music, with purposeful, focused perception.
4. Moving to music: clapping, conducting, tapping, and dancing.
5. Creating short pieces, from simple, improvised phrases and ostinati to songs and instrumental compositions.

[2]Charles Leonhard, and Robert House, *Foundations and Principles of Music Education* New York: McGraw-Hill, 1972, p. 143.

[3]Louise K. Myers, *Teaching Children Music in the Elementary School* Engelwood Cliffs, N. J.: Prentice Hall 1956, p. 18.

Affective Area:
1. Demonstrating growth in musical value judgments.
2. Showing a more positive attitude toward music.
3. Applying skills gained in class to new musical experiences.
4. Tolerating the taste and values of others.
5. Displaying an increased willingness to participate in classroom activities.
6. Demonstrating performance sensitivity to even simple routines and experiences in class.[4]

Many objectives at this level coincide with the objectives of the other arts of instruction. The advantage of "aesthetic education" as a unifying concept can readily be seen in general program guidance. But consider the program at the action level, where the teacher enters the room and disseminates information.

General Music

The school music program generally starts in kindergarten, either with a classroom teacher playing recordings and leading children in the singing of songs or with the music specialist involving the children on a weekly or biweekly basis in the classroom. At this age (5 or 6 years old), children are capable of matching pitches within their voice ranges, clapping rhythms, singing limited-range songs learned by rote, and moving to music.

Programs of "general" music extend from the kindergarten level through fifth, sixth, eighth, or ninth grade, depending on the school district. Activities and materials have been developed for these classes by music book series companies such as Ginn and Silver Burdett. These activities include singing, listening, playing rhythm instruments, and creative activities. Since the general music curriculum is most often a required course of study for *all* students, efforts have been made to design the instruction in an enjoyable, easy-to-accomplish form. This approach contrasts with the older notion that music in the schools should teach people to read music so that they might sing in church choirs. The music programs of today have a much broader approach and attend to the "valuing" of music much more closely than did the earlier "singing schools."

The general music program has been implemented in the public schools in several ways. The best model, from the music educators' point

[4]Donald Metz, *Teaching General Music in Grades Six Through Nine* (Columbus, Ohio: Charles Merrill, 1980), p. 11.

of view, is to have the music specialist in each school work with children on a daily basis. Because of financial problems, few of these models remain in school systems. The variations that have resulted include spreading the teachers' time between two, three, or four school buildings. The teacher still is the music teacher and prepares classroom presentations, but the number of students these teachers see in one week can be well over 500. At best, teachers in this situation normally see each child twice a week for about twenty minutes a session.

The second model for general music instruction is that of the music supervisor who prepares materials for classroom teachers to present to the children. The classroom teacher's musical background obviously limits this model. If the third-grade teacher has a background that includes piano performance, the children may gain a sufficient amount of information and enthusiasm from music. If the teacher has no musical background, the music activities may result in poor training for the children; even worse, they may develop a negative attitude toward music gained indirectly through a reticent and ill-prepared teacher. A hardworking music supervisor can overcome many of the teacher variables by preparing materials that require little musical background of the classroom teacher. Needless to say, these experiences cannot be as rich as those developed and implemented by the music teacher. (At least, music educators suffer under this notion.)

A third model for music instruction in general music leaves instruction solely to the classroom teacher with no support from the music specialist. Again, the background of the classroom teacher shapes the quality of the music instruction. A major disadvantage in this model is that curriculum continuity is left to chance. Only the lucky student will have an exciting music experience at each grade level. Continuity is also limited by having no specialist develop a sequence for the instruction. Nevertheless, even this instruction in music is better than totally avoiding the subject, although some would argue this point.

Within these three modes of general music instruction, several methodologies are used. The Kodaly, Orff, and other general music approaches have a following of dedicated teachers. The teachers are, for the most part, *music* teachers. Classroom teachers have neither the time nor the skills to become involved in music teaching such as that defined by Kodaly. At any rate, the methods used in the majority of schools are eclectic collections of materials from several approaches. The purpose of this text, as we stated initially, is not to recommend techniques of teaching but to consider the "what" and "why" in teaching music.

Elementary classroom teachers have a body of instructional materials that have been developed by textbook companies to integrate the singing, listening, and playing experiences of children in a manner that can be managed without formal background instruction in music. These activities are well planned, with organized teachers' manuals for suggested activities. Most states require some basic instruction in the arts for the elementary classroom teacher. This requirement normally takes the form of one or two introductory courses in the "arts," predominately the visual arts and music, with an accompanying course in basic teaching methods in the arts.

With these approaches to staffing music instruction in the public schools, at first glance one is led to believe that the task is being managed to some degree and that all is not lost to science, mathematics, and reading. Perhaps the weakest link in music education is the lack of a systematic curriculum. The instruction is all too often left to the chance that the elementary teacher has some interest in music and can convey that interest to children; the chance that the music teacher can work with a large number of children and teach them to understand and appreciate music, and the chance that the really superior teacher will remain in the lower grades to work with children at this critical age of development.

Without question, children develop musical skills at an early age. Several studies cited by Shuter[5] indicate that children form their underlying abilities for music before they enter formal schooling. Shuter summarizes her findings as follows:

> To sum up, the first essential condition favoring the full development of musical ability in the earliest years is opportunity to hear music. No doubt it is highly desirable that some of this music should be made by a parent or other person of whom the child is fond. But if the parents cannot play or sing, they can at least try to listen to music with enjoyment and attention, and show appreciation of music and musicians. Before he is old enough for formal music lessons, the child can be encouraged to make his own music, with his own voice and with whatever sound-producing facilities his environment can offer. . . .

As evidence of the concern that researchers have for the age of beginning instruction, consider a survey of fifteen hundred members of the Incorporated Society of Musicians (England), a sample that represented 35 percent of the membership. Among musicians who had absolute (perfect) pitch, the average age for beginning music instruction was 6.1 years; the average age of initial instruction for students who did not have perfect pitch was 7.0. Figure 2.1 gives a clear picture of the relationship between age of beginning music instruction and absolute pitch.

The question remains as we review the general music offerings in American schools: Do we offer too little, too late? Studies indicate an early formative development of music skills, and so more emphasis must be placed on music training in kindergarten through third grade. Unfor-

[5]Rosamund Shuter, *The Psychology of Musical Ability* (London: Methuen, 1968), p. 76.

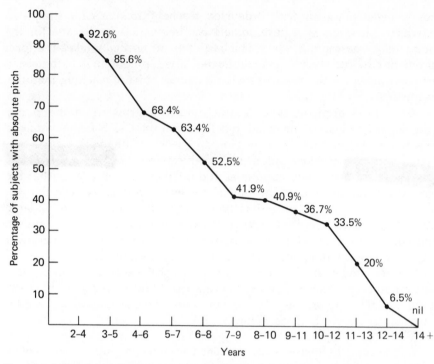

Figure 2.1 Relationship of Age of Beginning Instruction to Absolute Pitch. *From Rosamund Shuter,* The Psychology of Musical Ability *(London: Methuen, 1968), p. 73.*

tunately, students often mature during this time of early musical development with little musical guidance. Research supports the Suzuki notion that children develop skills in music between the ages of three and six. Perhaps more important, these skills are necessary to later musical development. To date, much more interest has been devoted to music programs at the high school level than in the primary grades. High school programs are generally organized to accommodate talented students who have survived the early music programs.

Most secondary schools have music programs for the common student population with general music programs for the middle school, junior high school, and high school students. Truly successful secondary school programs are far less prevalent than the required elementary school programs in general music, but they do exist. Most students who come to the university to major in music education were never channeled into the general music classrooms of junior and senior high schools.

"Talented" students are offered opportunities to develop their skills (normally in performance), but all students should be offered opportunities for musical growth as part of general education. Several states have started considering music skill development as part of the "basic skills" so much discussed in education, although few states have seen fit to mandate instruction in the arts as a basic skill or equate the need for such instruction with the need for traditional subjects.

The tendency has been to develop additional high school programs in integrated arts or the humanities rather than in music alone. This decision has been influenced by the idea that the fine arts have some cohesive quality that will allow for transfer of information from art form to art form. This notion is a higher-level connection, that of human expression, than the idea that Impressionistic paintings are closely tied to Impressionistic music. In this light, general music is really general education and part of general arts education.

The reasons why so little has been done at the junior high school and high school levels are many. Teachers can "lay blame" on the crowded curriculum, the subjects that students must take, the counselors' concerns about college entrance requirements, the parents' lack of interest in music, the budget, the lack of music staff, and so on. Most high schools have an instrumental teacher (usually a band director) and a choral director. Any additional staff usually have assigned duties in one of these performance areas as well, which leaves instruction in the secondary general music to teachers whose training has been very specific—and not in general music instruction.

The number of students enrolling in music education with a specialty in general music teaching is very small. Although some students later shift to general music, the initial enrollment is normally in a performance-related area—choral or instrumental. When one considers this pattern, it is not surprising for the college music major to be a product of the performance side of the high school curriculum. To date, neither author has talked about a career in teaching music to a student who was not involved at some time in musical performance. Students from the general education (music) curriculum have selected other major fields of interest, or so it would seem.

If general education in music or general music emphasis declines in importance in high school, consider the problem of learning about music after graduating from high school. Junior colleges and universities certainly offer music appreciation courses, which can be used to fulfill humanities or arts requirements in liberal arts degree programs for matriculated students. But what about the member of the community who is not attending school in a formal degree program?

In considering the music curriculum in other settings (e.g., adult education or continuing education or education in "lifelong" learning), opportunities to learn about music diminish drastically. Just as there are fewer general music courses in high schools than there are in elementary schools, far fewer opportunities exist for the adult to learn about music in a general way in adult education. After surveying course offerings by high schools in adult education and community college course offerings for the "nonmatriculated" student, we found very few courses aimed at developing an understanding and appreciation of music. The music courses that do exist for adults tend to be of the basic-skills type, such as beginning folk guitar or group instruction in piano, with only some junior and community colleges offering courses in music appreciation such as American Music, Music of Black America, or Introduction to American Jazz.

In recent years, state arts councils have fostered an interest in the arts in the community at large. These programs stem from efforts at community awareness of opportunities in the arts. As these efforts are strengthened with financial support, various recreation and park districts have also become involved in developing arts programs. For the most part, parks and recreation programs have addressed a younger population. Several park department programs are being developed for adults, a trend that should continue during the next five to ten years. The idea that education extends far beyond schooling can be seen here directly.

Music educators should heed the shift in population age within the United States and develop quality programs for "students" of any age. Lifelong learning can be an exciting teaching area, since the student participants elect to become involved in a learning experience without state educational requirements. Elementary general music programs are mandated by state guidelines and high school programs are mandated by tradition. Instructional programs at the postsecondary school level have fallen to chance. These programs include offerings by secondary school districts, junior college school districts, parks and recreation departments, and some community center enrichment programs. The last named would include courses offered by art institutions, museums, and performing arts centers.

A broader definition of general music is called for when we consider continuing and general education. Those who view general music as instruction for children aged five through fourteen must rethink the role of music in the community. This role can be greatly expanded through adult instruction. This lifelong learning model will require new materials, new methods of teaching and planning on the part of music educators. It is not hard to realize that a forty-five-year-old student enrolling in a music skills class will not be satisfied by singing "Go Tell Aunt Rhodie" from a level-one songbook series.

General music instruction can be instrumental in heightening community interest and support of the arts. Since it is difficult to support something one does not understand, a higher level of community understanding of the arts and music will aid in raising interest in arts programs on a community level. We later discuss the involvement teachers must have in this larger community, but for now, consider the broader view of general music in community and continuing education in the arts.

Recommendations for a General Music Curriculum

As the readers visit public schools as part of their training, some measure of quality will be made. Some evaluative criteria will be established by the readers themselves, the professors teaching the college courses, or the teachers being observed. The totality of a general music curriculum is nearly impossible to observe in one or two visits to a classroom, but such is the usual observation schedule. Repeated visits will reveal many more teacher-student interactions, some student development, and more of the curriculum scope and sequence, but not the total program structure or intent.

Most teachers have choices in selecting the materials and activities they offer their students. These activities normally stem from the teacher's own interests and strengths. For instance, a teacher with limited vocal skills will probably emphasize activities that do not require singing to the students. Such decisions shape instruction for children. This is not to say that the instruction is not complete, but we do note that this teacher will spend more time with listening activities, instrument performance, and creative activities.

Most general music classrooms are geared to one age and grade level, with the pace set for the average student. The curriculum does not have an accelerated general music class to allow gifted children to explore music more fully, although some effort to support such programs has begun in recent years. The curriculum assumes approximately eight years of instruction, but of more interest is that the exit level is attained independent of the starting grade. It seems that most students have the same exit-level skills no matter when instruction begins. Evidence of this phenomenon is noted when a fifth-grade student begins general music instruction and is not considered to be behind in schooling.

Based upon evidence collected by Shuter and others, we must voice a strong recommendation for earlier high-quality instruction for children. The unevenness of general music offerings for preschool, kindergarten, and primary grade students must be resolved if we are to improve the musical skills and perceptions for the general student population. If this task cannot be accomplished on a broad basis, then a viable curriculum must be established to accommodate children at various skill levels in each entry level of music instruction. We will later find that early training has a marked result on performance skills. Systematic training is needed to develop music appreciation and a level of music values across time.

Two components should be stressed in the development of general music instruction: *early instruction* and *sequenced instruction*. The components of a general music program should include instruction that is sequenced and progresses logically from level to level. Instruction in most music programs has centered on the following areas:

General Music Curriculum Components

I. Knowledge and Perception of the Structural Elements of Music
   a. Melody
   b. Rhythm
   c. Harmony
   d. Form
   e. Dynamics
   f. Timbre
   g. Non-tonal music techniques
II. Development of Music Skills
   a. Listening
   b. Singing
   c. Reading
   d. Playing classroom instruments
   e. Moving to music
   f. Writing music notation and composing
III. Knowledge of Musical Heritage
   a. Learning about
     1. composers
     2. periods of music
     3. folk and ethnic music
     4. musical instruments
   b. Learning to identify
     1. music by period
     2. music by composer
     3. standard repertoire of songs and music
   c. Learning to perform
     1. folk and patriotic songs
     2. simple dances to music

Music Performance: Choral

The success story in music education is told and advertised by the performance capabilities of school ensembles—be they instrumental or vocal. To investigate the validity of this statement, one need only engage a stranger in conversation about the *quality* of music instruction in the local public schools. The response, if any is offered, is most likely given in the terms of awards, contest winnings, and publicity earned by high school ensembles.

Two major divisions in school musical performance are choral and instrumental ensembles. The choral program has grown naturally from the general music experiences in the intermediate grades with the formation of fourth- and fifth-grade choirs. In the middle and junior high schools continued choral experiences are often less strongly organized.

The major development of anything that can be considered a curriculum rather than a choral activity can be found only in the high school. At this level, students can choose among various choral experiences including glee clubs, madrigals, ensembles, mixed choruses, swing choirs, barbershop quartets, and various levels of "select" choirs. There is an opportunity to sing music of various levels of sophistication and style. This is usually the first time the vocal music student is auditioned, that is, selected for membership based on ability rather than age or grade level or desire.

That students have an opportunity to audition and progress through a series of levels of performance may indicate that the changing needs of students are being met. All too often, this is not the case; many students have the option only of singing in the same choir for three or four years —hence the old saying, "Yes, I had one year of choral training, three times." The better choral programs have well considered, structural instructional models that permit students to learn more about music and experience a broader range of music each year. The damning observation that some choral groups sing only the required state contest music all year stands as true in some cases. Such a situation reveals a disregard for students' educational needs.

The age level for introductory choral experiences normally begins around nine years of age. Fourth-grade mixed choruses can be found; fifth-grade choruses are more commonplace. These activities are normally scheduled outside of the regular general music class and even outside of the school day. On rare occasions, the high school or junior high school choral director may make time to work with children in the intermediate grades chorus, but the duty usually falls to a general music teacher.

In addition to the school programs in choral music, other community activities are available to children of the same age. Children's choirs are commonplace in churches and in community-sponsored programs. Boys' choirs have enjoyed popularity for years and are often supported by churches and choral societies. The reason for this popularity is the quality and quantity of music written for this medium.

As children mature, selecting voices for choruses and consequently choral activities for children becomes somewhat more difficult. By the time the male student enters middle school or junior high school, the changing voice (or the unchanged voice) is emerging as a phenomenon that must be resolved. Even when most boys have unchanged voices, for instance, in fifth and sixth grades, they often abhor being called "sopranos." In mixed choruses, boys with unchanged voices will continue to participate only if the conductor is sensitive to the problems of the changing voice and the fragility of some boys' egos.

Since general music is offered from kindergarten through eighth grade in most school systems, elective participation in chorus can be added to a student's schedule rather easily. Continued participation in choral music comes to the test when the student moves from the elementary school to the middle school or from the junior high school to the high school. As with all changes from level to level, students are counseled into new study schedules before they know how difficult the new work load and school situation may be. High school choral programs, while offering the student many options, may lose potential students simply through counseling. In most schools, students can participate in select choirs that require auditions or sing in a nonselect group such as a freshman chorus. Although such entry-level choirs pick up rather droll nicknames, the training in such choruses is often very good. Such nonselect choirs give the student a chance to continue participation in music performance while they allow the choral director to assess the student's singing ability and correct deficiencies of technique.

Another importance of the nonselect choral group cannot be overemphasized. The choral program far excels the instrumental program in allowing for participation by less talented or less polished performers. That the concert choir is a select group limits participation to those who have previous experience and some musical ability.

The choral curriculum should have two sides, which reflect the role of high school music. This dichotomy begins to emerge in late middle school or junior high school and follows through the senior year in high school. On the one hand are the nonselect opportunities to learn more about music and participate in music performances; on the other hand are musical performance experiences for the musically talented student.

We would be remiss in not acknowledging the role that choral music departments take on once a year or so in working with the theatre department, the art department, and others in presenting the "school musical." This activity, for it is indeed an activity, has never become a stable part of the school music program. The educational value of such theatrical productions has been argued nearly as much as the educational value of a marching band. While it is necessary to have good singers in a good theater chorus to stage a broadway musical, this activity is not an essential of the music curriculum per se. It is, however, an important

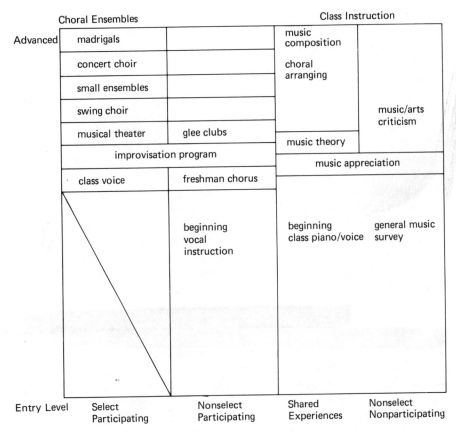

Figure 2.2 Choral Music Curriculum.

motivational and community relations activity when accomplished skill-fully.

Consider the relationships in the curriculum outline that includes the outgrowth of the choral activities from a general music class. Note the structured voice class in the choral activities for the senior high school found in the curriculum outlined in figure 2.2.

Recommendations for the Choral Music Curriculum

The major question, as one reviews a choral curriculum outline, is the actual content of each activity in class. This curriculum assumes that students in the high school receive no additional music training. This is most often the case and should result in the inclusion of music teaching within the choral performance area. We strongly suggest that choral groups and vocal performance should not displace the general music classroom. By design, a choral program allows development of skills required for singing in ensembles, develops an intimate knowledge of choral literature group performance, and brings the participants in front of the public in performance activities. Again, students involved in the better choral programs have opportunities to broaden their knowledge about music theater, composing, and musical judgments. Whether these opportunities become part of the performances or whether they are part of a separate class is a curriculum decision. In most cases, students cannot participate in a performance group and also take classes in music appreciation and/or theory. If this is the case, choral teachers must do more than conduct the ensemble rehearsal. Better choral directors allot time to listening, discussing, reviewing, and comparing music and music performances.

Perhaps more stress should be placed on the learning of vocal skills. In our curriculum, we have included a voice class. Although this is not a requirement of a good curriculum, attention must be placed on more than group singing or ·choral materials. Since most choral directors are intimately aware of the performance abilities of their students through auditioning and other testing, the voice classes should attend to correcting common problems of tone production, diction, pitch placement, and development of range, as well as develop the ability to sing alone.

A major concern of the authors is that children may sing well as preschoolers and then develop strange approaches, techniques, and habits as they progress through general music classes. If not carefully guided, the singers may become self-conscious, not support the tone, or sing with rigid face muscles and closed mouths. These concerns are voiced not so much about students who manage to participate in choral activities but about that group of students that is nonselected (nonparticipatory) and for the most part nonsinging. If we charge a choral director at a junior high school with a mission, perhaps it should be to foster some skills for the nonselect students in the public schools.

Carrying this to the postsecondary school level, we find a population in the United States who mutter, sing off pitch, and have great difficulty reading music. Good examples of this phenomenon can be found any Sunday morning in any church in the country. It is rare that one stands next to a truly well trained singer in a church congregation, one of the few places that the American public does sing. Consider how difficult it is to get strangers to join in song even around a campfire in a national park. We are fast losing a tradition of singing in this country, and we will be poorer for it.

Opportunities to continue in participatory ensembles are available in most communities. The choral student who graduates from high school has the opportunity to sing in church choirs, community choral societies, barbershop quartets, and perhaps even a community music theater association. These people have more chances to continue their association with music than the large group in the population—those nonselected nonparticipants.

Consider the difficulties a fifty-year-old hardware store salesman would have in learning to sing. Our salesman last sang in grade school where he learned a few rote songs. He never learned to read music and never developed a good singing voice. His vocal experiences have been relegated to singing popular songs in the shower. Where does he turn to join a choral ensemble or, for that matter, even to learn basic vocal techniques? Perhaps some church choir would tolerate his membership, but the repertoire of church choirs is specific and utilitarian. The curriculum must offer a series of entry-level courses for postsecondary school adults to "pick up the pieces" and begin to participate in musical performance.

Although we do not assume that 90 percent of the population is yearning to participate in music ensembles, some vehicle should be in place to allow the mature adult to continue music education. As we indicated in describing general music, the most intimate involvement of the mature adult in music is as a listener, a critic, a perceiver, a consumer. To fully appreciate choral music, some basic knowledge of performance in choral literature is helpful. The vocal curriculum, as does the general music curriculum, extends from the school through adult continuing education.

Music Performance: Instrumental

Closely akin to choral performance objectives are those of the instrumental music program. Perhaps the most visible music program to the populace, the instrumental music program has managed to rally community support for music in the schools. Consider the number of community members who see marching bands each year. This exposure to "high school music" is greater than any other form of school music endeavor. These observations are easily validated by attending any football game or parade, then attending an indoor concert by any high school music ensemble. Support for the high school marching band extends to a community pride and identity.

Instrumental performance programs can be reviewed dichotomously as "band programs" and "orchestra programs." The programs based in the band area include the marching band (football band) cited above, the concert band, the wind ensemble, the jazz band, wind-brass chamber music, percussion ensemble, pep band, and wind-brass-percussion instruction. Stage band programs have the same opportunity for student growth as has been mentioned for the choral program.

The orchestral area of the instrumental performance program includes string orchestra, string chamber music, "studio" orchestra, symphony orchestra, and string instruction. The orchestral program often has an early beginning with string instruction for very young children, while recruiting of students for these parallels recruiting for the band program.

Instrumental programs have developed levels of instruction that can be considered a curriculum. The instrumental curriculum progresses somewhat differently, however, from the choral performance curriculum. Where choral performance emerges from the general music classroom as an activity with fourth- or fifth-grade choruses, the instrumental program begins with specified instruction classes at varying levels. This difference is significant in that students are grouped by ability level from the beginning of the instrumental instruction sequence. The distinction here is that we do not have fifth-grade instrumental music, sixth-grade instrumental music; we have beginning winds class, beginning strings class, or beginning brass class with students enrolled from various class levels. If this logical beginning to instructional sequencing were continued throughout the instrumental curriculum, students could progress logically through an eight- or nine-year sequence. Unfortunately, this is not always the case.

Although the choral program offers a broader curriculum for student participants at the high school than at the elementary level, the instrumental program seems inverted. The best sequencing of instruction in instrumental music is found at the elementary and intermediate levels. As students progress to high school, fewer options are open to continue sequenced instruction. In all too many high schools, the only available music instruction is an activity—that of the marching band in the early fall, followed by concert band. The case is even worse for aspiring string students. Even in communities that have strong beginning string programs, the junior high school or high school student often finds no string teacher, no string instruction, and no string ensembles at these levels. Again, the ironic situation is all too prevalent in which we have good beginning programs to involve large numbers of students, only to be followed by unstructured activities or no program.

To accommodate an optimum level of student performance, instrumental ensembles should be available to provide opportunities to "learn" through participation. Some high schools have organized "reading" ensembles (band and orchestras) for students to improve reading skills and to allow student conductors to stand before their peers and conduct. These opportunities should be the rule rather than the exception. Although the size of the school has much to do with the scope of such programs, even high schools of a few hundred students have been able to develop band and orchestral experiences that provide continuing "musical development" and an understanding of musical aesthetics.

Band Programs

With concert bands in over twenty-three thousand schools[6] in the country, band programs seem to have a security not enjoyed by other segments of music education in the schools. Most instrumental programs engage students in learning to play instruments during the fourth, fifth, and sixth grades. This elementary school beginning is recommended by most educators as optimum for the musical development of students. Selected programs have been started during seventh grade (as students start the 7–9 junior high school) or even as late as ninth grade (for those systems that have four-year high schools). The timing of initial instruction in instrumental music often coincides with the division of grades between elementary/middle school/junior high school/and high school.

The trend in the last few years has been to replace the junior high school with a middle school. The rationale for this change is that for social reasons students are better grouped in a grade 6–8 arrangement than a grade 7–9 arrangement. The recent decline in student population has also allowed for more freedom in making decisions about student placement, without the press of overpopulated classrooms.

The impact that rearranging school levels has had on the music program is significant. Consider a music program that starts in fifth grade. If students were started in the instrumental program, they would move to a new school after the first year of instruction. Each move a student makes from school to school interrupts his or her musical training to some degree. The interruption is more significant when the student must change teachers, school districts, or both. In some states, each level of instruction is controlled by a different school board and consequently different teaching staffs.

In addition, there has been an alarming tendency for school boards to delay the start of instrumental instruction to the sixth grade when middle schools are adopted. Apparently, they reason that a program involving only one grade level is not enough of a program to be worth the administrative trouble. This is in stark contrast to the music program of the Baltimore County (Maryland) schools in which every third-grade student in the system studies one woodwind instrument, one brass instrument, percussion, and violin for six weeks in an exploratory unit.

It is not our place to pass judgment on the most appropriate school grouping of grade levels, but some groupings are considerably better for structuring instrumental instruction than others. Perhaps the easiest structure for the music teacher would have been the old K–8 and 9–12 arrangement where beginning students could work with the same teacher for a period of three or four years at the elementary school level. These

---

[6]Figures supplied by the American Music Conference.

programs now seem to be few and far between. A close approximation of this system can be found in the "unit" district in which all instruction K–12 is controlled in a consolidated school district. These situations tend to be in smaller communities, which make use of staff at more than one level. The music teacher may work with the elementary school band, the junior high school band, and the high school band. This teacher may be charged with the choral and instrumental program or with band and orchestral program for all three levels.

With the conversion to middle schools, two phenomena emerged. Grade school instrumental programs were diluted by removing one class of students (the sixth graders, who played with some facility), and the middle school programs could not be compared with the old junior high school programs (which included the ninth-grade class). The performance abilities of elementary and middle school groups suffered as a result. Needless to say, the 7–9 junior high school yields some superb instrumental performance groups. This level of playing ability is difficult to achieve with a 7–8 intermediate school in which only two grade levels participate.

The impact on the high school has been somewhat less than on the other two segments of the school system. The three-year high school certainly has had a smaller population to draw upon than the four-year high school for performance participants. The effect of early instruction on the development and experience of students before reaching high school has not been thoroughly investigated. Whether students are better prepared to enter high school programs by a K–5 and 6–8 program or a K–6 and 7–9 program is a question that has not been answered. In the opinion of the authors, the level of performance in large ensembles is better in the K–6 and 7–9 program or the K–8 and 9–12 program.

Most of us are aware of the early age at which some children become involved with string instruction. String instruction lends itself to class instruction for children as young as age three. These classes are not part of a public school offering, and the students quickly become a problem for the school system when they appear at the front door of the elementary school with two or three years of experience in playing violin. School programs usually begin in the fourth or fifth grade. With no activities or violin instruction available, the Suzuki violinist who started at age three has no option except to continue outside instruction until the school system catches up with his early beginning. It could be four or five years before the student's classmates even touch a violin. While public education is not charged with offering unique programs for talented children, we lose too many students by not being able to offer instruction and activities to challenge individuals.

Unless structured out-of-school activities are readily available for children who begin violin at such an early age, many will drop out of string performance after a short time and not renew their interest in their later school years.

Scope of Instruction

The instrumental programs in elementary school have consisted of instrumental classes, small ensembles, and performance experience in large ensembles (band or orchestra). Students in most cases are encouraged to play solos, usually to participate in solo contests and festivals sponsored by local or state music organizations. Instruction at the elementary school is in addition to the general music program and is scheduled separately. Students generally are assigned instructional classes based on their developing abilities. A strong instrumental program should offer two or three levels of instruction for children in wind class, brass class, percussion class, and string class. Curriculum offerings are noted in figure 2.3.

The Middle/Junior High School Instrumental Curriculum

The development of the middle school instrumental program has largely parallelled that of the elementary school program. The middle school program, whch must interface with the feeder schools at the elementary level, normally offers intermediate and elementary instruction. Middle schools with no feeder schools have programs to start students with entry-level band instrument instruction. Somewhat more tenuous is the question of a string program at the middle school. If beginning string programs do not exist at the elementary school, they are less likely to exist at the middle school. The string program should allow for students to begin instruction at the middle school level and even at the high school level.

There are several approaches to teaching students in instrumental groups. Some programs have grouped students in "like-instrument classes"; some give each student a "private" lesson each week; and some offer instruction to all beginners in a "heterogeneous" class where woodwinds, brass, and even percussion students learn to play together at the beginning level. If managed properly, instruction can be of high quality in any of these three settings. The reader should note the curriculum outlined in figure 2.3 of the homogeneous type where instruments are grouped for classes of brass instruments, woodwind instruments, and so forth.

A typical middle school curriculum or junior high school program

Class Instruction				Ensemble Experience	
Beginning Year	strings	winds	brass	percussion	beginning band	beginning orch.
Intermediate	strings	winds	brass	percussion	concert band	full orchestra (winds, brass, percussion selected by audition).
	string orch.	small ensembles				
Advanced	strings	winds	brass	percussion		
	small ensembles					

Figure 2.3 Three-Year Instrumental Program (5–7 or 4–6).

must relate well to the elementary program in instrumental music. The junior high programs in instrumental music normally allow for beginning instruction for students in either seventh or eighth grade. This option is important for students who have not yet had the opportunity to begin instrumental instruction or have not taken advantage of available instruction. The junior high school student population should also have students with strong backgrounds in music performance when one considers that some ninth graders have up to five years of playing experience on their instruments. If this is the case, student ensembles should be quite respectable in performance quality.

A vast amount of jazz band literature has been arranged and composed for the younger jazz student, and many junior high schools have incorporated jazz into their curriculum. This literature does not require the high range and endurance found in music written for high school and professional bands. Although student performers on piano, bass, and set drums (the rhythm instruments) are sometimes hard to find at the junior high school level, student interest is usually high in jazz and jazz ensemble participation. The rationale that supports jazz studies for junior high school students is based on the creative approach to music. One of the few means of approaching improvisation for instrumentalists is provided by the jazz program. Allowing students to express themselves musically by creating "solos" is an important part of musical development.

Apart from the addition of the jazz component to the curriculum, the junior high school curriculum looks much like the middle school program. Various levels of instruction must be available for students of varying performance abilities. In many states, students have completed their general music requirements before entering junior high school. Although the completion of general music requirements may offer some flexibility in student scheduling, it places an added constant burden on the instrumental program. Again, as with the choral curriculum outlines, we have not specified content of each class. It is important that students learn more than fingerings, bowings, and major scales in the instrumental course offerings. The objective of the performance program should be the same as that of the choral program, that of a musically independent performer.

The High School Instrumental Curriculum

In instrumental music, fewer instructional options seem to be open at the high school level than at the elementary or middle school level. The assumption made by many high school curriculum planners is that students interested in instrumental music have had earlier opportunities, hence do not require remedial training or beginning instruction. There *are*, however, students who would like to begin to learn to play as late as the ninth and tenth grades, but these options are often not part of the high school curriculum. In many high schools, the insistent student may be given an opportunity for individual instruction to accelerate from beginner stage to a level where he or she can "join the band." The problem with individual instruction is that it is a stopgap measure in most cases. While this kind of private turoring can be used for one, two, or even ten students, the high school director does not have time to instruct fifty or sixty beginning students on an individual basis.

A survey by the American Music Conference indicated that 85 percent of schools have concert bands, but it also showed that only 22 percent of the schools had orchestras. There are many reasons that orchestras have not fared as well in the high shool curriculum as the bands, including instrument popularity, recruiting, and lack of an orchestral tradition in a majority of the newer high schools. The goal of the curriculum developer should be to attain balance in available instruction. Beginners as well as advanced students must be accommodated; both string and wind band instruction must be offered.

An instrumental program can become distorted by any of several parts of that program. Two activities come to mind immediately: marching bands and jazz bands. The marching band has found a place in many high school curricula and serves purposes that extend far beyond music instruction. Many music educators have attacked marching bands for having no purpose or place in music education because of the approach some band directors take in fielding a marching show. The recent popularity of corps-style marching and the propensity for bands to rehearse one contest presentation throughout an entire year have added substance to critics' concerns about the direction of instrumental programs in general. It is true that an unrealistic amount of a band director's time can be consumed in preparing for maching contests, festivals, and football half-time shows. One means of evaluating balance in an instrumental program is to review the curriculum of a high school band program during the fall term. If the only activity scheduled for students is marching band, the program is not being directed toward musical goals. A musically directed high school program will include small ensemble performance, class lessons, and concert band rehearsals during the marching season. If these activities can be scheduled, the band director has been able to place the marching band in a proper perspective.

Another activity that can dominate an instrumental program in the high school is the jazz band. The jazz band has wide popular appeal not only to the student participants, but also to the general student body. The music performed appeals to the student listener in general. The limited scope of many jazz band programs involves a very small nucleus of students. These students may receive excellent instruction in performance in the jazz medium. Consider, however, that perhaps eighteen to twenty students are involved in one jazz band program in a school that may enroll as many as three thousand students. An industrious teacher may have two jazz bands, but even doubling the number (40 students) is a poor showing among the number of students that may be interested in jazz. Many school systems forestall any involvement in jazz, improvisation, or both until high school, if they offer it at all. One reason for this hesitation may be found in the materials that were first available for high school jazz bands (then usually called "stage bands"). Materials were often professional jazz arrangements that made high-range demands on the brass players, causing teachers to be very selective in the group's makeup.

The major shortcomings of the jazz "program" in the public schools are threefold. First is the fact that few students are permitted in the program. If students do not or cannot play a "jazz" instrument (piano, bass, drums, saxophone, trumpet, trombone, or guitar), their involvement is very limited. An occasional tuba, flute, or horn player may be asked to join the ensemble for one or two numbers per concert, but the major impact of the program is for "jazz instruments." What of the oboe player, the violinist, or the cellist? These instruments have been used in jazz ensembles, but are not included in a normal instrumentation for most jazz programs in junior or senior high school. A viable jazz program must be open to all interested students.

Second, jazz programs often fail to encourage students to participate in jazz improvisation. Often, students play notes written for a jazz ensemble without learning simple principles of improvisation. In this regard, jazz programs do no more than concert bands or concert orchestra programs; perhaps not less, but not more. The educational strength of jazz instruction is its ability to encourage improvisation. The added experience of playing jazz rhythms is not enough justification to have jazz ensembles without including improvisation.

The third shortcoming of many jazz programs is the single emphasis on performance. It is the unique jazz program that offers instruction in jazz literature and jazz history or that even makes the subjects a part of the jazz experience in the schools. Just as many students play in the high school orchestra for four years without any sense of music's history, so may young jazz students remain ignorant of Charlie Parker and Dizzy Gillespie.

Jazz as a component of an instrumental music program should allow for improvisation classes, some experience in listening to jazz and learning jazz history, and open opportunities for selected students to learn to arrange music in a jazz idiom. Again, these opportunities must be available to all interested students.

Recommendation for the Instrumental Music Curriculum

A high school instrumental curriculum is outlined in figure 2.4, which shows the various components that can be offered in the high school. Limitations of staff, physical facilities, and financial support may make some components impractical. In these cases, the content of separate courses such as music appreciation should be synthesized in the instrumental rehearsal room.

Teaching assignments in the high school are allocated in a slightly different manner than they are in the elementary schools. If class piano is to be taught at the high school level, the instrumental or choral director more than likely will wind up teaching the course. This is also true of group guitar lessons. We have placed class piano and class guitar under the instrumental rubric simply because they are instruments, not because they must be staffed by the band or orchestra director. In surveying high school curricula, we find that several school districts hire specialists to

	Bands	Orchestras	Class Instruction	
Advanced	wind ens.	chamber orchestra	music composition	
	concert band	concert orchestra	music arranging	
	small ensemble programs			
	jazz band	studio orchestra	jazz literature	
	marching inter. band	string orch.	music theory	music and arts criticism
			music appreciation	
	improvisation program		improvisation guitar/piano	music theory
	class lesson program		class lessons piano/guitar entry level	music and arts appreciation
		Beginning Instrumental Instruction		general music survey
Entry Level	Select, Participating	Nonselect, Participating	Shared Experiences	Nonselect, Nonparticipating

Figure 2.4 Instrumental Music Curriculum in High School.

teach class piano. While these programs are not widespread, when they do appear, they have been very successful in involving large numbers of students. Ideally, a high school of three thousand students would have a music staff of five or more full-time music faculty. Rarely will you find this to be the case.

Adult education in instrumental music exists in programs offered by high schools, community colleges, and some park districts, but is not as widespread as the course offerings in general music. The opportunity for a middle-aged person to sign up for beginning orchestra is almost non-existent; chances to sign up for beginning band instrument instruction are only slightly better.

As we have suggested with general music and choral music, adult education in instrumental music will gain more emphasis in the coming years. Research has indicated that beginning students in instrumental music can be successful.[7] Although some problems develop as adults mature, such as problems with dentures and bifocals, older people can be successful in beginning programs. Teaching techniques may need to be slightly altered for adults because their ability to grasp concepts and principles is somewhat higher than that of the beginning elementary school student. On the other hand, adults may lag behind younger students in some aspects of physical skill development.

It is evident that there is a growing interest in instrumental music for adults. The music educator should be prepared to work with students varying in age from five years on up. The same curriculum should exist for the adult beginner as for the high school beginner. The assumption cannot be made that adults have had prior instrumental music experience or even prior general music instruction.

Recommendations for the Music Education Curriculum

Having reviewed the general, choral, and instrumental programs separately, we have an insight into how each segment of the music curriculum should function. While we can assess the strengths and weaknesses of the general program separately, the quality of the choral activities, and the number of students in intermediate band at a high school, to gain a good perspective of the health of music education in a community each component must be considered as part of a whole. One strong component does not make up for deficiencies in other areas.

[7]John M. Burley, *A Feasibility Study of Structured Instruction in Instrumental Music for Adult Beginners* (Ed.D. dissertation, University of Illinois, 1980).

We can point to successful programs in the public schools in general music, instrumental music, or choral music. The examples are many: a Kodaly program with children more advanced in ear training than are most college students; a high school orchestra that performs better than many community orchestras; a small ensemble that involves every student in the instrumental program with monthly recitals; a beginning adult band that performs on television; and the list could go on.

But a curriculum must be reviewed in terms of how it affects *all* students in the particular school system or community. As a matter of fact, a school with a strong marching band program may have a poor general music program as an indirect result. If the public is led to believe that the quality of a music curriculum can be measured by the precision of a marching band, fiscal support for the remainder of the program may suffer. The band director who continues to be concerned about the general education of students in the arts (and music) will not make the mistake of misdirecting public opinion and evaluation of the music program.

Staffing should allow for the instruction of the nonselect students, those who are not in the music performance programs. Too often, the one or two music teachers in the high school have more to teach than can be managed even when working only with the "select," participating students. Staffing and teacher load assignments are a direct indication of the strength of a program. Although a few notable high schools have more than ten music staff members, most high schools have two or perhaps three teachers with very specific duties, usually in performance. If high school teachers must make a decision, based upon time constraints, they will choose to work with selected performance students; those students in the general education sector will suffer from a lack of course offerings.

Being realistic about the cost of instruction, we cannot expect many high schools to have a staff of ten music teachers, but we should press to have enough instructional time to offer a balanced curriculum. If we do not, rest assured that no one else will.

Another consideration in music curriculum development is whether the course offerings become part of an arts education program, not an isolated group of courses for select students, as we caution above. Much has been written about "arts in general education" in recent years that directly affects course offerings in music. These programs, to date, have capitalized on the success of the music program, pointing to it as a significant part of the arts. The greatest effect that such programs will have is on the nonselect, nonparticipating students. To educate the general student body and hence the general population in the arts is a noble goal.

Music programs should be directed to goals and objectives that allow for the acquisition of musical knowledge and skills that truly reflect the nature of the musical art. This topic is addressed more fully in chapter 5, which discusses an approach to musical meaning and the relationship of aesthetics to education.

The success and impact of a music program relies heavily on the teacher who continues it. The teacher's qualities, musical background, personality, and teaching skills have more to do with the success of the program than any formal curriculum plan.

We are all aware of the importance of the individual teacher in the curriculum. The next chapter investigates the components of that person, the preparation required for successful music teaching, teaching skills, and attitude toward students and teachers. Good teachers rise above poor curriculum outlines, whereas poor teaching can destroy the best educational plans.

Questions for Discussion

1. Interview selected local music teachers to determine the objectives of the programs. Do the programs have similar goals and objectives? Establish how the goals and objectives were developed.
2. Determine community interest in school music programs by interviewing people outside the school system. What perceptions do townspeople have of the quality of music instruction? Did they recall general music instruction in their experience? Their children's experience?
3. Review with your classmates the number of schools with small ensemble programs for instrumental and choral participants. Did the experiences extend through the year? Were state contests the motivation for the student involvement?
4. Define the difference between the sequencing of instruction for the choral music programs and the instrumental music programs. Do you think that both programs should be patterned in the same manner? If so, why?

Recommended Readings

Bergethon, Bjornar, and Boardman, Eunice. *Music Growth in the Elementary School.* 4th ed. New York: Holt, Rinehart and Winston, 1979.

Bessom, Malcolm Alphonse Tatarunis, and Forcucci, Samuel. *Teaching Music in Today's Secondary Schools, A Creative Approach to Contemporary Music Education.* New York: Holt, Rinehart and Winston, 1980.

Burley, John. "*A Feasibility Study of Structured Instruction in Instrumental Music for the Adult Beginner,*" Ed.D. dissertions, University of Illinois, 1980.

Green, Elizabeth. *Teaching Stringed Instruments in Classes.* Engelwood Cliffs, N.J.: Prentice-Hall, 1966.

nhard, Charles, and House, Robert. *Foundations and Principles of Music Educa-tion.* New York: McGraw-Hill, 1972.

Metz, Donald. *Teaching General Music in Grades Six through Nine.* Columbus, Ohio: Charles Merrill, 1980.

Myers, Louise. *Teaching Children in the Elementary School.* Engelwood Cliffs, N.J.: Prentice-Hall, 1956.

Shuter, Rosamund. *The Psychology of Musical Ability.* London: Methuen, 1968.

3/the teacher in music education

And gladly woulde he learne, and gladly teche . . . —Chaucer

As a teacher, you will become part of a long tradition. Although the details, methods, and materials of teaching have changed over the centuries, some constant threads of the tradition seem immutable. In his description of the Oxford Scholar from the Canterbury Tales, Chaucer depicts a teaching profession that really has not changed much since those early days. Teachers learn. Constantly and continually, they acquire new knowledge and skills, new techniques and methods, new dreams and aspirations. The knowledge they seek is not necessarily motivated by utility or practicality; a good deal of it is knowledge for the sake of knowledge. Learning is its own reward for teachers. In short, they learn "gladly," an important model for their students. They also offer this knowledge to others gladly, realizing that the very act of teaching is rewarding. The emphasis in Chaucer's description is on attitude, or in more contemporary terms, on mind-set.

Teaching is far more than an occupation; it is a profession. To characterize a profession (as opposed to a job) we would list components such as constant high-level performance, continual renewal, systematic effort, accountability, and independence. Perhaps independence is valued most by members of professions, for without the opportunity to make independent decisions, teaching would quickly become a chore. Some assert that teachers in the public schools are not independent. After all, curriculum guides, textbooks (often chosen by others), duties assigned by a principal, and attendance keeping are all part of the teacher's world. These guidelines and duties are neither independent nor professional in nature. They sound as if all of the decisions have been made for teachers elsewhere. Yet, once the classroom door is closed, the *teacher* makes the decisions, and those day-to-day classroom decisions have the most impact on learning. At what stage of learning is the student? What is the one key phrase I can utter that will somehow "turn on the light" for him? What should I do to keep my students on task? Teachers make these and thousands more *professional* decisions constantly. When all is said and done, we know great teachers exist who can make even the most mundane outmoded textbook "work." This chapter examines the role of the teacher in music education and outlines the preparation that future teachers need to enter the profession.

Scholarship

Teachers should be scholars. The idea sounds formidable, carrying images of dusty libraries, lonely rare-book rooms, and the like; however, modern scholarship rarely fits this stereotype. Scholarship, like so many other topics in this book, is more an attitude than a set of actions. You, as university students, are now afforded the rare opportunity to build in yourselves a set of scholarly attitudes that will serve you and your future students for the rest of your life. There are certain characteristics of a scholar that we hope will become a part of you, allowing you to deal with future decision making with much more ease.

Expertise

A scholar is generally characterized as a person who has mastery of a specific range of human knowledge. In our case, this knowledge base is music and education. More than that, the true scholar has a context within which the specialized knowledge fits. He or she has a good general knowledge of the human condition and knows something about almost everything. *Most important*, the scholar knows the difference between specialized knowledge and general knowledge. A scholar knows what he or she knows, and prefers to admit ignorance of other things. This is one of

general + specific knowledge

the toughest problems to face a new teacher. Suddenly assuming the role of "expert" is a heady experience. It is far too easy to get carried away, losing scholarly integrity. In matters of knowledge, honesty is the best policy. If you do not know something, admit it and then go find the answer. Your students will think no less of you. Indeed, they will appreciate your honesty and return it in kind.

We address the preparation you should consider in two areas: (1) specialized knowledge in music and teaching; and (2) general knowledge, which provides a context or framework for your expertise or specialized knowledge.

General Education

As a university student, you are in a position that would be envied by a large segment of the population. You are free to seek knowledge for its own sake, unfettered by the demands of practicality. While some students are in programs that have highly structured curricula, consider the wide choice students are afforded within curricular requirements. There are history requirements but which history course will you take? There are general education course requirements in the social sciences, English, and the natural sciences; and in most colleges and universities, these can be met in a variety of ways. Many students question whether they should be "wasting their time" in courses they feel have little "relevance" to their future as music teachers. Although we do not want to dictate a weighty treatise on the values of a "liberal" education, consider general education as an important part of your preparation as a music teacher.

What makes a teacher *interesting*, someone who is able to engage the attention of students both in and out of class? Of the many potential factors, of most importance seems the ability of the teacher to relate what he or she and the students are doing in the music classroom to the world at large, to life in general. Far from a mere euphemistic notion, a broad knowledge base holds real practicality for teachers of any subject. This assertion is based on three arguments. First, dull, narrow people make dull, narrow teachers. While you are and will be highly committed to the value of music in the lives of children, do not fall into the trap of being a "music freak" who is unwilling or unable to hold an intelligent conversation with a tenth-grade science student. You may never be as able as the science teacher to deal with authority in the sciences, but you should be able to ask meaningful questions and understand a bit of what your students are telling you as they discuss their activities and interests in this field. (Of course, the science teacher should be able to talk about music as well.) Your ability to engage in this sort of discourse greatly increases your credibility as a mature adult for the students in your charge.

The second advantage to a broad base of knowledge stems from the realization that you are a *teacher* first and a music teacher second. Music teachers often have difficulty accepting this idea if they become too wrapped up in their daily musical dealings with students. We have previously discussed the power of role modeling. Several models should be presented to children by the music teacher. The "musician" model is a powerful teaching aid in making musical progress with your children; other and equally powerful models exist as well. Personal models of life-long learning, of dedication to a task, and of the personal satisfaction of being a well-informed citizen are all models that teachers hold up for others to imitate. These notions may seem rather overblown ideals at first glance, but they are nonetheless true. If you are to be a *professional* educator, rather than a music learning mechanic who merely diagnoses and "fixes" music learning problems, you will have to accept responsibility for advancing the general goals of education and those of the parents and community that pay your salary. If you are to present a positive role model that shows students "learning is good" and "education is good," you must prepare yourself while you have the opportunities. Become the "educated" person that you and society wish to present as a model for children.

The third reason for gaining breadth of knowledge in your undergraduate education and in your life as a teacher is practical. You will be expected to function as a member of a "team" of professionals within a school system. To be effective on this team, indeed to be accepted at all by other professionals in your school, you must have an understanding of what *they* are trying to accomplish. Successfully teaching music often requires cooperation from the administration and your fellow teachers. Your interest in their work and your ability to converse with them about *their* goals and *their* subject matter will be vital. You cannot fake it. Your knowledge and concern must be genuine, or your success is liable to be shallow and short-lived.

For some music teachers, most of their schooling was irrelevant and joyless, except for the hours spent in music classes. These people may find it difficult to realize that this is not true for everyone. Because we enjoyed music, we became musicians. Natural human inclinations force people to induce others to follow their lead and, by doing so, to affirm that they were "right" all along with their career choices and that the rest of education really is of less importance. Our caution is never to denigrate another professional educator to students, administration, or other faculty. Never try to make your music program seem better by making all other subjects seem worse. In the end, you will be the loser, and your students with you.

Evidence-Based Decision Making

One characteristic of scholars, as a group, is systematic decision making. As a scholar-teacher you will be called on for thousands of decisions each week. Nowhere is education more individualized than in music teaching, a fact that increases the number of decisions a music teacher must make. Individualization, creating a different educational program for each student according to his or her particular educational needs, is a process of continual trial and evaluation. As a teacher, you will have to be able to behave as a scholar does and rely on *evidence* for your decisions rather than on whim. This *systematic* decision making is one feature that raises schooling above education in general. To fully participate in this decision making, a teacher must be able to identify and evaluate learning problems quickly. The choice of solutions or teaching strategies teachers apply must be based on evidence from experience, research, and reading. Amassing this evidence base is an activity that does not cease when one graduates from college, nor five nor ten years into the teaching career. Good teachers, like other good scholars, are always seeking new evidence, new knowledge, and new methods for making their decisions.

Tenacity

Tenacity is another scholarly quality that teachers must develop. Most good teachers hold beliefs (evidence-based, we hope) and hold them strongly (tenaciously). Rather than flit from one educational fad to another, these teachers perform their usual decision making in a consistent manner while consciously looking for evidence that they might be wrong. Teachers can be found, of course, who make the undesirable leap from tenacity to dogma. The dogmatic person is one who refuses to give rational consideration to evidence that is not in line with his or her beliefs. While being a dogmatist is personally comforting (nothing bothers you, you *know* you are always right), it is devastating to the learning process. The advice is clear: Decide what you believe is right, based upon evidence; perform your actions in a manner consistent with those beliefs, while always maintaining a touch of skepticism.

Personal Qualities

Why should a person want to teach? We often hear the assertion that someone enters a teaching profession becuase he or she "loves children."

If you find in your student teaching interactions with students that you really do not love children as much as you thought, do not despair. *Loving* children is not the sole criterion for teaching. The successful professional teacher sometimes loves children and their eagerness to learn—but not always. Far more important than loving children is to love the adults the children will become. Never forget that your most important product is a well-schooled population of adults.

As a prospective teacher, it is important that you be able to at least *tolerate* children, and if possible it is desirable that you like and enjoy them. If you *do not* tolerate them, or if you *dislike* children, you will quickly find that they easily sense your negative feelings.

How does a potential teacher decide how well he tolerates children? Remember the evidence-based decision making we mentioned? You guessed it—find a summer job as a camp counselor, lifeguard, or part-time but regular volunteer in a school to see if you still enjoy children. The objective is to interact with children on a daily basis for a long period of time, not just in spurts. We advise you to do this early in your undergraduate program, before you invest a full four years in university-level teacher training. If you find that you just cannot stand children, if you find that your temper is shorter than you knew, if you find that children's fidgeting drives you up the wall, do your potential future victims a favor: Become an accountant.

Stages of Concern in a Teacher's Career

Significant research has been conducted on the general pattern of teachers' professional lives. Our purpose here is to inform you of some results of this research to enable you to plan and not be discouraged by the gremlins that may sneak out of the bushes to snare you along your path to becoming a teacher. Like children growing up, teachers go through a number of predictable stages every time they begin something new—a new curriculum, a new teaching method, or a new set of teaching materials.[1] As a beginning teacher, you will go through the same stages, perhaps even more markedly because virtually everything you do will be new as you accept your first teaching position. To begin this discussion, we must define a term, *concerns*. Gene Hall, a leader in research in educational change, put it this way:

---

[1]The information on teacher concerns in this section is adapted from the work of Gene Hall, Shirley Hord, and Susan F. Loucks in the Procedures for Adopting Educational Innovations Program, Research and Development Center for Teacher Education, University of Texas at Austin.

The term "concerns" is used to represent a composite description of the various motivations, perceptions, attitudes, feelings and mental gyrations experienced by a person in relation to an innovation. [In your case, the innovation is music teaching.] The concept was coined by Fuller in research on the shift in concerns experienced by undergraduate education majors in relation to teaching. Fuller proposed that the student teacher's most intense concerns progressed from being unfocused on the task of teaching to a more egocentric orientation related to teaching, to a focus upon the job itself, and, finally, to a focus upon the consequences of their teaching for students.[2]

Hall's work has concentrated on the development of the original Fuller model for application to educational innovation in general.[3] We have modified Hall's model by applying it once again to Fuller's intended audience (see figure 3.1).

Stages of Concern	Expressions of Concern
Impact	
6 Refocusing	I have some ideas about music teaching that would work even better.
5 Collaboration	I am concerned about relating what I am doing to what other music teachers are doing.
Task	
4 Consequence	How is this brand of music teaching affecting my students?
3 Management	I seem to be spending all my time getting material ready and just keeping things running smoothly.
Self	
2 Personal	How will being a music teacher affect me?
1 Informational	I would like to know more about music teaching as a career.
0 Awareness	I just want to play my horn.

Figure 3.1 Stages of Concern: Typical Expressions of Concern about Teaching. *Adapted from G. E. Hall, Shirley M. Hord, and S. F. Loucks, "Concerns Based Consulting Workshop," (Research and Development Center for Teacher Education, University of Texas at Austin, n.d.), p. 5.*

[2]Gene E. Hall, "The Concerns-Based Approach to Facilitating Change," *Education Horizons*, Summer 1979, p. 203.

[3]G.E. Hall and S.F. Loucks, "Teacher Concerns as a Basis for Facilitating and Personalizing Staff Development," *Teachers College Record* 80, no. 1 (1978): 36–53.

Awareness

The first stage of teacher concern is *awareness*. At this level, potential teachers have not really considered teaching as a life's work. Typically, they express that "I don't know anything about music education, and I don't much care to know. I am concerned with other things right now." In many cases we hear the music student affirm, "I just want to play my horn." Perhaps you went through this stage, perhaps not. In many cases, the decision to consider music education as a career is dictated by circumstance: a perceived uncertainty about one's ability to succeed in some other musical endeavor or perhaps the modeling of a powerful teacher with whom you have had contact. Once past this initial consideration, once the decision has been reached that "well, maybe . . . ," the future teacher quickly moves to the next level of concern.

Information

The *information* level is where many undergraduates in music education find themselves. Teaching is at least a possibility and the task is to seek out more information, as much information as possible. Indeed, an overview is one of the reasons you are reading this text. Most students do not worry about the personal aspects of becoming teachers; they concentrate on teaching in an impersonal and selfless manner. Questions arise as to the general characteristics of the profession: What do teachers do and what are the requirements for teacher certification.

Personal

At the *personal* level, the future teacher is uncertain about the demands of teaching and his or her adequacies to meet those demands. This uncertainty will be realized and recognized by your state of terror the night before you are to do your first full day's teaching during the student experience. At this level, teachers become concerned about financial well-being and the community status implications of the profession. Potential conflicts in their own value systems as they begin to teach become a major concern: Will the teaching position demand that you do things that conflict with your ideals, beliefs, and values?

Management

Management concerns deal with the efficiency, organization, management, and scheduling required in teaching. "What do I do next Tuesday?" quickly gives way to "What do I do Wednesday and Thursday?" and so on. Many teachers hang at this management level for years and progress only slowly to more mature levels of teaching. There is no way to completely eliminate management concerns except by experience, but you *can* apply yourself *before* you are forced to perform day and day out by gathering as much information as possible to aid you in these organizational requirements for teaching. The importance of management is discussed later in this chapter, but for now, set up in your mind the idea that before you become truly effective as a teacher, you will have to develop the ability to keep things running smoothly.

Consequence

"Mature" teaching really begins at the *consequence* level as the teacher focuses on the impact of music education on the students. The teacher further assesses the impact of his or her teaching on the students. Teachers typically become concerned with the place of music in the lives of their students, with evaluation of student achievement and progress, and with changes necessary to fine tune the teaching to increase student success. Music teachers in performance are under the gun from the beginning to evaluate student performance in terms of its musical quality; teachers at the consequence level are evaluating beyond this requirement. They evaluate the effect that the fine performance has on the lives of their students. The teachers ask if the effort on the students' part is worth it in the long run, if the constant rehearsals and practicing are doing harm to other educational endeavors, and if the student is getting lasting or only momentary benefit. Some teachers rise to this level of maturity only late in their careers. Some never attain this level, struggling with personal and management concerns until they retire or leave the profession.

Collaboration

The focus at the *collaboration* level shifts to coordination and sharing with other music educators. Many leaders in our professional organizations and many college music education faculty are engaged in these concerns. How can I share what I know and have learned with others? How can I, in turn, learn from them? This is the level of the *master teacher*, who can not only direct student studies but also can aid teachers with insights and knowledge about various teaching problems.

Refocusing

At this *refocusing* level, teachers become creative in their approach to instruction. They have examined the consequences of their teaching on students and have fine tuned their basic approaches. They have shared what they know and have learned from others at the collaboration level. Often teachers reach this level by deciding that the only thing that will make their teaching better is some radical and innovative new approach. They have the security and experience to judge the evidence and decide that chances for success with a new approach are good, and they proceed accordingly.

In applying this model of the stages of concerns that teachers express, one must understand that at any one time, most teachers exhibit some concerns at all the levels. Most teachers find their concerns are concentrated at one or two particular levels. Future teachers should realize that people differ in their rates of progress from one stage to another. Some may move quickly into mature teaching, whereas others never progress beyond level two (personal) or three (management). As you move through your career in teaching, keep these levels in mind, assess frankly your stage of development, and by identifying your level of concerns, deal with them systematically. Above all, do not worry if you find that after two or three years of teaching, your concerns are still mostly self and task concerns rather than concerns about students and fellow faculty members.

Learning the Craft

A great deal of uncertainty plagues a person who begins to take courses "required" to become a music teacher. At first glance, some of the courses, or parts of them at least, seem of borderline relevance. While there is no way that a text such as this can give specific recommendations concerning every course on every campus (the variation is simply too great), there are a number of things we can say that may help you decide the importance of the courses in your program. At times in this discussion, you may feel that *everything* is important, and indeed that may be so. You will find some courses easier than others, find some fun and some drudgery; but do not fall into the trap of assuming that the ease or difficulty of a particular skill development has any bearing on its eventual importance. You may find the easiest things, and thus the things you like the most, are far less important to your success in teaching than others; then again, perhaps not.

Musical Skills Courses

We cannot say enough about the importance of any course that helps improve your skills and knowledge concerning your craft, that of music. Our eventual goal is to develop *musician* teachers. Pedagogues, yes; educators, yes; interesting, well-rounded persons, yes; but first and foremost, we hope to develop musicians. The course group we have named "musical skills" falls into three categories: performance, history, and theory.

Performance. The performance courses are usually easiest for most students to understand because they are most directly connected to the role of the "musician" to which they aspire. The courses, as a group, directly connect the experience of a musician with the substance of music. By direct interaction with musical materials, we develop the fluency necessary to better understand music and the teaching of music.

Your ability as a performer, instrumentalist or vocalist with a high degree of skill will accomplish several things for you as a teacher that are of direct practical application. First, your performance ability will serve as a model for your students and, even though it sounds corny, as an inspiration to your students. For the vocal music teacher, singing is an important and handy way to directly model for your students. If you are a mediocre singer, you will be unable to model successfully.

For a band or orchestra director, the situation is not so simple, since it is hard to model the violin part to the *Impressario Overture* if your principal applied instrument is trombone. (Besides, it's a nuisance to be picking up the instrument all the time.) Yet even here the study of trombone can be useful, for it supplies the necessary experience to make musical choices and decisions that are the basis for performance judgments.

Debate continues about whether teachers absolutely need to continue their performance once they enter the profession. After all, if they already possess the musical judgment skills necessary to cope with their performing groups, it may be doubtful that they will learn a great deal more by practicing every day. As the beginning teacher quickly finds, there are so many other things to do—preparing scores, lesson plans, concert publicity materials, and the like—despite what Chaucer says about "gladly learning." The fact is that if you continue to practice and to perform either as a member of a dance band or chorus or civic opera, your students will know it. They will know it and will believe you when you get excited about how great a thing music is as part of one's life. They will believe you when you admonish them about the importance of practice. They will believe you when you tell them that through musical study, they can have something that will stay with them the rest of their lives. Now, they *may* still believe you if you put the horn away the day you graduated, but your job will be easier, and you will be much more credible, if you remain a functioning musician.

Participation in performing groups in your musical training is also an excellent way to hone your skills as a performer. Two additional side benefits can accrue as you participate in performance groups. Through modeling, you can learn a good deal about rehearsal technique if you apply yourself and listen while the conductor is speaking to the other sections of the group. In this situation you find yourself trying to model someone else's techniques. There are numerous techniques and methods to model, so by working under a number of conductors, you will learn many different approaches to musical and performance problems. You will gain additional knowledge about the context of music by performing a wide range of musical styles. (The importance of context will also be discussed as part of music history and music theory.) Consider the assumption that the more music you know, the more music you know. Try to experience as much music as you possibly can in the most direct way you possibly can—by performing it.

Jazz performance in our schools has risen in quality and quantity during the last decade. If you can learn jazz performance, jazz history, and jazz literature, we encourage you to do so. Not only does jazz represent an important body of American musical literature, but the job you may want after graduation may hinge on your ability to run a successful jazz program. Through the efforts of such groups as the National Association of Jazz Educators, many schools in the country include both jazz band and swing choir as a regular part of the curriculum, on a par with concert band and mixed choir. Jazz improvisation, both vocal and instrumental, is an excellent way to improve performance ability and your knowledge of musical structure.

Many university students who did not have the benefit of early learning in jazz through their high school programs are reluctant to attempt these skills at college. Perhaps they know they are good at "legitimate" performance and know the demands of that performance, and feel they should stick to what they know best. The real reason may be because learning jazz improvisation, like learning any skill, reduces one to a beginner level again. If one can perform Mozart well, it may be difficult to put up with the bad early sounds created while learning to play the blues. A certain embarrassment sets in as you admit to anyone who can hear you that there are some things you cannot do well. We contend that it is better to be embarrassed now than later when your students come to you requesting that you start a jazz band or swing choir and you have to admit that your preparation is incomplete and thus you can be of little help to the students.

Theory and Sight Singing. Music theory courses and sight singing are sticking points for a large number of students. In most cases, failure in these courses does not reflect a lack of native ability (traditional harmony can be successfully taught to a normally intelligent ninth grader), but a lack of serious application on the part of the student. The two groups of students who seem to have the greatest difficulty are singers (even in sight singing) and percussionists. These students usually have trouble because of the way in which they have been prepared before entering college. Many singers have never been taught to read music properly, and some have gotten most of their information by rote. Percussionists rarely have had to deal with reading pitches or listening to intonation, unless by some chance they were started on mallet instruments. Even marimba and xylophone students have never had concerns about playing in tune.

Students have difficulty at times realizing the significance of theory courses, thinking that their superficial wizardry on the clarinet proves their point. They can and have performed without a knowledge of music theory, and sometimes quite well. What these students fail to ask is, "How much would the performance improve if I had a better understanding of the form, structure, and harmonic content of the piece?" Theoretical studies form the basis for a major part of learning the context of music, and that context is of supreme importance to the understanding of musical style.

Sight singing, on the other hand, is a skill that is directly useful in the life of every musician. Not only is it useful to be able to sing a line in the score as a model for your students (without picking up the trombone again), but a question arises in the minds of some if a person cannot sight sing: Can he (or she) really hear well enough to be called a true musician? That sight singing is a rigorous course of study in every major conservatory in Europe and America speaks to its importance. Throughout your career you will be engaged in music performance with children, even in a general music classroom. If you are ever to become an efficient rehearser, you *must* be able to hear errors, detecting the difference in what you hear from the printed score. Many students claim that they can do this in spite of their poor sight-singing ability, yet we have never seen one who actually can do this. Before the complexities of hearing an entire score can be approached, mastery must be gained over a single melodic line.

Various colleges and conservatories use different methods of teaching sight singing. Some use solfeggio, where "C" is also "**do**," and all sharpened ed or flatted pitches are sung as accidentals. Some use the "tonic sol-fa" method, where the tonic of the key signature of the music becomes "do" and only notes outside the key are sung as accidentals. Some methods make use of scale degrees—one-three-five, for example—while other methods use no syllables. The important point is that any of these systems can be effectively learned and used. All of us in music education have seen entering graduate students hamstrung by their inability to sight sing. If your college or university is willing to graduate you even though you are deficient in this skill, say thank you, take your diploma, and then find someone to teach you to sight sing. Whatever your path to effective sight singing—be it private instruction, self-instruction, or university class instruction—this skill is critical to your success at working with students in music.

Music History. The study of the history of music is fascinating. In this part of the university curriculum you learn the circumstances of change in the development of music. The study of musical change, which keeps the arts alive, relates events in society to music from one era to the next. The direct benefit to you is that your history and literature courses should make you more fully aware of the context of music and allow you to judge the music in terms of its style and its interpretation. For instrumentalists, history of music courses are often their only introduction to vocal literature. For singers, understanding the evolution of the sonata can also be a revelation. Only through knowing musical context can one gain from experience in a wide range of musical styles and periods and begin to understand how musical thought "works."

One obvious benefit of music history is to make one aware of more and more potentially useful pieces, but this benefit is far overshadowed by that of being able to think more musically. The practical side of studying musical context is that of "performance practices." These courses are normally offered at the upper level of music history, beyond the first year of study required of most students. If undergraduate students were more attentive to the style and practices used in the performance of pieces by period, many of the performance debacles we hear at the high school level would not occur. We have all attended concerts in which tempos were much too fast, instrumentation was not properly balanced, or the dynamics were not properly attended to. Too often, these errors in musical judgment (context) stem from the conductor-teacher who has been ill prepared to rehearse and present the music selected for performance.

Other obvious applications of a background in music history are discussing music with students in the class and writing program notes for a concert. The teacher should have the background to discuss the development of music in a historical sense with students: in short, relating musical context to the students. The undergraduate student often feels forced to study music history and becomes determined not to foist such information on his or her charges. The result is tragic. The student's attitude as an undergraduate blocks a large area of knowledge about music from further exploration, and the pervasive attitude carried to children closes this field of knowledge to more students. Unfortunately, many students in a high school orchestra would be hard pressed to tell you whether Mozart wrote music that predated the music of Beethoven—hardly a scholarly approach.

Conducting Courses. Music conducting courses were not established to generate an army of Toscaninis. The objective of these courses is to educate good, solid, followable, unswerving conductors, not the florid professional who stands in front of an orchestra that often would do as well without him and displays wild gesticulations aimed at the impressionable patron in the third row. This caricature is, of course, unfair, but do keep in mind that even the most highly stylized conductors suddenly can become *very* plain and precise when the music gets complex and the orchestra starts to have trouble.

In conducting classes you will learn the rudiments of conducting: score reading, score preparations and rehearsal techniques. Like becoming a good singer, becoming a good conductor takes practice. You will get some practice conducting other members of the class, but not nearly enough to do well. A great deal of discussion as to the advisability of practicing conducting to a record has continued for years. Some maintain that it encourages sloppiness because the record never changes tempo and the miscues never result in disaster. Others contend that practice with a recording is definitely better than no practice if the student dwells on the basics of good, expressive beat with cuing and the mechanics of the baton. Ask your conducting teacher which method he prefers for your practice.

Score-reading skills can be practiced with a recording. Understanding a musical score while following a performance aids in the preparation of future scores for rehearsal. Watching live performances with an open score, a student should become sensitive to difficult sections for the conductor. At what times must the conductor be particularly aware of possible problems with the performers?

Rehearsal techniques are included at some universities as a component of music methods courses. We see the proper structuring and sequencing of a rehearsal as closely akin to conducting ability: the pace of the rehearsal, the decision to stop and rehearse, the decision to ignore minor errors in performance, and quick decisions that require training. We compare this skill, one which all conductors must accomplish, to that of teaching a child a new fingering or a new note name. Rehearsal techniques vary in pace as a direct result of the performance quality of the participants in the ensemble. In some situations the conductor is well advised to maintain a steady pace, with few interruptions; in others, frequent stops seem to be the only means to a successful performance.

The student who enrolls in a conducting class only to·work on a four-beat pattern is ignoring a large component of conducting. Only through outside work in watching conductors conduct, conductors rehearse, and teachers conduct rehearsals of students in an educational setting can a student develop the requisite skills to become a music educator actively involved in performance.

Keyboard Skills. Piano skills (keyboard) are tremendously practical acquisitions for the music educator. For the teacher of general music, the piano serves for both the accompaniment of class performance and the demonstration of musical ideas. For the teacher of instrumental music, the ability to accompany simple solos will encourage students to perform solo literature. For the teacher of choral music, it is often impossible to have a rehearsal accompanist present every time you need one. In addition to good general piano technique, music teachers need to be able to improvise accompaniments for both instrumentalists and singers, given only a melody line. This skill requires that the teacher have an excellent knowledge of harmony and ties together the piano class and theory class.

Courses in keyboard skills are offered on most campuses and take several forms. On some campuses, students with no piano or keyboard background may enroll in class piano for rudimentary training in playing scales, harmonies, and simple accompaniments. Often these skills are attached to the keyboard part of the music theory class. If such skills are taught as part of music theory, the major thrust of instruction is toward understanding skills and harmony, not the ability to accompany young children. Added to these two areas of piano instruction is the private piano lesson. While this may seem the best of all possible worlds, the student must be aware that learning only piano literature will not adequately prepare him or her to be a music teacher. Excellent instruction is available on a one-to-one basis in the private lesson, but the piano teacher must be particularly aware of the purpose a music education student has in studying keyboard instruments: to gain facility at a tool that can be used in the classroom.

The skills that can be used to advantage in the keyboard area include the ability to transpose as one accompanies students. The flexibility this offers the teacher is to be able to accompany instruments as diverse as a horn in F or a tuba in double B-flat. A teacher who is accompanying a singer or chorus should be able to accomplish simple transpositions to match the range of the singer(s).

A higher-order keyboard skill is that of sight-reading musical scores. This requires somewhat more ability than playing music written for piano, since the visual arrangement of the music makes it more difficult to read. This task is even more difficult when reading a transposed instrumental score than a choral score.

The ability to "read through" a large number of pieces allows the teacher to review new literature. The alternative is to hum through one line at a time, hoping to grasp some mental image of what the music might sound like when you hear more than one part at a time. Teachers have been found so lacking in this ability that many publishers have resorted to recording short excerpts of their music to which teachers can listen. The problem with this process is that publishers record the music they are most interested in selling. The teacher's selection, then, is limited by the available recordings furnished by the publisher.

Once you apply yourself assiduously to the study of piano, you will find that you have a tool that you will use virtually every day that you teach music. If you neglect the study of piano, you will be as much at odds as a mechanic without his wrenches.

Music Education Courses (Tools of the Trade).   A large segment of your curriculum in music education is composed of courses designed to inform you about your chosen career. These offerings have a wide range on most campuses, some optional and some obligatory. While no set of courses can give you all the answers, most music education professors work hard to make their offerings stimulating and practical.

The majority of courses in music education are "methods and materials" courses, and as the name suggests, they prepare you for teaching by giving you a background in the methodology (pedagogy) of teaching and the wide range of materials and musical literature used in the schools. No matter what your eventual teaching goal, you should try to make yourself a well-rounded music teacher. The methods of the general music classroom, for example, are superb for use in performance classes in certain situations. You should be acquainted with the methods and job of your counterpart in instrumental music if you plan to be a future choral director, and vice versa. Not only will you be better able to "fill in" if the need arises, but your appreciation and understanding of the complexities of the other teacher's job will enable you to help create a consistent, well-focused music curriculum for all students at all levels.

At times, especially in smaller school districts, teachers are expected to teach the full range of musical course offerings. There are still a great number of school districts that employ one person as band director, choral director, and orchestra director. Often this person may be required to teach one or two periods a day at the middle school or the elementary school. If you cannot do all this, and do it well, you reduce your marketability significantly. A willingness to adapt, while desirable, is different from a real set of skills that you can use. Good advice is to prepare yourself as broadly as possible in the area of teaching methods.

The methods courses you will take should establish a set of philosophies, goals, and objectives to guide you in your teaching. As well, you will be asked to prepare and present carefully prepared sample lessons. On most campuses, these are given under the name "microteaching" and are small, easily handled lessons taught to one's classmates and critiqued by both professors and students. A few years ago it was rare to find sophomores and juniors teaching in the public schools, but current trends in more and more states require "early field experience." This field experience allows students to get their first taste of how a teacher functions working with children in classrooms.

For instrumentalists, skills classes offer aid in learning to play all the instruments they will eventually teach. Many in the profession consider these classes to be the most important courses in the curriculum for here many of the problems beginning students face can be experienced by the teacher-to-be. At times, students in these classes resist practicing the instruments, fearing damage will be done to the embouchures used in performing on their major instruments. Let us assure these students that this is nonsense. In the first place, the amount of practice that one will allot to other instruments will be slight in comparison to the thousands of hours spent on the principal instrument. There may be some temporary discomfort, but no permanent damage will occur. Second, if one wants to become a teacher, there is no way to demonstrate a proper embouchure for an instrument *except* by demonstrating it. These skills are critical to band and orchestra directors, as well as to teachers of beginning instrumentalists.

Showing a beginner (and all teachers teach beginners at one point or another) "how to do it" has no substitute. Showing how, as we have indicated, is modeling and is our most powerful method of teaching and communicating. As an experiment, try to explain to someone how to bake bread, assuming that the person you are teaching has never been in a kitchen and knows absolutely nothing about it. You cannot say, "Put six cups of flour in a bowl," if the person does not know what *flour*, *cup*, or *bowl* mean. Imagine the sheer enormity of that task. If you could *show* the person, however, it would be easy. The situation is analogous to the beginning trumpet student. You could say, "Place the mouthpiece in the center of your lips and buzz" if the student knew what *buzzing* meant, or for that matter, what a *mouthpiece* was. The fact is that your new student probably will know nothing—absolutely nothing. By demonstrating competently and producing a good, characteristic tone, the teacher will be able to bring him along quickly.

In addition to techniques and methods courses, the instrumentalist should learn about the complexities of care and maintenance of various instruments. Although knowledge is to be gained about caring for instruments, the thrust at this point is one of administration. Both choral and instrumental teachers are confronted with administrative details ranging from grading students and financing tours to purchasing equipment, uniforms, and choir robes to obtaining releases for travel and all the other thousands of details that go into being a music teacher. (It has been said that most of the music teacher's time is spent doing things that are distinctly unmusical, such as the administrative details just mentioned.) We have a piece of advice that sounds rather childish, although in truth, it seems to work for many. As you progress through music education courses, keep careful loose-leaf notebooks, one for each area of study. One notebook should be maintained for administration, one for literature, one for teaching techniques, and so on. These notebooks should grow to accumulate not just the wisdom of your professors but also lesson plans, goals, and objective statements that you so carefully work out for class. Become an ardent reader of professional journals. Articles that will aid you in the future should be clipped and saved.

There is one orchestra director we know whose notebooks go back many years. If he has a problem with a trill fingering, he knows precisely where to go for helpful information. If he wants to know something about library record systems, he has a notebook on cataloguing systems with forms he has gathered from his colleagues. His notebooks on instrumental music and music catalogues are nothing short of amazing. We venture to say that he could provide the name of the publisher and the price for virtually everything published in music. While some may feel that this orchestra director has gone too far, he is an excellent and efficient teacher because he never has to search for information—he can and does devote his time to teaching of students.

The purpose of methods classes, then, is to synthesize information about how to teach and to support prospective teachers with information that is critical to their functioning as a professional. Teachers must escape the low-level information-gathering concerns we discussed earlier. The logical beginning for this process are methods courses in music education. Professors supply valuable information, demonstrate how to teach in a variety of situations, and allow students to teach under controlled conditions in methods courses. Consider the potential usefulness of the information as you select courses in general music methods, instrumental methods, choral methods, junior high school methods, or Orff techniques, Kodaly techniques, and other specialized methods courses taught by music education faculty.

Education Courses

A majority of music education curricula require students to enroll in courses staffed by a department or college of education. Known generally as "professional education courses," they comprise the common core or approach for all teachers. These courses structure academic knowledge of children and how they grow, develop, and learn. Students should gain an understanding of the history and philosophy of our educational system and begin to assert an identity as teachers. Many programs direct attention to "educational media" that range from file projects to tape recorders.

Another large segment of coursework offered by the education faculty deals with tests and general evaluation techniques. A particularly relevant group of skills may be those dealing with handicapped students, especially now that many of these students are mainstreamed into the regular classrooms of our public schools.

The term "mainstreamed" brings up another facet of the coursework in education: learning to speak the language. Like many other professional fields, education has developed its own terminology. To some, this language is an important means of clear communication among professionals; to others, it remains only jargon. No matter which you consider it, it is the language that will be expected in communicating with the principal, the school board, and supervisors. The courses one completes in the education department should give fluency in this "education" language.

Student Teaching.   Far and away the most valuable part of the preparation in music education is the time spent in the school, functioning and behaving as a teacher; still supervised and guided, yes, but as a teacher nonetheless. Student teaching, which usually occurs in the senior year, is valuable for at least three reasons. First, it provides the student with regular, continuing, professional contact with children and teaching. Many who thought they would be teachers change their minds after the experience, whereas others are excited and enthused by it. Just as one learns to play the clarinet by practicing the clarinet, so one learns to be a teacher by practicing teaching. Only through practicing will you be ready to go out and teach on your own.

The second reason that student teaching is important is that it allows you to prove to yourself, and to the profession, that you are competent. Despite the artificiality of the student teaching situation, it remains the best test available for your future performance as a teacher. Student teaching is rigorous and important; nobody wants to hire someone with a C in student teaching. The evaluation made during the student teaching process is important to students who pass student teaching and students who fail. This evaluative hurdle is critical in the selection of competent teachers for the future. Many students find that they are not able to cope with teaching during the student teaching process. This self-selection process is as important as the formalized grading imposed on student teachers. Students who do well, achieve high grades, and enjoy teaching have had the first successful teaching experiences in this process.

The third reason for the importance of student teaching is to introduce young educators to the life of a teacher. It is one thing to prepare for a class presentation and go out to a local elementary school, teach it, and then see a professor for comments. It is quite another matter to teach all day, every day, and look to the accomplishments of the students to tell how well you have done.

Something as important as this teaching experience should not be entered into lightly. The selection of the school and teacher with whom you work is of supreme importance. We suggest that students get involved early. Investigate available student teaching sites and centers used by the university. Talk to other students who have taught in each center; see if you can arrange a visit to several schools. Most departments will honor students' wishes concerning placement in a particular school district for student teaching if possible. Participate in the selection process, or place blind faith in your professors and assume responsibility for the consequences.

On some campuses there is a choice in the manner in which student teaching can be undertaken. Some schools permit students to teach part-time for a year rather than full-time for a semester. Some colleges do not allow students to go far from campus and have students return to campus each day. The best situation for student teaching is to do it full-time, away from campus, living in the community in which you teach. The other situations are just too far removed from reality to be meaningful in the introduction to teaching.

The current trend in student teaching, as we have mentioned, is to place students in schools during the sophomore and junior years in conjunction with education courses or music education methods courses. These opportunities to visit schools and work with children and teachers may aid university students in making connections between discussions of methodology in the classroom and seeing teachers implement various methodologies.

Another variation on student teaching experiences is that of the internship. Proposed as parallel to the medical intern, these programs would place students in an intern program for one year after graduation to aid them during their first year of teaching. Cost constraints in both college budgets and school districts make these programs more and more difficult to find. Professional teachers associations (including teacher unions) have also started to limit the number of student teachers that can be accommodated by a given student teaching center each year. These are matters to be discussed as students approach the senior year and plan to student teach.

Electives

Electives are those cherished portions of the curriculum that seem to vaporize before the music education student's very eyes. A well-planned curriculum will allow 10 to 15 percent of the required credits for a degree program to fall into the elective category. To the authors' knowledge, no music education degree in this country has this number of electives available for students to choose courses in general education or in music. The fact that so few electives are available to students in music education is based on the high number of requirements for teacher certification. When students complete requirements for certification in most states, they are left with few elective hours in a degree program.

It is not our purpose to prescribe the last vestige of student decisions but to suggest that these credits not be left to random choice because of a college timetable or sequence of course offerings. This valuable portion of the undergraduate degree, if used carefully, can offer students an expertise that can make them unique among their fellow students. The writers have known music education students who have minored in English education, math education, physical education, electrical engineering, physics, and computer science. Most of the students who pursued these minor fields of expertise began with a careful consideration of their electives and matched them to their interests outside the field of music.

Areas of concern to the educational profession include working with handicapped children, children in special education, and technology in education. These are all fields in which the students can become involved through elective courses in the degree program. As we said earlier, one aim undergraduates should have in considering courses is that of their future marketability while searching for a teaching position. Teachers with distinctive transcripts who can do the normal job of teaching music plus hold interests in innovative areas certainly have an advantage.

The other avenue for selecting electives is that of concentrating efforts in one specific field. Rather than broaden themselves, some students elect to specialize and become expert in one field. The serious undergraduate student who looks forward to employment as a high school band director should concentrate time not only in conducting but in marching band techniques, jazz band techniques, and perhaps instrument repair and some educational administration courses.

Let us close this discussion by simply stating that students who complete minimum requirements for a degree and take inconsequential electives will have more difficulty in convincing future employers of their seriousness about teaching.

The Music Educator

In discussing each component of an undergraduate curriculum, we have chosen not to place a relative value on the various components. While it is easy for us to say that keyboard instruction is valued and education courses are valuable, we have not tossed a coin and suggested that learning to improvise on piano is more important than learning the educational views of Plato and Socrates. Our warning has consistently been that teachers tend to lean toward the practical side (the *doing* side) of teaching while neglecting broader issues. No less is this true for students, for students can easily see the value in learning to test voices for high school choir as something that is practical and critical to their survival as music teachers. Students may have more difficulty in agreeing with our suggested scholarly approach to the profession.

In closing this chapter, we restate the concern that the profession be led, guided, and molded by scholars. Discussing the value of music in an educational system, scholars have a better chance at placing music into context than do teaching technicians whose only concerns are rehearsing, performing, and recruiting. Each candidate for an undergraduate degree in music education holds the potential for true scholarship. Through striving for higher levels of intellectual understanding, teachers will be more effective, the profession will be healthier, students will gain a valued model, and the community will profit from an enlightened youth. The chapter that follows details the development of music education in recent times. These developments have not taken place as a result of lackluster teachers with no creative or intellectual interests.

Questions for Discussion

1. Select a teacher you have either observed or have had as a teacher in class and assess the levels of concern the teacher exhibits through his or her actions. Knowing the teaching situation in which this person is working, is the teacher effective working with these levels of concern?
2. Considering the areas outlined as important to music education students, which areas do you feel are adequately covered through requirements in your degree program? Are courses available to you in all areas discussed?
3. Discuss with your professor or other teachers the degree program they completed. What strengths and weaknesses did they see in their program as compared to the program in which you are enrolled?
4. What value do you see in learning evaluation techniques for the general student population? Do IQ tests have any bearing on how you will teach music?

5. In reviewing all the teachers you can recall in high school and college, what percentage would you judge as articulate scholars? Is your attitude any different toward these teachers in retrospect? Toward any other teachers you have had in the past?

Recommended Readings

Hall, Gene E. "The Concerns-Based Approach to Facilitating Change," *Education Horizons,* Summer, 1979, p. 203.

————, and Loucks, Susan. "Teacher Concerns as a Basis for Facilitating and Personalizing Staff Development," *Teachers College Record* 80, no. 1 (1978): 36–53.

4/the development of music education

In chapter 1, a general discussion of education and schooling suggested that socialization is one of the primary reasons for these institutions. The discussion also pointed out the differences between education (in a broad sense) and schooling (in a specific sense). The societal aspects of education cannot be overemphasized. Education is a form of human interaction that has been institutionalized (or designed or programmed) to accomplish social functions of specific purpose.

The broad purpose of education is clear, and always has been. If the student of education can grasp the broad social purposes of education, specific tasks in teaching are more easily ordered. If the student of teaching uses only current, specific objectives to guide actions in the classroom, the result may be a vacillating teaching style based on current trends, fads, and "pop" psychosocial theory.

Education as a Social Process

Education is a social process made possible through human relationships. Although the specifics of educational content may differ from culture to culture, the dependence of individuals upon others for learning does not. Humans are not born with the knowledge to survive and assimilate a culture; they acquire it through one form or another of teaching and learning. In a sense, education is a communicative process. We have defined education as a continuing process in which a person learns a way of life. The process continues from birth to death through interactions with one's family, peer groups, the social community, and schools.

Schooling was also defined as a more formal institution in which some part of the educational process occurs in our present society. Much of the educational process has been given over to the schools. Many of the topics once considered proprietary to the home and family environment have been thrust upon the schools in recent years. Included are such controversial topics as sex education, ethics, values education, consumer education, and other subjects that cannot be categorized as "three Rs" or "basic skills." A continuing argument about school prayers and religion in the schools is another example of educational topics that are difficult to resolve in the American schooling system.

Defining the specifics of schooling in the United States is difficult without considering a particular community, since local schools boards and members of the community determine the school "curriculum." A general discussion, then, must include the social dimensions of education that are important and are generally designated as appropriate topics for a school curriculum. The social purposes of schooling include (1) cultural transmission, (2) vocational preparation, and (3) socialization.

Cultural Transmission

The *cultural* component is a process of communicating the society's heritage. Without this transmission of culture, each generation would have to start without the advantage of previous knowledge. Culture depends on a continuum of knowledge, beliefs, and values.

The transmission of beliefs and values is critical to a society. For example, a value such as monogamy is transmitted by the culture; it acts to promote social stability. Many beliefs that define the quality of life are keys to the prevention of social chaos.

The transmission of values is something easily demonstrated in music education. Copland's "Billy the Kid Suite" and Brahms Symphony no. 3 are valued as "works of art"; the music teacher transmits the idea of "art" effectively or ineffectively to students. Neither of these cultural objects holds the same cultural value for the South American Indian. The values attached to art objects vary widely from culture to culture.

Cultural transmission in the American educational system is accomplished through interaction among members of elected school boards, family members, teachers, and school administrators. The cultural content of the curriculum is less clearly defined than any other area of the school curriculum. Many beliefs and values are fostered in the family and may coincide with those of the society at large. In some cases, the school acts as a forum for students to weigh their beliefs against those commonly held by society.

In an important sense, the arts are excellent mirrors of the society that encourages them. Indeed, one of the best ways for students to understand the functioning values of a culture is through the study of artworks that a society produces. A true understanding of the Japanese, for example, cannot be attained through study of the country's social mores, economic system, and political history alone; also needed is some study of the unique Japanese aesthetic, which in large measure defines the culture's point of view. A true understanding of other cultures is also impossible without a discussion of the aesthetics of the culture. The systematic study of theater, the visual arts, dance, and music (with all their variants in our pluralistic society) is a proper function of American schooling.

Vocational Preparation

A second purpose for education is vocational preparation. Throughout history, the "educational system" has transmitted survival skills to the young. In earlier days these skills included hunting, personal defense, and shelter building; skills were transmitted by the family or the tribe. As the notion of a *vocation* or work apart from the family developed, the educational system responded with apprenticeships, guild training, and eventually technical schools. In America today, the task of preparing students to "make a living" is vested in the formal schooling system more often than in the family or society at large.

Transmitting skills from generation to generation becomes more complex as one considers modern societies with computer processing, automobile transportation, and mega environments. No one person can develop all the skills needed to be totally self-sufficient in such a complex society. Schooling is essential because no one person can transmit *all* that is considered important in the culture. The parent or family is ill-equipped to teach children the necessary skills to learn a vocation in today's society. Fewer and fewer children follow the vocation of their parents. Rather than take advantage of the opportunity to learn a skill from parents, children turn to the schools for vocational training in an area that is often beyond the family's experience.

With little training for "job placement" remaining in the home, the secondary schools have taken on the task of vocational training. Although some of this training may begin in the earlier grades, most such training has been concentrated in the secondary schools and, more recently, in the community colleges.

The secondary school has developed a three-level curriculum for students that encompasses the academic, general, and technical tracks. All three curricula are often offered in the same school but have different purposes. The academic curriculum does little to prepare the student for a vocation; instead, it prepares the student for advanced studies at the university level. Most people reading this text are products of an academic curriculum. Students working in the arts are most often from the ranks of the "academic" track.

The general curriculum and the technical track of secondary schooling have been extended in recent years to the community college. The student in the general curriculum normally does not receive the foreign language and classics background of the academic, nor the technical training in woodworking, metalworking, agriculture, or business that technical students select. The two-year degrees developed in junior and community colleges reflect another level of vocational preparation generated by the American society. Laboratory technicians, computer operators, and highly skilled mechanics are now trained in an "extended curriculum." A shortage of skilled workers has pushed apprentice-level training into the secondary school and junior college. Junior college curricula include courses in welding, heavy equipment maintenance, dental hygiene, and avionics. As the reader can surmise, these vocational curricula also include elective work in the arts.

Vocational preparation affects the secondary school arts program in a direct manner. Many of the intensive music performance programs in high schools defend their programs on the basis of vocational preparation. The attitude at these institutions is that students should have the opportunity to learn performance skills sufficient to compete in the professional world upon completion of high school. With the intense pace of many of these programs, students do develop to a high level of musicianship. Most students, however, also continue their work at the university level before attempting to enter the professional world as musicians. In this regard, the music program is perhaps the strongest of any in the arts. While some visual arts programs excel in preprofessional training, theater and dance lag far behind.

One question we must ask as we review the music curriculum is, "Should the primary purpose of high school music be vocational preparation?" If it is, we have failed to meet this goal. If all students enrolled in instrumental and choral music performance groups pursued vocations as musicians, we would have few of the citizenry left in the audience. Programs that hold such aims tend to be highly selective and highly competitive. These programs also exclude many students who have average or below-average performance abilities.

Socialization

The *socialization* dimension of schooling is essential to the cohesiveness of society. Members of any society must learn to interact on a day-to-day basis, and many of these interactions are learned in the controlled environment of the schools. The first time that some children compete for attention, toys, or space is in the classroom. Learning to interact with others occurs, for most children, in nursery school, kindergarten, or first grade. The promotion of peer-group interactions is important, for through such interactions children are exposed to the experiences, values, and beliefs of others in society. These contacts are a broadening influence on the child's perception of the world.

The school allows the child to explore social interactions outside the family unit. The formation of friendships with other children of the same age is a direct outgrowth of the process. Grade school children form "clubs" of common interest. These interactions also encompass boy-girl relationships since most schools in the United States bring children of both sexes into the same school. This is a valuable function of the socialization process.

The schools must also be considered a "place" to put children—a ten- to twelve-year nursery. Although many teachers recognize this as a real function of the schools, many members of society do not understand the impact that schools, and children in schools, have on the economy. During contract discussions between teachers and school boards, the point can be made that schools are efficient caretakers of children during the parents' working day. Add to this the number of potential workers kept out of the job market by being in schools and colleges, and one begins to see the integral place of schools in the economy of the country. With the number of working mothers increasing yearly, schools play a part in the financial success of the family. If working parents had to pay for child care for school-age children, a large proportion of their incomes would go for caretaking.

The economic impact of schools is best noted at the upper end of the schooling ladder. Enrollments in community and junior colleges interact directly with the level of unemployment. When unemployment is high, junior college enrollments are high; when jobs are easily attainable, junior college enrollments suffer. Students return to school during high unemployment cycles to learn new skills to find better jobs or broaden their skills to become more attractive to employers. This interaction is an ongoing societal process.

Music Education as a Social Process

In considering the arts as a portion of the social function of schooling, some parallels are easily drawn. Perhaps the easiest purpose to relate is the "place that the arts hold in society." If the purposes of education are understood in a social setting, then the purpose of the arts in society, and consequently the purpose of the arts in schooling, should follow in a logical manner.

The reasons given by music teachers for having "music in the schools" have some base in the social structure of the community. Too often, however, music teachers assume that the community conforms to their view of the purpose of music and the importance of music in the lives of children. Careful inspection of these stated and intended purposes must be examined by arts educators, and the community at large.

As with education in general, a definition of the role of music in schools is difficult without input from the community. Some communities support music instruction as a integral part of the curriculum, while others barely meet the "state" requirements of music instruction, if any exist. A discussion of the societal role of music can focus on the same components as that of schooling: *cultural, vocational,* and *social.*

Music in the Culture

Music teachers have clearly defined curricula in music in order to transmit the musical heritage of America. This *cultural* justification of music instruction is valid and complies with the general discussion of the social puposes of schooling. Difficulties arise only when the content of the curriculum does not reflect what the community considers to be part of the cultural heritage. If a finite body of information on and about music could be collected for the schooling process that everyone agreed was requisite to understanding American society, there would be little discussion of the reasons for music instruction or the purposes of spending monies on such instruction.

In trying to transmit values and beliefs about music, reflect on the importance of music to the nonmusician members of society. Do they need to know or recognize the Mozart Symphony in G Minor, K550? Must they appreciate opera? What part of the culture that is music should become part of schooling? The music teacher will include much more in an answer than will the general populace. If teachers do not accomplish some level of the cultural transmission process, the art of music will drop from the cultural makeup of what we know as society.

Most people have heard of Beethoven's Fifth Symphony and know about string quartets. Few of these people could not identify the symphony on hearing it played or tell the instrumentation of the string quartet. The questions most often used in an evaluation of music programs seem to be fact oriented. A large portion of the society makes music part of its daily life through listening to radio, television, and sound recordings. This interaction with the arts (music) is a real and significant *part* of the culture. The music that composes the diet for the "average" listener varies as much as the population. Black children commonly listen to different music than white children do. Country and Western music has regional followings and can be considered "folk music." This use of music as a part of daily societal influence is too often ignored by educators. Teachers must understand that music is part of the culture and has a broad acceptance.

Music in Vocational Preparation

The vocational aspect of music education exists in the performance-based sector of schooling. Many music programs in instrumental and choral music are performance-based, meaning the primary goals are to (1) develop an excellent performance environment; (2) train students to be successful, competent musicians; and (3) select "talented" students for the music program.

This inverse listing of goals points to a selection process in many performance-oriented music programs. The first step is to select *only* talented children, using some criteria for admission into the "program." These students then become the chosen few who will be trained to become "competent" musicians. The teacher works hard to develop performance situations to foster the musical growth of student performers. This approach is, certainly, vocational education (schooling). Students selected to participate in the music performance programs in most high schools have the opportunity to continue their training at the university level or enter directly into music performance as a vocation.

Music performance programs are skill oriented. The music teacher, committed to developing musicianship through performance, has a clear definition of the purpose and objectives of the program. The question of performance goals is easily answered and evaluation is constant: Can the children play or sing the materials in the curriculum?

In broadening the question to include all children in the schools, what skills should members of society acquire in the school music curriculum? Should everyone be able to sing in tune, recognize a Sousa march, or distinguish the difference between a violin and a violin-cello? *Perception skills* are considered part of most school curricula and should be developed into *listening skills* for the student. The ability to be a critical listener should be a result of a school curriculum, but it is separate from the question of vocational education.

Music in Socialization

From a social viewpoint, the music curriculum seems more clearly defined in terms of performance and vocational preparation than in terms of a general cultural transmission to society. Consider the final layer of complicity, that of the social process in music instruction. The social dimension of the music classroom has long been recognized by teachers. From grade school to university, music has been used as a vehicle to facilitate social interaction and learning. Music has been used as a component of social studies, history, geography, and foreign language curricula, to name a few.

The social dimension of schooling certainly extends to the music classroom. A number of students participate in music ensembles for the close social interactions that occur among fellow performers. Without question, activities such as marching band, jazz band, and swing choir engender this group social interaction and identity. Students who participate in such performances tend to identify with the group and gain peer recognition from this involvement. To ignore this component of the student involvement in the music program is to miss a major reason for student involvement in music activities.

The Development of Music Instruction

Schooling in America had its beginnings in 1630 in Puritan New England. Our country's education system is unique for it is not directed by the national central government. The United States is one of the few countries to have educational control at the local level (towns and municipalities). At first, this approach was a reaction to the government control of European schools and authoritarian churches. This tradition was strengthened by the isolation of most communities in America during the seventeenth century.

The early settlers along the Atlantic coast developed forms of government that grew out of democratically deciding to do things for themselves rather than leave decisions to others. Views of local autonomy were trans-ferred to the educational systems as they were developed. As early as 1642, the Massachusetts Bay Colony passed ordinances requiring each town to provide school expenses from town funds. Since these towns were supported by tax revenues, the early American school systems be-came the first really public schools in the world.

The pattern established in Massachusetts became a model for the col-onies, and by the time of the American Revolution, the precedent was established based upon the principle that the schooling of the youth was essential to the well-being of the country. An extension of this logic asserted that the state has an obligation to provide an "education at pub-lic expense." For an excellent overview of the history of American educa-tion as it applies to music education, one should read the detailed and colorful account presented by Birge.[1]

Although it is tempting to present a general account of the history of music education in this text, the student is referred to other sources for this information. Our purpose is to review general trends in education as they apply to music education without detailing specific dates and places. Early history is of interest, but the trends and developments in education that will most affect your teaching have occurred since 1920.

In 1929 the federal government renamed the Department of Education (founded in 1867) the U.S. Office of Education. This office was charged with the collection and publication of factual information concerning edu-cational practices in different parts of the country and with the general promotion of public education. In 1939 this office became part of the Federal Security Agency and, in 1953, part of the Department of Health, Education, and Welfare. In 1980 the Carter administration created a new Department of Education; recognizing the importance of American schools to the society, President Carter gave education a cabinet-level voice to aid in the formulation of U.S. policy. Throughout these changes, the basic commitment of the government to local autonomy in education-al matters largely remained. Although some have attacked federal policy in education as intrusive, the curriculum remains the responsibility of the states and local school systems. This decentralization is, as it was in the seventeenth-century, unique among nations of the world.

Educational Principles and Psychology

With the emergence of educational psychology at the turn of the century, several experimental movements in education became popular. The work

---

[1]Edward Bailey Birge, *History of Public School Music in the United States* (Washington, D.C.: Music Educators National Conference, 1966).

of William James, considered the father of American educational psychology, was stated as a behavioristic view in his *Principles and Talks to Teachers on Psychology*. The premise, now well known, was that man should be considered a living organism with instinctive reactions to his environment. The potential of educational psychology grew as educators began considering the growing body of knowledge about human behavior.

During the 1920s, the work of Sigmund Freud had an impact on a group of educators. This limited influence caused changes in the classroom atmosphere and diminished the authoritarian climate of the schools. The acceptance of psychoanalysis as a viable endeavor represented a new, scientific approach to human growth and the learning process.

Following William James, philosopher John Dewey defended functionalism, the view that human beings are products of both heredity and environment. To put his theories to the test, Dewey directed the Laboratory Schools of the University of Chicago. His theories grew to a philosophy of education, and Dewey was an active participant in the Progressive Education movement. The basis of Progressive Education was democratic education through individual activities. The Progressive Education Association, founded in 1919, promoted freer, more individualized schooling. Few guidelines were given, since the group held that experimental approaches should be tried in teaching.

In reviewing the history of education, one can see that schooling was aided and shaped by philosophers, psychologists, professional association, and interest groups. The effect of any one movement or individual would be hard to isolate. In like manner, in considering historical developments in music education, we must conclude that a large number of forces affected the development of music teaching. The development of "serious" music in American society, the first symphony orchestra, and the first touring music ensembles all had their impact on the acceptance of music in the school curriculum. To separate musical development in America from music education would be as difficult as separating music education from the development of the public schools.

Change in the schooling process tends to be slow; public education, however, was broadened steadily to include more curriculum offerings through the 1920s and '30s. The conclusion of World War I saw a great increase in high school bands and orchestra programs as musicians returned from the military. As the number of high school bands increased, the number of professional bands seemed to decline. The famous Sousa band was dissolved in 1925, leaving band music to the public schools.

Music programs became more specialized, and performance programs centered on the talented student. The 1930s saw the growth of national solo and ensemble competitions. Begun in 1934, these contests ran until

1941 when the travel restrictions of World War II made continuing the festivals impossible. In the district and state finals of the 1940 national music contests, some 10,000 bands, orchestras, and choruses participated, along with over 15,000 instrumental soloists.[2]

The adoption of the GI Bill after World War II ensured a plentiful supply of teachers. Music programs expanded again, primarily in choral and instrumental performance. The general music program changed also, as can be seen in the music textbooks of those days, which show that more emphasis was placed on musical activities apart from singing. With "curriculum" expansion, preparing students to sing in church choirs was no longer a primary objective, and the interest of teachers turned to other music-related information and activities. The emphasis on music reading for all elementary students, which had diminished since the 1930s, was not replaced by any single system of music training.

Several trends in general music have been evident since 1940. The methods applied to music teaching in Hungary by Kodály have taken hold in a growing number of schools. Teachers have been trained in the Kodály approach through established Kodály institutes, which base their training on a singing model with a return to solfege.

General music teachers have become familiar with the work of Carl Orff and his approach to training children in music. Music teachers have adopted Orff materials and adapted them to their own teaching styles and to the American educational system. Combining aspects of Orff and Kodály approaches to teaching perhaps typifies the American music teacher. One criticism of this eclectic approach is that teachers use parts of many teaching methods and philosophies but have no logical or "complete" system or method.

In instrumental music, popular approaches have included the Suzuki method of teaching violin. This method was established in Japan by Shinichi Suzuki as part of his Talent Education Program. The Americanized version has been successful within limits, but again, American teachers have taken great liberties with many of Suzuki's philosophies and methods. The authors note that the most successful American Suzuki programs are those that remain fairly faithful to the original.

Beginning in the 1960s, when the increasing number of students exceeded the capabilities of the music programs to teach *all* students, the music program became more selective than before. It was a comfortable position indeed. Why select less qualified students when only a limited number of students can participate in a program? In this matter, the music teachers made the same decisions that a football coach would make.

[2]*National School Music Competition Festivals, 1940 Reports* (Chicago: National School Band, Orchestra, and Vocal Associations, 1940).

With the selection of better students and the rejection of weaker students in performance programs, the quality of music performances improved. The key to maintaining a "successful" music program in the late 1960s was the production of a highly regarded music performance program. Usually the instrumental music performance program overshadowed the choral program, but the critical ingredient for both was performance.

Music Education Since the 1960s

With the enormous increase in the number of students attending public schools and a liberal public attitude toward government involvement in education, the 1960s brought support in the form of large federal and foundation grants to develop better music curriculum materials. Perhaps the best known of these projects was the Contemporary Music Project for Creativity in Music Education. This 1963 program, known in its abbreviated form as CMP, led to what has become the "comprehensive musicianship" approach. CMP encouraged the development of music teaching and learning that was integrated in presentation. Individual disciplines of history, theory, analysis, and performance became components of surprisingly broad courses of study.

The first major funding from the Office of Education directed toward the improvement of the music curriculum sponsored the Yale Seminar in Music Education in 1963. The Yale conference laid the groundwork for a ten-year program of music curriculum revision. In all, the U.S. Office of Education funded sixty-four projects in music education, which varied in duration from one to five years. The scope of these projects ranged from simple pilot studies to large curriculum development efforts. Reimer states, "Perhaps more than any other single event, the Yale conference of 1963 demonstrated the inevitable movement of music education in the 'schooling decade'—that revolutionary period of school reform beginning with Sputnik in 1957 and ending some ten years later."[3] The membership at the seminar included thirty-one participants (11 theorists/composers, 4 conductors, 3 musicologists, 1 public school administrator, 2 performers, 3 college music administrators, 5 public or private school teachers, 1 music critic, and 1 educator). Recommendations included a call for a broader base of repertory for public school instruction and a greater emphasis on creativity. One result of the Yale conference surfaced seven years later as the Juilliard Repertory Project, which generated cur-

[3]Bennett Reimer, "The Yale Conference: A Critical Review," *Council for Research in Music Education*, Bulletin no. 60 (Fall 1979): 5.

riculum materials for the elementary school.[4]

Also in 1964, the Office of Education funded the National Conference on New Uses of Educational Media in Music. At this conference, which was typical of funded seminars and conferences of the 1960s, multimedia devices were displayed with suggested applications for the music curriculum.

The 1965 Manhattanville Music Curriculum Program was directed by Ronald B. Thomas. This program was generated in response to the Yale Seminar's call for a more creative approach to music education. The MMCP was based on a composition model in which students, regardless of age, were given limited compositional tools and sound sources and asked to compose, then perform, and finally analyze the music developed in the classroom. Although Thomas developed his curriculum in a creative atmosphere, many of his ideas were drawn from techniques used by teachers in public schools throughout the country. The resulting approach was a creative model in which children expressed themselves through the music they composed and performed. Another significant future of the MMCP was its effort at utilizing a then popular educational theory, the "spiral curriculum" of Jerome Bruner.

Two large conferences on music education, both sponsored by the federal government, took place in 1966: the Ohio State Conference on Research in Music Education and the International Seminar on the Education of Music Teachers. This same year saw the first phase of the "Development and Trial of a Two Year Program in String Instruction" by Paul Rolland. This project was continued through 1970 and generated instructional materials, films, and teachers' manuals. This curriculum for violin students is based on principles of movement that allow students to play with little tension and to progress rapidly during the first two years of instruction.

In addition to the Yale Seminar and the Manhattanville Project, the Tanglewood Symposium of 1967 is perhaps the most often mentioned federally funded project of the 1960s. The members attending the symposium, which was sponsored by Music Educators National Conference at Tanglewood, Massachusetts, drafted the *Tanglewood Declaration*, which reinforced the view "that education must have as major goals the art of living, the building of personal identity, and nurturing creativity. Since the study of music can contribute much to these ends, we now call for music to be placed in the core of the school curriculum."[5]

There was a positive atmosphere during the 1960s, with an abundance

[4]Fahrer Alison and Paul A. Harry, *Juilliard Repertory Library* (Cincinnati: Canyon Press, 1970).

[5]Robert A. Choate, ed., *Documentary Report of the Tanglewood Symposium* (Washington, D.C.: Music Educators National Conference, 1968), p. 139.

of federal funding available to universities and schools interested in trying new ideas. Young composers had a chance to work with high school students on completion of their university work and were supported for one or two years. The arts flourished in education, as education flourished with millions of dollars of support from foundations and federal sources. During this time the federal government also established regional research and development laboratories to work with the Office of Education. These laboratories were charged with investigating the best educational research and theory through implementing consumer-level materials. Some funded programs were conceived only as pilot projects, a "what if" concept with no predetermined outcome. Many of the teachers that you, the reader, had in high school, were products of this "schooling decade." This was also the period of the new math and other experimental programs. Programs in many diverse fields were supported by the National Science Foundation, the National Endowment for the Arts, the National Endowment for the Humanities, or the Office of Education.

As federal administrations changed, policies toward education changed with them. In the early 1970s, American educators began the widespread adoption of a new educational setting that originated in the English primary schools: the "open classroom." The open classroom allowed for individual effort in a much less formal environment. Open education encouraged students to work individually or in small groups. Rarely were any two groups working on the same material at the same level. Teachers were trained to work in open classrooms, but some teachers could not cope with the noise level, the increased activity, and the seeming lack of structure of this new approach.

Even school architecture was altered to allow for the open learning environment. Elementary schools contained large common areas for student activity with smaller modules surrounding them for individual work. Many curriculum materials developed in the 1960s were employed in new "media centers" and activity centers. The publishers of school textbooks developed learning packets and study modules for individualized instruction.

Music education responded to open education with individualized listening stations and with workbooks and cassette tapes for independent study. Music teachers had to rethink their classroom management techniques to allow for this new freedom of activity. Teachers spent countless hours devising musical activities in lessons that could be used in small-group settings. As with most major changes in education, teachers who were adaptable, energetic, and imaginative succeeded in creating an exciting and productive classroom experience for their students.

One area of music instruction that did not fit the open classroom model was music performance. Those teachers who conducted successful music performance groups did so by isolating students in separate rooms in a traditional music classroom. Of further concern was the beginning instrumental program. The noise level generated by beginning instrumental students necessitated isolating student groups from the large common areas of the open classroom.

Some school systems that adopted the open classroom concept, and even constructed new buildings to accommodate it, abandoned the concept after a few years. Although the movement spread extensively on the elementary school level, few high schools engaged in this approach to education. Modular scheduling for high schools was one attempt at allowing high school students some flexibility in the open school concept.

By the fall of 1972 a nationwide effort to improve school programs was established under the concept of educational accountability. A cooperative accountability project, a three-year study, was initiated in April 1972 and was financed by funds from the Elementary and Secondary Education Act of 1965. Its purpose was to establish the best possible match between education and accountability: to lay down broad guidelines and specific programs under which education could make a meaningful accounting of itself both internally and externally.[6] Primarily, accountability calls for the assessment of established goals and performance-oriented objectives. High energy costs and other skyrocketing operational costs of schools in the mid-1970s increased the necessity for cost-effective education. Any saving made by closing schools or reducing staff was more than offset by the rising inflation.

As costs continue to rise, administrators frantically looked for means to document fair return on expenditures by the taxpayers. They did this often not by choice but under duress from the legislature. By 1974 twenty-three states had enacted laws addressing educational accountability.

Heightening the anxieties of the education community, taxpayers resisted increased educational costs. School board referenda for increased funds were defeated regularly in the 1970s. Schools also came under attack for a failure to educate students. Test scores declined. School systems were sued by high school graduates who were illiterate. The blame was no longer placed on the student who had failed; the entire educational system was held accountable.

It was at this point that a frustrated cry for solutions brought us the "back to basics" movement. Usually defined as reading, writing, and computations, the "basic skills" are relatively easy to measure. Declining test scores, complaints of ill-prepared college freshmen, and the experiences of employers (including the U.S. armed forces) indicate that stu-

[6]John Cooksey, "An Accountability Report for Music Education," *Council for Research in Music Education*, Bulletin no. 36 (Spring 1974): 6–7.

dents simply are not performing at satisfactory levels in basic skills.

Some researchers blame this lack of performance on television; some blame general social conditions. Some attack the "new math." Some in the population of recently desegregrated schools, both black and white, blame the disruption caused by busing. The rather simplistic solution proposed by leaders of "back to basics" is to remove distractions and increase instructional time in reading, writing, and computation. To do this, "frill" subjects must be reduced or removed from the schools. Unfortunately, music and art instruction are prime targets for this reduction.

We propose another cause and another solution. During the 1960s and '70s, the nature of what children do in schools began to change. From copying questions off the chalk board and the answering them in writing, American schools entered a "fill-in-the-blank" generation. It was easier for the teacher and easier for the student. Some curriculum developers became enamored with "experiential objectives" in which the goal was not observable change in the student but merely "going through" a set of experiences. *But children are not plants.* They do not learn efficiently by osmosis.

What is needed in American schools is not a return to the basics; we never really stopped teaching basic skills. What is needed is a return to *rigor*, both in general education and in music education. We note that performance programs of high quality, even those that place unreasonable demands on students in terms of practice and rehearsal time (maybe especially those programs) are not under attack by basic skills advocates. They are of obvious high quality. Attacking these programs is almost unthinkable in a culture that sprang from the Protestant work ethic. What is needed is a new rigor in general music. Only then will musical study achieve its goals, and only then will it rightly compete for space in the curriculum.

The Current Role of the Music Educator

Music educators must seriously consider two new avenues of music instruction. As the cost of education continues to rise, the allocation of funds from school budgets will be directed toward successful programs, especially those that involve many students. Subjects perceived as "basic" to becoming a productive member of society will have first consideration in this diminishing funding of public education. Although the number of school-age children is predicted to drop in this decade, the cost of schooling will rise. Efforts to reduce this cost will cause the repeated review of educational programs in the arts as well as in all other areas of the curriculum. By broadening the definition of music education to include lifelong learning and recreational music, we can enlarge the student population in music education.

Higher education in America has moved from a selective educational institution to a mass education model. The development of junior and community colleges has advanced training in education and made it available to nearly everyone in society. This mass education tendency has developed with little impact on the arts. The two-year certificate in technical training rarely includes arts courses. A two-year arts certificate is available in music at some schools, however.

Lifelong learning implies continued education for the citizenry. Whether this education takes place in a public school, a community college, a university, a community center, or a park should be of little concern to the music educator of the 1980s. This new breed of music educator must be prepared to work with students of any age and in the public schools or the community at large.

There will continue to be many "bandwagon" movements in education. The discerning teacher must choose carefully where to place his or her energy. Many of the fads in teaching last for a short time and are replaced with new fads or more stable solutions. In considering the social aspects of schooling and of music education, the reader should consider our aging population, the diminishing school-age population, and fewer financial resources. With some adjustments in music education, the coming years can be as productive as the highly financed 1960s.

Summary of Major Trends

In reviewing the development of music education, one can see that music instruction started as a general curriculum component in the colonies and became very specialized. Some trends in music education that follow the development of schooling since 1900 can be summarized as follows:

1. Programs have expanded as student populations have increased at all levels of instruction from 1900 through 1975.
2. Universities and higher education institutions are changing from selective education to mass education institutions.
3. The connection between more education (schooling) and financial well-being is becoming clearer.
4. New technology-based industries have increased the importance of adult education. As equal education opportunities are promoted, the growth of technical schools and community colleges will continue.

5. The population in the United States is aging and will continue to age for the next twenty-five years. In addition, the number of school-age children will decrease by 6 million students by the year 2000.

In reviewing current trends in education and music education, one sees numerous problems that must be solved:

1. Education is expensive with costs requiring vast portions of the gross national product. Although it is possible to lower costs with modern teaching methods, the profession is labor-intensive, and it is difficult to trim costs beyond a certain point. The per pupil cost of education will continue to rise.
2. New inventions such as cable television, satellite communication, videodisc, videotape, and computers are being used to reach children more efficiently and could reduce educational costs in the future.
3. Systems of lifelong education are being investigated to determine how to organize lifelong learning; retraining will become more and more important in the future.
4. Concerns for individualized instruction for students with learning disabilities will grow to include many more students in the schools as individualized instruction for the reduced student population becomes feasible.

Two points should be noted as one looks forward and discusses trends. First, education changes slowly. The adoption of the "new math" was never completed; it was discarded by many schools before some school systems even adopted it. Having technological aids for teachers and schools does not mean that they will be accepted quickly by the profession. This resistance to change will continue to impede the progress and implementation of many "new" methodologies or technologies.

Consider the number of teachers that have not investigated the Orff approach or tried any of the available materials. The question is not whether to use the Orff materials or not, it is whether the teacher investigated the possible application of the materials to his or her situation—and Orff has been with us for twenty years. Only when a number of teachers become excited about a methodology do they band together to "spread the word" about the great new find. Such has been the case with Orff and Kodály in the past decade. Yet, progress is still slow.

The second point all educators must consider is the current state of the profession. Too many educators label twenty-year-old methods as "current." Projects funded in the 1960s can hardly be considered current, yet many of these projects are still being heralded as new ideas. This situation only reinforces the point of the slowness of educational change.

Your interest in new ideas and your willingness to consider new methods should remain with you throughout your teaching career. If you lay these aside, your teaching techniques will not develop during your tenure as a teacher.

Questions for Discussion

1. Discuss the vocational considerations of students in a school music program who wish to become rock singers.
2. What music literature would you consider important for *all* students to learn as part of the socialization process of education?
3. What effect will individualization have on large music ensembles in the future?
4. Review the Tanglewood Report and discuss the declaration and its effect on school music as you know it today.

Recommended Readings

Birge, Edward B. *History of Public School Music in the United States*. Washington D.C.: Music Educators National Conference, 1966.

Choate, Robert A. *Documentary Report of the Tanglewood Symposium*, Washington, D.C. Music Educators National Conference, 1968.

Cooksey, John. "An Accountability Report for Music Education," *Council for Research in Music Education*, Bulletin no. 36, Spring 1974.

part
three

5/the acquisition of musical meaning

Among some musicians, and unfortunately among many music teachers as well, the notion has arisen that music and the other arts are separate from the ordinary flow of life. They view the arts as entities that require special skills and insights that only a "talented" few are capable of acquiring. If one were to ask these people what special things art supplies, they would answer that the arts are "up there" somewhere. They have placed artworks, artists, and those who are regular consumers of art on a high pedestal, insulated by a mystical space from ordinary existence. While pedestal sitting may be comfortable for those with ballooning egos, most people would agree that this unnatural position is not an acceptable stance for educational practice in a democratic society.

Yet school policies have been affected by this position, with select choirs, bands, and orchestras the only widely available form of music schooling after age fourteen or so. Our performance-oriented music curriculum makes it painfully evident to a large portion of the school population that music study is for others, not for them; they just "don't have it." Have *what*? That ill-defined something, "talent." Ask the student in the hall, or the man on the street, and you will find that he considers the art world to be a rarefied never-never land, a place where he has no stake, where he feels strange and lost, a place populated by people with whom he has no experience and to whom he bears no allegiance.

The consequences of this disenfranchisement of the population is evident in the society shaped by it. Lack of *public* support from ordinary citizens (the "great unwashed" to many in the arts community) can be seen in the percentage of the population that attend concerts, dance recitals, or museums. Attendance is "up" at most museums, and tickets are hard to obtain for many symphony orchestras, but the *percentage* of the population supporting the arts remains less than impressive. If this situation is ever to be remedied, it is up to the only institution that has a systematic chance to affect the attitudes of the population: the schools. Conventional wisdom and psychological research tell us that a lack of knowledge and understanding breeds fear and distrust. To remove this fear, the schools must attack the problem of the lack of true understanding of the arts as vigorously as they attack other societal problems. For the arts to flourish, the population must be schooled to understand that the arts are a nourishing part of day-to-day existence. In chapter 1 we maintained that any rationale for the inclusion of music in the schools must rely on those things that music can accomplish and that nothing else can. This chapter establishes a way of examining the meaning of music drawn from philosophy and psychology, which will be a natural and useful tool for the everyday curricular decision making of teachers.

The Pervasiveness of Music

When one begins to examine music and its *raison d'être*, an immediate observation can be made: Music is virtually ubiquitous. Music forms a fundamental part of the fabric of culture. So obvious is this fact that many students simply accept the existence of music as "natural" without ever asking the important questions raised by the presence of music: Why did human beings "invent" music? Why does music exist in virtually every culture? Why is music so important to us that it is almost impossible to envision life without it?

At some point in the progression from music student to music teacher, each must find answers to these and other questions. All must assert some rationale for music teaching—some strong set of beliefs on which music educators may build sound educational practice and on which they can rely in defense of music's place in an overcrowded curriculum. Most persons reading this chapter have already made a major commitment to schooling youngsters in music; in many cases, this decision has been reached almost as a matter of convenience. Many have known music as a powerful part of life, and have doubtless enjoyed their experience with it; they have been around music teachers and know something of the profession—from the student side at least. For these reasons, many music education students expect the transition into the profession to be an easy one, certainly easier than starting "cold" in exploration of some other life work. Reasons of convenience, however, are hardly potent enough for so major a decision. We hope that establishing a firm understanding of the power and usefulness of music will provide strength for the future music teacher and underscore this commitment to music schooling.

School time is limited. Any field of study becomes a part of the curriculum only at the expense of some other field of study. By asserting that children should study music, teachers must be aware that they are asserting that children should *not* study something else. In the past, many music teachers have simply assumed that music should form a part of the curriculum; music's worth is obvious to them. Hoping that students would somehow come to the same conclusion, teachers have floated along, never addressing the issue of why we teach music.

To what end has this set of assumptions brought us? If one were objective in judging the situation as it now stands, perhaps the nagging fear that music really *does not* deserve space in the curriculum might be justified. If music teaching were accomplishing a great deal, there would be more support for it. We would not find that 80 percent of the secondary school students in this country regard the study of music so lightly that it loses in the competition for space on their schedule cards. We would not find school boards and parents so willing to sacrifice music programs whenever there is a budget crunch.

These failures are a direct result of the confusion and misunderstanding of the educational establishment concerning the best and truest role of music in human existence. While we cannot explore all the theories concerning the importance of music to humanity in a general text, we can begin such an exploration by setting out some major points.

Music exists because it is useful to human beings. This premise is borne out in the realization that music exists in cultures that are struggling even to survive. In societies where simple food gathering takes precedence over all else, where the survival of the species is under constant threat, in the midst of famine, drought, and physical attack on the lives of the tribe, music not only exists but seems to hold a special place. The position that music is some sort of cultural "frill" and serves no real purpose is unsupportable under such circumstances. If music were not essential to humankind, it would cease to exist when the lives of the people making it were threatened. The objective evidence tells us this is not true. The literature of anthropology and ethnomusicology is rife with examples of music's essential place in life. The Anuak tribe in Ethiopia, for example, exhibits an active and even growing musical culture, despite a genocidal war against them with which they are ill-equipped to cope.[1] Somehow these people, faced with virtual extinction, still find time to engage in musical activity. Music must fill some special need for them, as indeed it does for all of us.

Music is used in many ways. Sorting them out may be helpful in our search for music's place in human existence. To begin, two conditions pertain in the presence of music: Music can be ignored, heard but not really intruding on conciousness, or music can be accepted. The first situation arises with "background music," such as is found in stores, elevators, airliners, and on radio programs that students switch on while studying. Music experienced in this way is hardly experienced at all. The function of background music is to block out or mask other noise, to cause people to stay longer in stores, or just to fill aural space without being obtrusive. This music is not an experience in itself but a support service for ordinary experience. Studies have indicated that music can cause people to spend more money in the marketplace as well as be more productive in the work place. But music existed long before its popular use as aural camouflage; music exists in cultures that have never heard of recorded sound. Background music is an artifact of our times and Western culture rather than a key to some fundamental truth about the power of music.

The other condition embodies listening in which music is accepted and received, at least enough to intrude on the listener's consciousness. A hierarchy of such music ranges from music that is merely part of an experience to music that is the whole experience. For example, music can be an adjunct to dance; here music is of secondary importance to the action it supports. Music in such circumstances is a *motivation*, a means rather than an end in itself. There is a hierarchy within this level of musical experience as well, from disco to ballroom, from "modern dance" to classical ballet; yet one basic attribute shared by dance forms is their *use* of music to further other experience.

Another kind of purely utilitarian music is ceremonial in function. "Signal experiences" in music include bugle calls and fanfares that announce the presence of some special person or a special event. In the foyer of the White House a harpist from the Marine Band performs music—often music by Bach, Saint-Saens, and others—but the performance of the music is functional. The function is a semiconscious signal to the occasion. Just as harp music itself is not ordinary, the experience

---

[1]David Osterlund, "Anuak Tribe of Southwestern Ethiopia: A Study of Its Music within the Context of Its Socio-economic Setting" (Ed.D. dissertation, University of Illinois, 1977).

associated with it here is not ordinary. The presence of the harp music serves to set the scene, to announce the occasion as special.

Imagine Westminster Abbey. The abbey itself is a multipurpose building used for all sorts of events. An event held there is raised from the ordinary just by its location. And the scene is not complete without music to define the event. Imagine the sound of a boys' choir coming from the nave; the event announced is most certainly a religious one. Now imagine the same abbey with the sound of trumpets proclaiming a fanfare: A state event is to take place. In both instances, the musical event is attached to another event. The music serves as a signal, a device for directing the consciousness of the listener.

Another use for music is as entertainment, or diversion. This use puts music in a class with baseball or stamp collecting. Most often it is for this kind of experience that pop and rock music exist. The musical experience is an "easy" one. It takes no great amount of thought or concentration and is readily available to all who would partake of it. The entertainment function of music has spawned an important industry in our culture, one that is too large to ignore. Mass culture affects all of us. Since teachers often use music as a teaching device that is principally associated with entertainment, we plan to return to this discussion later. For the present, the student is admonished to separate the musical material from its function. Musical entertainment per se is not a proper function of schooling. Entertainment is readily accessible to students without the intervention of the schools. To be blunt, entertainment is obvious; systematic schooling in the obvious is a waste of precious time.

Another function of music is what we might call "sensory massage." Just as physical massage feels good without any particular profundity, so music at times "feels good" as it provides the sensory stimulation important to our well-being. You have doubtless listened to music, alone or with close friends, at high-volume levels. The pure sensory stimulation of such an experience fills a natural and proper human need. The popularity of drug use in such settings to increase sensory stimulation, while officially reprehensible, is at least understandable. Related to this use of music are lasaria, light shows, and the "sensory overkill" discos of the late 1970s.

The effect of such stimulation is both physical and emotional. Heart rate may increase; there are changes in perspiration rate and eye pupil size. The listener can become emotionally "charged" or, if the music is more tame, relaxed and preoccupied. In one sense, this massaging is related to entertainment; it is natural and requires no particular training to enjoy music in this way. Try listening to Debussy's "La Mer" some night when you are feeling particularly mellow; or to Moussorgski's "Night on Bald Mountain" if you need a recharge. The stimulation is undeniable.

The last way in which music used is as an entity in itself—as an object that has intrinsic value without recourse to outside events or settings. This is the way in which music is experienced when it is perceived as art. The human fascination with art has long preoccupied philosophers, who have realized that the mere existence in a culture of certain objects that are revered as "art" is of great importance in the overall scheme of things. Art objects are purely the product of human intellect and action, and yet these objects have assumed an importance that rivals the significance of powerful natural forces. The search for "truth" concerning music and the other arts forms an entire branch of philosophy.

The diverse philosophical stances that exist about the nature of art can fill a lifetime of study. We have chosen to brush lightly against some of the major classifications of aesthetic thought, presenting a middle-of-the road position drawn principally from the twentieth-century view of aesthetics called "expressionism." We have chosen this path because expressionism is readily accessible to most teachers and can form a basis for further questioning and study for the more interested student. It is essential that students have at least some well substantiated view of music as art on which to base teaching decisions. Expressionism can form such a basis at an intuitive level that is impossible with many of the other aesthetic positions.

The Shared Qualities of Music and Life

What is it that attracts us to great music? How does it function? Why does music form so natural a part of human existence? Why does it seem to enrich our lives? Is music an intellectual undertaking? Is it emotional? Does music communicate? If music does communicate, what does it "talk about"?

The central assertion of most aesthetic positions is that music and the other arts possess *meaning*. Were the converse true, were music meaningless, it could not be in any way "understood." The question immediately raised by this assertion—"What does music *mean*?"—has prompted Olympiads of verbal gymnastics from musicians and philosophers. Aaron Copland maintains that "the semanticist who investigates the meaning of words, or even the meaning of meaning, has an easy time of it by comparison with the hardy soul who ventures forth in quest of music's meaning."[2]

An initial confusion exists in addressing this problem because the word "meaning" brings to mind the most common conveyor of meaning,

---

[2]Aaron Copland, *Music and Imagination* (New York: Mentor Books, 1952), p. 21.

language. Speech and the written word are symbol systems, groups of symbols structured according to certain laws of grammar, syntax, and usage into a temporal stream. Because both music and language possess the power to communicate, because both exist "through time," and because both are governed by sets of rules, some romantically inclined writers have called music "the universal language." Most contemporary thinkers deem this notion as false for several important reasons. A major one is the failure of music to function as a complete and efficient communication system.

Susanne Langer notes that meaning exists at two levels.[3] The first, or *denotative*, level is that of common communication. This level we shall call "direct meaning." Use of direct meaning in communication enables us to cause others to recall totally shared experiences with the object, event, or condition expressed by the peculiar combination of sounds that form a word or string of words. Direct meaning is the stuff of everyday speech. Take, for example, the linguistic representation "motorcycle." All of us, because of long direct association of the symbol and object, have a clear denotative meaning for motorcycle, a "definition": a two-wheeled vehicle, powered by a motor, and possessing handlebars and a prominent gas tank which the rider straddles. If we could not symbolize these shared experiences, we could not communicate. Symbols such as words, diagrams, and pictures are portable and easily altered by the addition of other symbols. If it were necessary to provide an actual motorcycle each time we wanted to communicate ideas about motorcycles, communication would become so laborious as to practically halt. If we had only lightweight motorcycles available, and wanted to communicate concerning larger machines, we would have to secure another motorcycle. We can, of course, modify or change the symbol "motorcycle" with other symbols: for example, "big motorcycle," or more specifically, "big black motorcycle" or "big black Triumph motorcycle."

At each step of the way, we become more specific, choosing more restrictive modifiers until we finally reach a *particular* motorcycle: "Marlon Brando's big black motorcycle in the motion picture *The Wild Ones*." This specificity is a characteristic of denotation or direct meaning.

Another meaning conveyed by "motorcycle" or any other word symbol is not based entirely on shared experience and thus varies from symbol user to symbol user. These are *connotative*, or "indirect meanings," based on association of the symbol with the unique mix of personal experience that each individual brings to the communication process. Connotations concern attitudes about and feelings toward the object, event, or condition symbolized. Consider the feelings engendered by the phrase "big black motorcycle" in a California camper who has been terrorized by

[3]Susanne K. Langer, *Philosophy in a New Key* (New York: Mentor Books, 1942).

members of Hell's Angels, or among those whose driving safety has been endangered by roving packs of cyclists. These personal experiences forever carry negative connotations associated with the *object* itself, and with the symbol (i.e., the word "motorcycle") used to communicate about the object.

On the other hand, to one of the authors the phrase "big black motorcycle" carries an entirely different set of connotations as a result of early experiences with "Brunhilde," a particularly beautiful 500 cc B.M.W. that provided him with transportation during his undergraduate days. To him the phrase connotes joy, freedom, openness, and power. Beyond these general connotations are the myriad of *feelingful* responses to the idea of motorcycle that stem from particular events that took place on the road with Brunhilde. The quiet solace of a fall afternoon in Virginia experienced aboard this bike is part of the *meaning* of the word "motorcycle."

At a midpoint between the direct meaning about steel and rubber entities that in a sense "are" motorcycles and the completely personal *indirect meanings* that also "are" motorcycles, there is the area we shall label shared or *assigned connotations.* These meanings may be feelingful responses dictated by societal convention. To most, for instance, there is a feeling of recklessness, engendered by media stories and shared observation, associated with motorcycles. To cyclists themselves there is the vulnerability or feeling of danger that common riding experiences have brought. Each culture or subculture possesses these shared feelings. Liberal Democrats may assign one connotation to the words "American flag" while conservative Republicans assign it another. These culturally determined shared connotations form an important part of symbol usage.

These three levels of meaning, then, exist in the symbol system of words and languages: *denotations* symbolize direct, concrete shared experiences; *connotations* symbolize personal feelingful or affective experiences; and *assigned connotations* symbolizes shared feelingful or affective experiences.

Fitting music as *meaning* into these categories of symbol usage is a logical next step. Although some dogmatists in music education flatly deny that music carries denotative meaning, both intuitive common sense and empirical investigation lead us to conclude otherwise. Through repeatedly reinforced common experiences, certain specific musical passages convey shared denotative meanings. Often these meanings are in the form of Romantic narrative, like those brought to mind by *Till Eulenspiegel's Merry Pranks,* or the immediate association of the *William Tell Overture* with the Lone Ranger. The associations are easy and natural for both children and adults. In part because of this ease, many teachers in the past have placed great reliance on the "listen to the music and write a story" approach to music education. The difficulty with this approach, of course, is that these denotative judgments are only a part (and most would agree a small part) of the meaning of music. Children accomplish them so easily that they are not worth time in systematic music schooling. Why teach what can be done easily without instruction?

Other denotative meanings inherent in music are technical or historical. Were you to hear a performance of a Pekin Opera, for example, you would immediately place it as at least "oriental," if not actually Chinese. This denotative response is not just *about* the music; it is indicative of music's ability to symbolize concrete information. In this case the information is cultural, but many judgments are possible. The kind of formal judgment that places the Vivaldi *Seasons* firmly in the midst of the Baroque is an example; so is the identification of a particular sound as a trumpet or of a chord as one having the dominant function. Some writers (Leonhard and Reimer among them) have characterized these responses as "unmusical." We cannot support this position. They *are* musical responses, but of a denotative sort; an intellectual response, true, but still part of the fabric of the meaning of music.

Some students, on observing that music is incapable of carrying denotative meaning to the same extent that language carries it, are led to believe that music carries no denotation. They mention that it would be impossible to write a piece of music that could direct a person to the local grocery store or describe in music the steps necessary to construct a building. So they reject the notion of musical denotation forthwith. Better is the approach that admits to music's denotative component but strongly notes that music accomplishes denotation poorly. Music is a far less efficient means of denotation than is language or pictographs.

We have formulated two suppositions. Music in itself must be useful to human beings, else it would not be so pervasive in culture; and music is a symbol system carrying meaning. Music's demonstrated failure as a good denotation method leads us inevitably to look more closely at music's connotative abilities (both shared and private) for a clue to its best role in life.

Connotation addresses that facet of human understanding called variously "the feelingful life" (Leonhard), "subjective reality" (Reimer), or "the sentient existence" (Langer). Humans attach special significance to emotive qualities. Argument might be made that the existence of feelings (symptomatic of values, ethics, morality, and so forth) sets human beings apart from machines and computers. All lives are full of examples of this existence of feelings. Think back to the last turning point in your life, the last major event that involved you totally. It might be the death of a parent, the birth of a child, the realization that you were finally and irrevocably in love, or even your entry into college. The chances are great that the qualities of the event that made it important, that set the event apart as one which endures in your memory, are the feelings that surrounded the event and not the objective occurrence.

Some logical groupings of these feelings involving partially shared experiences have been set into categories called *emotions*. Love, hate, fear and the rest are major divisions of the emotive existence. These categories are at best representative only of the middle level of symbol use we have called "shared connotation." They are gross distinctions; for the close examination of feeling, for the fine tuning of the communicative process, they are not adequate.

To truly express the myriad subtle and ongoing states of feeling humans have invented music and other arts. The rather trite observation that no two persons get the same thing out of a musical performance is true. Each person brings a particular mix of experience to the musical situation against which judgments are made. Connotations are personal; they are unique to each individual.

Some aestheticians have gone to great length in attempting to prove that humans possess a *need* to symbolize feeling, this drive for symbolic representation being as strong as the biological drives for food, territory, and reproduction. While the logical argument of this need provided by Langer and her followers is an interesting intellectual diversion, it is hardly a necessary step in arguing the role of music in life. That the emotive life is an important part of the human condition is self-evident and requires no proof beyond simple observation. Music and the other arts exist not to fill a drive for symbolization but because they are directly and easily *useful*. In some ways art exists as a matter of convenience. Real-life circumstances from ordinary experience that give rise to rich emotive experience are not easy to come by. Just as the word symbol "motorcycle" is more portable and handier than the object itself, so is the art symbol more portable and easier to come by than the feelings expressed by it.

The Acquisition of Meaning

In searching for an explanation as to how musical entities come to have meaning, we are immediately struck by the cogency of a supposition put forth by William James. In sorting out the relative importance of various thought processes, James came to the conclusion that *association by similarity* is the fundamental process of human reasoning. For instance, consider being presented with an object you have never before experienced, some new thing in your life. The object is a clock. You have, of course, experienced thousands of other clocks, but never this particular clock. How do you know it is a clock? You do so by making a judgment of its similarities and dissimilarities to other objects that are clocks—perhaps this new object has two hands and a round face with twelve numerals on it. Imagine now another instrument that possesses none of the attributes of clocks in your experience: The case is a five-foot-tall blob shape covered with felt; it has neither hands nor face, but rather, blinking lights. It *is* a clock because it marks time, although you do not judge it to be a clock because it is not in any way similar to other clocks in your experience. The object carries no "meaning" of clock for you.

This fundamental process of similarity judgment is one important way in which meanings happen. Were we to present the following linguistic symbol to you—"General Mbombugassa"—you would doubtless judge it to be representative of some African military officer because it is similar in form to other symbols you know to be such. This is not the only way symbols gain meaning—we might, for instance, *assign* the meaning "clock" to the phrase "General Mbombugassa" by defining it so—but similarity of form is one of the major modes of meaning. In speaking to this point in psychological terms, Carroll and Wish state:

> What occurs is that two stimuli (which may be the "same" physical stimulus at two points in time) are perceptually very "similar" and are thus treated "as if" identical. That is, perception acts to group stimuli into more-or-less homogeneous classes based on degree of similarity. Without this ability to perceive the non-identical stimuli as similar, the perceptual world would forever be the "blooming, buzzing confusion" of completely unique and unrelated events of which James speaks. . . .[4]

Similarities do not go unnoticed by us. We have said that music tells us of feelings and have implied that feelings may be the "meaning" of music. How does music come to mean a particular feeling state? Some expressionist philosophers have concluded that music and meaning are *similar in form* and that this similarity is the key to understanding one through examination of the other. Thus Leonhard and House conclude that "great music does not give us moods and emotions, but insights into the form and structure of human feeling."[5] Langer has stated that "the pattern of music is that of the same form (as feeling) worked out in pure, measured sound and silence. Music is the tonal analogue of the emotive life. . . ."[6] These and other writings of speculative aesthetics would seem to indicate that music expresses feelingfulness directly, that a musical passage means the same, in terms of feelings, as some real-world event.

According to our theory, the beginning of the acquisition of meaning by musical structures is dependent on some realization, either conscious

---

[4]J.D. Carroll and M. Wish, "Multidimensional Perceptual Models and Measurement Methods," in *Handbook of Perception*, vol. 2: *Psychophysical Judgment and Measurement*, eds. E.C. Carterette and M.P. Friedman (New York: Academic Press, 1974), p. 392.

[5]Charles Leonhard and Robert House, *Foundations and Principles of Music Education* (New York: McGraw-Hill, 1974), p. 93.

[6]Susanne K. Langer, *Feeling and Form* (New York: Scribner's, 1953), p. 27.

or unconscious, of the similarity of form between the musical passage or work and some complex feeling state in the experience of the perceiver. The feeling state because it has been engendered in the perceiver by a major event in his or her life, is perceived as significant. The realization that the musical event is of the same general forms as the feeling state prompts the listener to ascribe the meaning and significance of the feeling state to the musical object.

A Model of Musical Meaning Acquisition

Some writers, notably Reimer,[7] have concluded that the process of aesthetic judgment making during which a listener derives meaning or significance from a musical experience is divided into two parts: perception and reaction. During the perception phase, the listener becomes aware of the parts of the musical composition and their relationship to one another. Broudy[8] has defined musical experience as the awareness of *sensory, formal, technical*, and *expressive* qualities of the musical work. The *sensory* qualities are those that directly affect the hearing, that is the highs and lows, louds and softs, textures, harmonies, and so forth, taken more or less singly. The *formal* qualities encompass the relationships of these elements to one another in some recognizable musical entity (form). At this level, the hearer is aware of key relationships, repetition, and so on. The *technical* qualities are imposed by the medium of the expression: music. In other words, in a musical composition certain devices (e.g., hue, color, and palpable form) are denied in favor of pitch, tempo, and so forth. The final qualities explained by Broudy are *expressive* qualities, and it is these that are deemed significant. The expressive qualities are the result of perception of the sensory, formal, and technical properties. If those perceptions do not occur fully, neither do the expressive qualities.

The "reaction" phase postulated by Reimer is concerned with the ways in which the listener relates these sensory, formal, technical, and expressive qualities to his or her life. Each life is different, and the relationships of musical qualities to life are different for each of us. Thus, Reimer concludes that the best mode for music education consists of teaching perception directly while fostering aesthetic reaction by providing an environment and attitude conducive to such reactions.

[7]Bennett Reimer, *A Philosophy of Music Education* (Englewood Cliffs, N.J.: Prentice-Hall, 1970).

[8]Harry Broudy, "Arts Education as Artistic Perception" (address to the Conference on the Foundation of Education, Lehigh University, 1974).

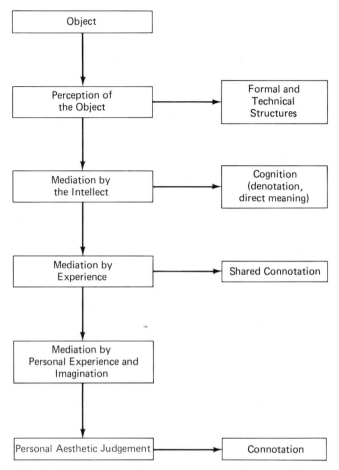

Figure 5.1 Deriving Musical Meaning.

To aid in reviewing these processes, look at figure 5.1. First, there must be the object itself; in the case of the musical art, a composition. This object must be in the form of sounds—real sounds from the environment, sounds translated from a musical score by the mind directly, sounds remembered from a previous hearing, or sounds provided by the imagination. These sounds are the physical "object" the listener will perceive.

The listener perceives this object (i.e., has it enter into his thought) where it is "processed." The intellect (cognitive processes of the mind) mediates the signals and makes judgments as to the formal and technical qualities of the music. The formal and technical meanings are not necessarily conscious, but they exist nonetheless. That a chord possesses the dominant function is not necessarily realized consciously nor necessarily "named." What is realized is the relationship of the sounds to each other, using the composition itself as context.

The next judgment is mediated by experience (in no small sense, by memory) as the formal structures of the work are placed in the context of all other formal structures previously in the experience of the listener. The judgment formation at this point in the process is of two kinds. The first is cognitive and allows us to make such judgments as "Oh, that is a Baroque piece" or "That is a saxophone playing jazz" as we compare the musical structure perceived to other musical structures we have experienced.

The second judgment formation is what we have deemed shared or assigned connotations. The mind ascribes certain general relationships between the shape of the piece and the shape of shared experience. Here we find listeners are able to say that the opening of Beethoven's Fifth Symphony is "forceful" or "domineering" or "ominous." Virtually no one would say that the opening of this piece is "light" or "frivolous." This similarity of judgment reflects the shared experience of all members of the culture. All of us have experienced the same rough categories of emotion, and to a certain extent the same musical environment (the major-minor Western European system). Thus we can come to some general agreements about the "meaning" carried by the music, noting that we do not necessarily do these things consciously. The music is a symbol that carries meaning just as a word carries meaning. If someone were to tell you a word firmly within your experience, such as "cow," you would not stop to figure out its meaning. The meaning would come to you automatically. The same holds true of the less complicated forms of musical expression. They are so firmly within your grasp that conscious thought is not necessary to derive meaning. Just as all persons have a different vocabulary of words with which they are familiar enough so that meaning occurs directly and immediately, so all persons have a musical framework —a different repertoire of musical forms that are immediately meaningful. Familiarity plays a large role in musical meaning formation.

The last part of the process imposes yet another mental process on the perceived and denotatively "understood" musical entity: the imagination, enriched by personal experience. This is the "aesthetic reaction" of which Reimer speaks. This portion of the process is purely personal and doubtless outside the realm of teaching.

Application to Music Teaching

If this model of musical meaning acquisition holds true, what are the implications for the systematic schooling of children? First, note that the cycle before the imagination assumes its role is largely dependent on structured, shared experience with various musical objects. The wider the context provided by shared experience, the more the potential for judgment making and the greater the meaning carried. This argues that a wide variety of musical styles and forms be provided for youngsters. Unlike some writers, however, we maintain that a systematic use of the music of other cultures is probably not indicated. The music of the Anuak in Africa is best understood in the context of Anuak life experiences, not our own. It would be inefficient teaching to be forced to provide the life experiences of another culture against which to make musical judgments before the music could be approached. In fact, it would be impossible. All that could reasonably be expected is that our students would impose a Western point of view on the music of other cultures. That this process would result in a significant or personally meaningful experience is almost beyond hope.

Instead, the teacher must pay close attention to widening the scope of experience of students within Western music. Notice that a great deal of the meaning of music is cognitively derived. The wider the cognitive base, the greater the chances for individual feelingful reaction. The imagination simply has more information to transform.

Viewed in this light, teaching musical form and structure, the place of a composition in historical context, or musical analysis skills, is definitely *not* a waste of time as long as each step of the way is related to the actual *sound* of the musical object. Thus, we should teach aural skills. If a composition by Mozart is being studied, it is *not* important that students know where Mozart wrote the piece or the political ramifications of his Masonic connections but it *is* important that students realize what qualities of sound make it similar to and different from other sounds in the wider context of Western music and in the narrower context of music of this historical period.

The emphasis of schooling in music must be placed on the acquisition of musical meaning. The qualities can be defined by numerous titles, terms, and categories; but the emphasis must be on a broadening musical experience. The components of musical experience are interlaced and important. Our stressing of the expressive qualities of music stems from a concern that they are too often overlooked as teachers struggle to "teach" and "test" for the acquisition of the formal and technical aspects of music only.

In keeping with our discussions of lifelong learning, the emphasis on broadening musical experiences gains much significance. If the student is taught in school the expressive qualities of music and the power of musical meaning, the adult will have a much clearer understanding and "appreciation" of music. We contend that opportunities to acquire the meaning of music by understanding the expressive qualities of music should be open to "students" of any age.

Theories of learning may aid the teacher in organizing the components of music into a logical sequence for learning. The acquisitions of musical meaning is dependent, in large part, on the sequencing of music materials in the affective and cognitive domains of the art of music. The chapters that follow outline current thought in these areas.

Questions for Discussion

1. What components of "aesthetic judgment" has Bennett Reimer identified as important?
2. Define "signal experiences" as discussed in utilitarian music. What place does this hold in a school music program?
3. Why should or should not music for entertainment (functional music) be a part of the school music curriculum?
4. Discuss music as a "universal language." What implications does this concept have for studying the music of other cultures?
5. Can the meaning of music be acquired without formal music instruction in classical music? Can you cite instances where individuals have knowledge of the purpose of music without extensive music training?

Recommended Readings

Broudy, Harry. *Enlightened Cherishing: An Essay on Aesthetic Education.* Urbana: University of Illinois Press, 1974.

Copland, Aaron. *Music and Imagination.* New York: Mentor Books, 1952.

Dewey, John. *Art as Experience,* New York: Capricorn Books, 1958.

Langer, Susanne, *Philosophy in a New Key.* New York: Mentor Books, 1942.

Leonhard, Charles, and House, Robert. *Foundations and Principles of Music Education.* New York: McGraw-Hill, 1974.

Meyer, Leonard B. *Emotion and Meaning in Music.* Chicago: University of Chicago Press, 1956.

Osterlund, David. "Anuak Tribe of Southwestern Ethiopia: A Study of Its Music Within the Context of Its Socio-economic Setting." Ed.D. dissertation, University of Illinois, 1977.

Reimer, Bennett. *A Philosophy of Music Education.* Engelwood Cliffs, N.J.: Prentice-Hall, 1970.

Sessions, Roger. *The Musical Experience of Composer, Performer, and Listener.* New York: Atheneum, 1962.

part
four

6/theories of musical learning and motivation

In an earlier discussion we made a distinction between education and schooling, pointing out that the latter is systematic and structured; organization contributes to the efficiency of the schooling system. Deciding how to structure experiences so that children might best learn from them is a challenge for both the administrator and the teacher.

Fortunately, teachers are not alone; a great deal of help is available. Indeed, some of the finest minds have devoted themselves to the problem of how children learn and how effective motivation for learning can be applied to the school setting. Future teachers need to heed these learning theorists early so that the principles involved can be considered during their methods class experiences.

The Learning Process

Consider the fifth-grade boy confronted with the problem of making a first sound on the flute. The teacher has given the boy the headjoint of the flute, has shown him how to hold it, and has demonstrated the proper embouchure. The child now formulates the problem: "What is the best way to go about making the sound I have heard?" He recalls all the things the teacher has shown him, purses his lips as best he can, blows, and—nothing. He tries again—still nothing. Taking the flute away for a moment, he reformulates the problem: "All I got was air; must be something wrong" and supposes a solution to it. Change the position of the lips, and blow harder, maybe. He tries, and behold! a small *"toot"* emerges. It is faint and airy, but it is a sound. Reinforced that he is on the right track, he again reformulates the problem, supposes another solution, and tries it out. This time there is more *"toot"* and less *"whoosh."* The process of reformulating problems and supposing and trying out solutions based on prior experiences continues. The boy is learning.

The educational theorist John Dewey presented a process of learning that is analogous to the situation just presented. First, actions on the part of human beings are caused by the realization that there is a problem to be solved—an obstacle, a barrier to accomplishing something. The problem may be fuzzy and ill-defined, but it is there nonetheless. The mind calls on past experiences and finally proposes a concrete solution, like: "What would happen if I tightened my lower lip a little?" Next the mind supposes an answer, based again on experiences up to this point, like: "There will be more sound." A frame of reference for success now exists. If the child tries the solution and his senses tell him that the supposition has a basis in reality, he is reinforced. The learning process of experimentation continues this way ad infinitum.

Notice some important points about this chain of events. The first is that it is a *process*. It goes on over time, with a beginning, a set of operations, and an end. Notice that at all stages, this learning process is based on experiences, and these experiences are developmental; they are based on those that have gone before. Notice that they have a final product, or end point: The behavior of the individual has changed. We can now attempt a definition of learning: *Learning is a developmental process, based on experience, that causes a change in behavior.*

Actually, the example of a beginning flute student is a bit more complex than it would at first seem. To help sort out the complexities, psychologists have divided the "mind" (as we will call the electrical churnings of the brain) into three domains. The first is known as the "cognitive," from the Latin *cognoscere*, "to know." The cognitive domain embraces all those things that experience has told the mind are true. If you thought you saw a person bouncing down a street on his head, the cognitive portion of your mind would react, for experience has shown you that this cannot be true. People just do not bounce down the street on their heads. The cognitive domain stores the truths that experience has taught us and compares them with observed stimuli. The flutist in our example now has some experience on which to base "knowing." If you asked him for an explanation, the things he told you would be from his cognitive domain.

The second domain is known as the "psychomotor," and the experience that the child with the flute has undergone has taught him some things here too. As the name implies, the psychomotor domain is concerned with the connection of the mind to motor skills. The child has learned "how it feels" to make a sound on the flute headjoint. The psychomotor portion of his mind "remembers" the way it set the muscles. A great deal of music teaching is involved with the psychomotor domain. Tone production in singing involves this domain, for instance, as well as fingerings on the clarinet or piano.

The last domain, known as the "affective," is particularly suited to learning through musical experiences. Here we find feelings, values, and all those myriad human qualities; here are love, hate, joy, and sadness. Our young flutist has been "affected" by his experience. The complex mixture of feelings of success, appreciation of self-worth, joy in the sound he has made, or sadness at its imperfection are all the result of learning in this domain.

But we have left a hole in the outline of the process. How did the child sense that part of the sound he produced was air and part was flutelike tone? How on the next attempt did he figure out that more was flutelike and less airy? At this point we must confront the problem of *perception*. We could say that "he heard it," but it is not that simple. For example, direct your attention to the sounds in a supposedly quiet room or to the radio that is playing while you study. The sounds you now sense were there all the time, falling on your hearing mechanism but not perceived. The same thing holds true in music. Musical perception is concerned, in part, with knowing *what* to hear.

While there is no real agreement as to what developmental stages children experience in musical perception, most psychologists agree that some sort of perceptual development takes place. Some development is maturational, which means it happens as a person gets older. Some of music perception doubtless is learned through sorting out experiences. If it seems to you that learning and perception are intertwined, you are correct. "Perception operates in learning, and learning affects all subsequent perception."[1]

---

[1]Charles Leonhard and Robert W. House, *Foundations and Principles of Music Education* (New York: McGraw-Hill, 1972), p. 110.

The totality of musical perception forms musical concepts in the mind. Some of the concepts children form early in life are such things as loud and soft, fast and slow, or high and low. Musical concepts can be conceived in either the cognitive or the affective domain, and both require the experiencing of musical stimuli throughout the learning process. With these concepts formed from experience, the child has a basis for making finer perceptions, and refined concepts are formed from them—concepts like duple meter, "dancelike," or "key-centeredness." Clearly any concept can occur only through perception; and once concepts are formed, they will affect subsequent perception. The thread that runs continuously through our discussion to this point is *experience*. If a child is to develop musical concepts he must *experience* music.

Experience must be structured to be efficient in schooling. If the teacher sits back and tries to let musical concepts form of their own account without structure, they probably will not. Another learning theorist, David Ausabel, has given us some clues to efficient schooling by defining a concept called "cognitive structure."[2] This theory postulates that perceptions grow and become organized into structures only when they are catalogued and labeled. Thus treated, they are placed into their proper niche in the growing cognitive structure. To facilitate this process, the child needs some prompting. The teacher's role is to provide "advance organizers," little clues that help find the right niche in the structure into which the perception is to be placed. Too often, information from the child's senses bombards his cognitive structure in a hit-or-miss fashion. Channeling information by categorizing, labeling, and organizing it aids in the quick assimilation of the new experience. Give the student a label for something he is experiencing, and his mind has a better chance of putting it in the right place. For our young flute player, this could be as simple as telling him that the example of lip placement he is shown by the teacher is "embouchure." Henceforth any information the child receives about lip placement, be it from perceiving the sounds he makes or from the nerves in his lip or from observation of his teacher, will be placed in the embouchure niche.

Though Ausabel concerned himself with structures in the cognitive domain, psychologists have identified similar structures in the affective and psychomotor domains as well. The affective or feeling part of existence is similarly learned. We can speak of concrete emotions, like love or anger, and be understood because there are large affective structures tying together lots of small feelings into large categories. As a psychomotor example, consider a soprano who is confronted with a high C on the vowel *ee*. Before attempting to sing the note, the psychomotor structure

---

[2]David P. Ausabel, *The Psychology of Meaningful Verbal Learning* (New York: Grune and Stratton, 1973).

of the mind will take over, setting the muscles in the throat and oral cavity to correspond with the category conception of high notes in general, and the substructures of high C, on that specific vowel. If the psychomotor structure is well built, the psychomotor portion of the mind "knows" that the passage will sound right even before it is uttered.

We must add a comment here concerning the rate at which these processes occur. The mind perceives a problem and sets up a solution and hypothetical result with tremendous speed, even in our problem-solving example of the fifth-grader with the headjoint. In the psychomotor domain the comparison of the muscle tension in the body and the psychomotor structure is virtually instantaneous.

Learning and Modeling

In chapter 1 we mentioned that a great deal of learning takes place through imitation. Psychologists call this "modeling," "copying behavior," or "matched dependent" behavior.[3] In presenting tasks for psychomotor skill development, music teachers often provide models of technical exercises. With the teacher demonstrating a skill like a trill or a sustained tone, the student attempts to copy the psychomotor responses to reproduce a similar trill or tone. Modeling a skill and requiring the student to drill repetitive technical studies is effective. The caution to teachers is not to forget the original purpose of the drill as *exercises*. All too often, students and teachers dwell upon the process (i.e., technical studies), forgetting that the reason for the technical studies was to aid the student in playing musically.

Many student performers move through a developmental stage in which technical skills in and of themselves are motivating. That students can play rapid passages or high notes is in itself rewarding, but the students must be reminded that the rapid execution of a three-octave scale holds little practical value and *no* musical value. In short, the development of musical performance skills (psychomotor skills) must be related directly to their application to the performance of music or, better stated, to the expressive performance of a music composition, not a technical drill.

Whereas any number of teacher behaviors can be modeled, either consciously or unconsciously, the most often cited examples are emotional and social behaviors. The reactions a teacher displays toward a piece of music, for example, are often copied by the students. Indeed, the entire

[3]N.E. Miller and J. Dollard, *Social Learning and Imitation* (New Haven: Yale University Press, 1941).

atmosphere a teacher sets for a classroom is often copied by the students. If the teacher approaches the classroom in a humorless way, or gives cues to students that the task of interacting with them is a job with little pleasure, the students will model this, and the atmosphere in the class will deteriorate rapidly.

Let us look at another example, one that is more closely related to music teaching. Most teachers would agree that it is important to have children learn to value concerts and musical performances. If the teacher displays a positive value system by talking about concerts, attending concerts, and so forth, the children will model that behavior. Teachers, if they expect their students to display changed behaviors, especially in matters of valuing, must display these behaviors themselves. And they must display them openly. The absence of particular actions by a teacher is as powerful a model as the presence of particular actions. If, for example, the teacher gives lip service to requiring that students get all work in on time and then is slow in returning it, the students will model the latter part of this behavior, resulting again in deterioration.

Modeling in social interaction is important for teachers. When you begin your teaching career, you will be confronted with some students you simply cannot stand. Teachers are human; they do not love every child. The important point is that if a teacher openly *displays* this dislike, the other students may model this behavior. While some advocate absolute "honesty" in dealing with student interactions, we do not. Honesty in these cases must be tempered with reason.

Development of Musical Skills

An important principle of learning has been expressed by Blair, Jones and Simpson:[4] "You learn to do what you do, and not something else." While this sounds obvious, educational practice shows us that many music teachers ignore this principle entirely. In chapter 5 we laid a foundation for music education based on the value and nature of music as an art. We concluded that music education should be aesthetic education. For this —the affective domain of learning—it is important to remember that Hannon Exercises, Rose Clarinet Studies, Arban Scales Studies, and O'Sevchik Violin Exercises *are not music*. These exercises for the development of psychomotor skills are means to affective ends. Recalling the Dewey model, learning becomes efficient only when the learner can formulate the problem that the learning is to solve. We must keep the musical

---

[4]Glenn M. Blair, R.S. Jones, and R.H. Simpson, *Educational Psychology* (New York: Macmillan) p. 115.

problems well enough defined so that both the teacher and the learner avoid wasted time.

A concern of many who observe student teachers (and even experienced teachers) is the choral warm-up exercise, a series of vocalises to which a choir is subjected day after day in a manner so routinized that is accomplished without any thought whatsoever. Ask a choral conductor why he uses certain warm-up exercises as opposed to others, and you may find that you get few rational replies. The teacher must clearly *define* an aesthetic objective and then adapt technical exercises to fill the aesthetic need. Students need to know the proper placement of vowels, for instance, but often the relationship of this to the expressive import of the music rehearsal that follows is not made clear to the students. They "learn to do what they do"—perform exercises perfectly.

Band directors have similar routine warm-ups. Observation tells us that by far the most popular warm-up exercise for a band is the mindless playing of unison scales, most often Bb major. To illustrate our point, compute an example of the total Bb scale production of school bands in a year and relate it to something we all understand—money. If it takes two minutes to play a Bb scale and its associated variations directed at no particular musical problem, and there are 75 band members, we could multiply that by the number of rehearsals in a year, say 180, and that again by the number of school bands in the nation (conservatively, 23,000), to arrive at the conclusion that 5,175,000 man-hours per year are spent playing Bb scales. At a rate of $3.50 an hour, that comes to $18,107,500.00 worth of Bb scales each and every year. General Motors should have it so good! This form of argument (*reductio ad absurdum*) is not entirely valid, but absurdity sometimes does provide perspective.

Sequencing of Musical Experiences

We can use our Dewey model and the Blair statement ("You learn to do what you do") to draw an important conclusion: Learning is based on experience and cannot occur efficiently without the active involvement of the individual. People learn by undergoing and becoming involved in specific musical experiences and musical problem-solving tasks. The order in which these tasks are presented is of crucial importance.

Consider, for example, the child who is confronted with a problem that is too difficult. Teachers at times expect students to understand problems almost by "magic," without any instructions. Evidence of this is can be seen in some beginning instrumental programs. The teacher's conceptual structure is so advanced that the component parts of counting rhythms, for example, are lost. The teacher is beyond the point of "counting" and fails to break down the task into easily grasped principles and concepts. The result is frustration on the part of the student.

Or consider the poor beginning percussionist who is placed on snare drum for reasons of convenience in heterogeneous instrument classes. After two or three weeks, the clarinetist and cornetist in the class are playing recognizable tunes. The percussionist is still playing single "taps." In another week, the flute players are coming forth with "Mary Had a Little Lamb," and the drummer is tap-tap-tap-tapping. It doesn't take long for the drummer to lose all sense of accomplishment; he may drop out. If the teacher had sequenced the learning of the percussion instruments properly, this would not occur. If the student had begun on a small marimba, for example, he would derive satisfaction from playing "Twinkle, Twinkle Little Star" right along with the rest of the class. The slow pace would be averted, and boredom would not set in.

To apply our eclectic learning theory approach, we need some scheme for sequencing instruction. Gagne[5] has listed five steps that should be included in instruction:

Gagne's Instructional Sequence

1. Inform the learner about the form of performance to be expected when the learning is completed.
2. Question the learner in a way that requires the recall of the previously learned concepts that apply to the task.
3. Use verbal cues to lead the learner through a sequence of concepts. This should result in the formation of a principle in the student's mind.
4. Ask the student to demonstrate one or more concrete instances of the task.
5. Require the student to make a verbal statement of the principle learned.

Leonhard and House call this sequence "synthesis-analysis-synthesis."[6] The first synthesis is the recall of the previously acquired concepts, which form a base for the new cognitive, affective, or psychomotor structure. This is accomplished by informing the student of the nature of the task's outcome (providing a context or "niche" in which to place the new learning), and questioning the student so that he can find within his own structure the proper niche with that label. The analysis

---

[5]Robert M. Gagne, *The Conditions of Learning* (New York: Holt, Rinehart and Winston, 1965), p. 5.

[6]Leonhard and House, *Foundations and Principles of Music Education*, p. 110.

phase consists in breaking down the new task into its proper order so that each step builds on the previous one. The resynthesis at the end of the cycle serves to check the new structure by making its use observable to the teacher. This final synthesis step also includes asking for a restatement of the learned principle in the student's own words; this again serves as a check, and may form the first synthesis step for the next piece of learning in the chain.

We mentioned that teachers often take certain knowledge for granted, which results in confusion for the learner. Gagne's process avoids that pitfall. When teaching a new rhythm task—thirty-second notes, for example—a teacher might begin by asking the student to recall counting quarter notes, eighth notes, and sixteenth notes. This is accomplished through questioning, not simply by "telling" the students. With the conceptual base firmly in hand, the student is then provided with the verbal cues that thirty-second notes are half as long as sixteenth notes; that the relationship between sixteenths and thirty-seconds is the same as that between quarters and eighths, and so forth. The learner is then required to demonstrate understanding in several musical settings. Finally, the student states the principle learned. The student has derived a principle: Beats may be subdivided.

The process of synthesis-analysis-synthesis does not have to be as detailed as the preceding example to achieve results. In an ensemble rehearsal the process may be accomplished by playing through an entire piece or a major section of a piece, analyzing the specific improvements needed, rehearsing them in isolation, and then resynthesizing by placing them in the original context by playing the major section again.

An advantage of this approach is that it aids in *retention* of the information. Resynthesis of the isolated knowledge serves to "anchor" the knowledge into the structure. Forgetting will always be a problem, but forgetting can be lessened by providing proper contexts for the new learning. To take an extreme example, most persons have at one time or another tried to memorize quantities of isolated information. A common example is represented by the new music student's need to learn the names of the lines and spaces of the staff. Resorting to a mnemonic device, "every-good-boy-does-fine," while providing no musical context is one approach; this saying (which is an example of *elaboration* in psychological terms) does aid in memory retention by providing a context for the new learning. Recall is improved even by such crude contextual associations. If the context is more closely related to the real task, rather than a contrived one as in our example, then retention is given better. A student who is prompted to recall the names of the notes as they are played begins to place the names into a musical context, and the proclivity toward forgetting is reduced even further.

Proper sequencing is vital to learning, but it is a time-consuming task for the teacher. Differences among students and school classes necessitate variations in instructional sequences. Success in teaching, as in anything else, requires planning and preparation. Too many music teachers do not take the time to plan rehearsals, to put the context into a logical sequence with clearly defined outcomes. These teachers rehearse their ensembles by playing through music and correcting difficulties only as they arise, mainly by rote. Inefficient at best, this mode of teaching at worst results in an almost total waste of time. A professional conductor would never think of going to a rehearsal without a rehearsal plan; to the professional, time is money.

Motivation

In any educational setting, in or out of school, motivation is essential to the efficiency of the learning experience. We define "motivation" as anything that causes an animal, including humans, to exhibit a particular behavior. Some motivators are at the physical or organic level; an example of this is the need for water. The absence of water causes a *drive* in the organism to provide the necessary missing ingredient. We earlier stated that one of the tasks for music teachers is the creation of a need for musical fulfillment in students. The result of the establishment of this need is the corresponding drive to experience music.

Closely linked to these base-level needs are higher-order motivators: incentives and motives. *Incentives* are things the organism wants—goals to be attained. Incentives may be concrete, such as a new trumpet to be gained from paper route proceeds; or abstract, such as a sense of satisfaction or pride. *Motives*, on the other hand, are essentially habits. Things that are done repeatedly tend to provide their own drives. This is the reason that habits are so hard to break; they are self-sustaining. Any voice teacher, for instance, knows how difficult it is to correct bad breathing habits once they have become established. Even though an *incentive* has been set up (a better vocal tone), the built-in drive of the habit (the *motive*) is stronger.

A useful motivation technique for teaching employs a process of reinforcement. When an act reduces or satisfies a need, the action is said to be *reinforced*. This process, if understood by the teacher, can be used effectively in motivating students. Blair, Simpson, and Jones put it this way:

> There is a little doubt that knowledge about the kinds of behaviors for which a youngster has been rewarded or from which he has received satisfaction will provide a teacher with the best possible tool for predicting future behavior.

Also, this knowledge should offer help in finding ways to change behavior, by changing the patterns of reinforcement.[7]

Based on the pioneering work of B.F. Skinner,[8] a system of operant behavior modification or conditioning has developed. The theory is simplicity itself: An animal presented with a reward for doing something will tend to do that something again. Early experiments included a pigeon pecking at two disks, one light and the other dark in color. Whenever the pigeon hit the dark disk with its beak, it was rewarded with a bit of grain. If the pigeon struck the light disk, it got nothing. It did not take long for the pigeon to exhibit behavior that involved pecking the dark disk exclusively.

This theory works with people as well, but despite the obvious nature of the principle, many teachers fail to incorporate systematic reinforcement in their teaching. The set of circumstances surrounding the process of reinforcement involves stimulus and response. A *stimulus*, in psychology, is generally described in terms of its function rather than its physical properties. That is, instead of describing the "thing" that is the stimulus, we describe the effects of the stimulus on behavior. We ask what effect the presentation of the stimulus will have on the probability of the behavior's recurrence. In common terms, a stimulus may make a behavior more likely to occur, less likely to occur, or have no effect. A stimulus that increases or accelerates the behavior is said to "strengthen" the behavior. The opposite, causing a decrease in the probability of recurrence of the behavior, is said to "weaken" the behavior.

Two things can be done with any stimulus. The stimulus can be presented, adding it to the situation, or taken away, subtracting it from the situation. We think of adding as a positive process, and so we label added stimuli *positive stimuli*. The stimuli we remove are *negative stimuli*. These distinctions are important later in the discussion, so remember that added stimuli are *positive* and subtracted ones are *negative*.

In like manner, there are two times when we can present or remove stimuli: (1) before and (2) after the behavior (the *response*) occurs. This may be confusing because in common thought we think of stimuli as always *preceding* a response. Keep in mind, however, that anything that affects the frequency of occurence of a behavior is a stimulus, no matter when it occurs.

An example may help clarify the situation. Imagine a child alone in a kitchen. The child spies a cabinet door and opens it curiously, almost by

---

[7]Blair, Jones, and Simpson, *Educational Psychology*, p. 115.

[8]B.F. Skinner, *Science and Human Behavior* (New York: Macmillan, 1953). This book is a summary by the author of his interpretation of organized social behavior as related to reinforced learning.

chance, and finds a bag of chocolate chips inside. In this situation, there are two stimuli. The first, or antecedent stimulus, is the sight of the cabinet. It precedes the response: opening the door. The second stimulus comes afterward: finding the chocolate. This consequent stimulus will likely influence the child to open that door again in the future. The child has an expectation of finding candy. Because the chocolate chips were *added* to the situation, they are a *positive* stimulus; because they cause an increase in the probability of opening the door, they are called a *reinforcer*. We have witnessed an example of "positive reinforcement." The opposite function of reinforcement is *punishment*. Most of us are all too familiar with that.

We direct our attention now to another example of reinforcement, this time in a musical setting. This example is drawn from an actual experiment. We will call the central character in this episode "Mr. Williams." He is a band director at a large university. In an effort to improve his rehearsals he has videotaped several of them to observe later. Being an honest and dedicated man, Mr. Williams objectively analyzes what he sees and comes to the awful conclusion that he would not want to play in his own band. The conductor is too negative. He has read up on things and discovered that, most of the time, positive statements reinforcing good playing habits are a more effective technique than negative ones. Try as he does, he cannot seem to make any improvement. Bad playing drives him wild, and he remains negative. He has a long-standing habit of negativism based on the model of the college band director he suffered through himself. When he hears a playing problem, his response is immediate and furious.[9] Frustrated, Mr. Williams goes to a colleague who is conversant with behavior modification techniques. The colleague offers to help. He rigs up a simple red light on the conductor's podium, out of sight of the players but where the conductor can observe it. When the red light flashes, it will serve as a reward, reinforcing the positive statements made by the band director. The colleague sits in the back of the room with the control button and watches. Whenever the conductor makes a positive statement, or even looks at someone in an approving way, the colleague presses the button and provides a reward.

Not that Mr. Williams ignores mistakes; it's just that he doesn't harp on them and belittle the miscreants. And he begins to praise good performance more and more. As this experiment progresses through several rehearsals, the improved playing of the band and the comfortable atmosphere, reflected in the faces of the players, serve as the reward in place

---

[9]The conductor has added a stimulus to the situation, but the stimulus is designed to cut off or discourage the behavior (bad playing) in the future. Because it is *added* stimulus, it is *positive*; because it tends to *extinguish* the bad playing, it is a *punishment*—the situation involves *positive punishment*.

of the light. Later videotapes and better performances indicate that the process has worked. Mr. William has modified his behavior through reward. The band has been rewarded as well, and starts to exhibit improved playing behavior—the situation is one of *positive reinforcement*.

The question undoubtedly raised is, "How the devil can a little red light possibly serve as a reinforcer for a highly educated and intelligent man like that?" The fact is that virtually *any* kind of *attention* that is contingent on a particular behavior, if it is not aversive, will reinforce that behavior.

Teachers sometimes fail to grasp the importance of this principle and give too much attention to students who misbehave. The attention serves as a reinforcer, and the misbehavior increases. In the meantime, the student who is behaving is ignored. The result is that to get any attention, a student must behave inappropriately. Another principle in behavior modification says that if a behavior is ignored, it tends to extinguish, or go away. Teachers should *ignore* behaviors they want extinguished and reinforce those they want strengthened.

Now consider *negative* reinforcement as a process we reinforce by removing an aversive stimulus. Take the example of a baby who is being stuck by a diaper pin. The baby will cry. The father removes the aversive pin, and the baby is content. The baby has learned that if there is something that he does not like (i.e., some aversive stimulus), he can let his father know about it, and father will come and fix it. We have *negatively reinforced* the crying behavior of the baby.

We have deliberately left for last the subject of punishment. A punishment is defined as any stimulus that tends to *decrease* the probability of a behavior. As was the case with reinforcement, punishment comes in both positive (adding to) and negative (removing from) forms.

The most obvious form of punishment is *positive punishment*, that is, the addition of an aversive stimulus to a situation. Spanking is one example, verbal attack is another. Without going into details, suffice it to say that positive punishment does not work as well as either positive or negative reinforcement in most school settings.

There is another kind of punishment, though; and while it may not work as well as reinforcement, it does have merit. *Negative punishment* is the removal of something that serves as a reward. Many of you may have been "grounded" for some misdeed when you were in high school. In this case, a reward—the keys to the family car, for instance—was removed from the situation. You probably remember that this sort of thing was somewhat effective.

Notice that with positive reinforcement and negative punishment we are achieving our goal of changed behavior without attacking or threatening people. We are manipulating only *rewards*, by adding or subtracting them. We either allow rewards (*positive reinforcement*), or we don't allow them (*negative punishment*). Aside from the humanitarian nature of such decisions, the bald fact is that studies indicate that either method is more effective than positive punishment.

One other principle of behavior modification needs to be pointed out. Educational theorists refer to something called a "reinforcement schedule," which is a timetable for providing a reinforcer. Time and again, studies[10] have shown that reinforcers applied occasionally, and at random times, work more effectively than those that occur every time the proper behavior is exhibited. For example, do not praise a child every time the child's behavior is appropriate. To do so would cause the child to stop striving, for reward would become a certainty, available anytime the child wanted it. If, on the other hand, a child is not *certain* that the reward will be present, he or she will keep trying in an effort to reassure himself (herself) that reward is still available, even though he (she) doesn't feel a compelling need to be rewarded at that particular moment. With its opposite counterpart of avoiding punishment (*avoidance behavior*), we have the two most fundamental and strongest drives in humans. Of all the theories given by educational psychology, this array of ideas about behavior modification is perhaps the most useful and easiest to apply in teaching.

The next three chapters investigate various intellectual endeavors as they apply to learning in music. Learning theories including motivation, reinforcement, and satisfaction of needs all have a role in each of these areas of learning.

We will find that an understanding of basic learning theory must be applied if successful teaching is to be accomplished, that modeling is extremely efficient and important to the learning process, and that the sequencing of instruction is critical. Even these techniques will be of little success if the student is not motivated to participate. Although all students will not be motivated to participate in the same musical activities, the techniques apply in all teaching situations and all areas of music instruction.

Questions for Discussion

1. What effect does forgetting have on the learning process? What steps can teachers take to counteract this persistent problem in learning? What unique problems in forgetting can you relate to music instruction?

---

[10]Clifford Madsen, R. Douglas Greer, and Charles H. Madsen, Jr., eds., *Research in Music Behaviors: Modifying Music Behavior in the Classroom* (New York: Teachers College Press, Columbia University, 1975). This text offers an overview of research conducted by Madsen and others in the field of behavior modification as it applies to music teaching.

2. Apply the Gagne instructional sequencing to a music instruction sequence. What difficulty is there in following this systematic process? What problems do you see in implementing such an approach to your teaching, if any?

3. List types of punishment that you have noticed in the music classroom. Are these punishments unique to the music teachers, or are they commonplace in schools? Does punishment take any different form in the performance rehearsal than in the general classroom? If so, why would this be the case?

4. Recall motivating experiences in your own music training. What techniques were not effective in motivating you to continue with music instruction? Are they techniques that you would like to see continued in your classroom? How many were positive and how many were negative reinforcers?

Recommended Readings

Ausabel, David P. *The Psychology of Meaningful Verbal Learning*. New York: Grune and Stratton, 1973.

Blair, Glenn; Jones, R.; and Simpson, R. *Educational Psychology*. New York: Macmillan, 1968.

Gagne, Robert. *The Conditions of Learning*. New York: Holt, Rinehart and Winston, 1965.

Hill, Winfred. *Learning: A Survey of Psychological Interpretations*. San Francisco: Chandler, 1963.

Madsen, Clifford; Greer, R. Douglas; and Madsen, Charles H. Jr., eds. *Research in Music Behaviors: Modifying Music Behavior in the Classroom*. New York: Teachers College Press, Columbia University, 1975.

Miller, N.E. and Dollard, J. *Social Learning and Imitation*. New Haven: Yale University Press, 1941.

Skinner, B.F. *Science and Human Behavior*. New York: Macmillan, 1953.

7/the cognitive component

The arts are fundamental modes of understanding and a way of knowing what the world is about; that is, a body of knowledge and a system of symbols.—Martin Engel, Arts and Humanities Advisor to the National Institute for Education

All human mental activity can be subsumed under three large categories. By convention, as much as anything else, these are called "domains" of knowledge and consist of the *cognitive* domain, the *psychomotor* domain, and the *affective* domain, representing activities in *knowing, moving,* and *valuing* respectively. In this and the next two chapters, we consider each domain in turn, discussing the content of the domain and the structure of knowledge in it.

Cognition

While each of the domains of knowledge involves the mind and its processes (mentation), the cognitive domain contains what is referred to in common usage as "thinking." Cognition is that mentation which serves to make sense of the world. It is the realm of ideas, names, relationships, and intellect.

Music educators have had an unusual history with respect to their emphasis on cognitive skills. Fifty years ago, a common goal of elementary general music was that all students learn to read musical notation. This understanding and translation of a symbol system is entirely a cognitive process. During the same period, goals for general music included the identification of specific musical works as to composer, title, and style period—another set of cognitive activities. The emphasis on knowing *about* music was so strong that many argued that the true nature of the art as an expressive medium was being neglected. The resulting emphasis on the aesthetic qualities of music as a basis for schooling extended into the 1980s; in this period, knowledge in and about the arts was downplayed.

We now note a resurgence of interest in cognition, although of a somewhat different sort. Since Lowenfield put forth his theories of creativity and human development, some have come to believe that the best rationale for education in the arts is not their aesthetic nature and their ability to enable children to explore the world of feeling, but rather their place in the fabric of general cognition. In discussing this newer view of the role of the arts in schools, Engel argues as follows:

> On the one hand is the position espousing the nomative and the ideal: "The arts are important and ought to be a central part of the curriculum." On the other hand is the voice of the descriptive and the real: "The arts are merely an enrichment and a luxury that can be eliminated from the school program." Unfortunately, both positions are correct, but for the wrong reasons. Neither the arts education advocates nor the budget-cutting administrators provide a rational basis for their position. For the purposes of education, then, the arts are either their own justification (which is to say they require no justification beyond the claim that art is intrinsically valuable and important) or the arts in education are the helping means to non-artistic ends. What is missing in both the justifying argument and the claim that no justification is possible or necessary is the possibility that the arts are not less than anything else deemed central to the curriculum of the school, that is, they are languages of comprehension, of thinking, of knowing, and of expressing information. Stating this position baldly: the arts, like other disciplines in the schools, are basically about knowledge.[1]

The truth about the arts in education probably lies somewhere between the position taken by those who have come to be identified as "aesthetic educators" and the "cognitivists." It may well be that we come to experience the aesthetic qualities of artwork in a purely cognitive process. At any rate, we believe that cognition will become the great issue of the next decade.

---

[1]Martin Engel, "An Informational Framework for Cognitive Research in Arts Education," *The Arts, Cognition, and Basic Skills*, ed. Stanley S. Madeja (St. Louis: CEMREL, 1978), p. 24.

How does the cognitive process make sense of things? What is "sense"? According to Dewey, the cognitive process works by moving the organism from a state of disturbance to one of stasis, or repose. It involves the construction of coherence—a web of relationships among objects, symbols, and ideas. Remember the "blooming, buzzing confusion" we described in talking about similarity judgments? The resolution of that confusion is the purview of cognition. The process is called *logic*.[2]

Logic, as defined by Dewey, is the end result of inquiry—the conscious or unconscious asking and answering of questions. At times, when listening to a piece of music, a musician can "catch" these questions as they go flying through his brain: "Who wrote that?" or "Why did he end the piece that way?" More often, the inquiry is made unconsciously, but it is made nevertheless. The existence of the question causes an unsettling effect, a disturbance. The disturbance can be resolved in only three ways. It can be *ignored* (something humans seem wont not to do). It can be settled by acquiring a state of *knowledge*. Or it can be answered metaphysically or by faith through *belief*.

These latter two terms, "knowledge" and "belief," are not good enough terms, according to Dewey. He maintains that what is reached in both cases is a state of "warranted assertability." This term is superior to the others because "it is free from the ambiguity of these . . . terms, and it involves reference to inquiry as that which warrants assertion."[3]

The point of this discussion for future educators is that the actions of teachers often cause and structure inquiry. For example, the presentation of an unsolved long-division problem presents a state of disturbance to the child. After learning the algorithm for long division, the child will quickly move to reach a state of warranted assertability by deriving an answer to the problem. At this point, learning ceases momentarily. The stasis state of warranted assertion has been reached, and the child has no motivation for further inquiry. But suppose the child presents the answer to the teacher, and the teacher says, "No. That answer is not correct. You forgot that you borrowed one from the tens place, here." Disturbance has arisen again, and the child works the problem over until another state of warranted assertability is reached. The child asserts that this new answer is true, warranted by the corrected application of the algorithm, and by the further statement of the teacher, "Yes. That is correct."

As you read the remainder of this chapter, which presents an outline of the component parts of the cognitive domain, try to ascertain how music teachers have unsettled you in the past—how they here removed the warrantedness from your assertions. Try to decide what musical in-

<hr/>

[2]John Dewey, *Logic: The Theory of Inquiry* (New York: Holt, Rinehart and Winston, 1938), passim.

[3]Ibid., p. 9.

formation you can cause students to acquire, and what kinds of problematic situations or questions you will present to students to accomplish this process. Remember that teachers can only teach. They cannot learn for their students. Learning takes place in the *students'* minds as a result of the problems *you* give them to solve and the order in which you present those problems. If the problems are too difficult, or in the wrong sequence, students may take the other option in place of warranted assertion. They may choose to ignore the problem and remain ignorant of music as a result.

Systematic Cognitive Skill Development

In an attempt to organize information to accelerate learning, the large curriculum projects of the 1960s emphasized the generation of new curricular materials. Many of these curriculum designs were based on behavioral objectives with measurable outcomes. Behavioral objectives, which state those changes in observable behavior in the learner that result from instruction, remain an important tool in understanding student progress. New methodologies were applied and evaluated in an attempt to synthesize information and sequence that information for the best use of time in the public school.

Teaching methodologies fall into two general categories: teacher-centered techniques and pupil-centered techniques. Both approaches are effective, but the degree of effectiveness depends on the content to be taught. A teacher-centered approach to instruction is useful for the synthesis of information; the teacher "makes sense" of the material and presents it to the students in a processed form. Music performance ensembles are nearly always teacher-centered. While some small ensembles can be pupil-centered, the fact that a conductor directs the rehearsal for bands, orchestras, and choruses makes much of music instruction centered on the teacher.

Programs in which the students assist in selecting subject matter and course objectives and aid in the evaluation of their progress are pupil-centered. The pupil-centered model works effectively in the "open school," which was developed in the early 1970s. Through the use of modular scheduling, individualized instruction, and an open atmosphere, students exercise a large degree of control over their learning. Several of the current general music textbook series for elementary schools contain large pupil-centered components.

The reader should keep in mind that no teaching situation is entirely teacher-centered or pupil-centered. Some blend of the two approaches is present in any music curriculum. Consider the approach taken by your professors in music education or in the music department of your university. How would you characterize your learning environment in applied music as opposed to music theory or class guitar instruction? Debating whether teacher-oriented or pupil-centered instruction is the correct way to teach is the purpose. Teaching method must be adapted to specific learning tasks to best use the teacher's and the student's time.

Teaching Techniques for Cognition

In considering techniques of teaching for cognitive outcomes, teachers have employed three major means of instruction: lecture technique, modeling technique, and discussion technique. Each technique has several variations in both form and usefulness for the music teacher. Knowing the underlying principles of these techniques should be of help as you prepare instruction in music.

Perhaps the most common technique of teaching at the college level is that of *lecturing*. Many of the classes you attend daily have large student enrollments, and so student and professor interaction would be difficult. The professor has circumvented this problem by simply lecturing to the class. Lecture technique is efficient and effective for presenting large amounts of cognitive material to a large group of students when time is limited. In a strict lecture situation, the professor or teacher simply presents material verbally with no interaction between student and teacher.

A variation on the lecture method involves *lecture with student recitation*. In this variation, the teacher begins the lecture with clear statements of objectives in an introduction, to create interest and maintain attention. The main body of the lecture presents the content in some organized manner. With the lecture-student recitation approach, the teacher interjects specific questions and then asks students for responses. The student response represents a built-in feedback mechanism to ascertain whether students understand the topic. In strict application, the teacher selects the student instead of asking for volunteers.

A lecture method can be used effectively in music when participation or performance is not critical. The lecture method works, but, as may be expected, it works with older students who have longer attention spans. The notion that a musicology professor *could* lecture to a fifth-grade general music class is plausible, but the instruction would probably not be as effective as some other method of teaching.

Modeling

Modeling is an effective instructional method in music performance. This method of teaching has some characteristics of the lecture, except that the teacher is physically demonstrating a technique or process instead of discussing it. Questions may be asked by students during the modeling session, or the teacher may ask the questions to be sure that the students comprehend the process being modeled. Modeling is an excellent teaching technique for presenting concepts that must be seen or heard to be understood. To convey the cognitive aspects of stringed instruments, it is much more effective for a teacher to display a violin and perhaps play the instrument for young children than to discuss the physical characteristics of the instrument or even show pictures of the instrument. That the student can see the bow move and the string vibrate has much more impact than discussion or lecture techniques on the subject of acoustics.

We have long been accused of talking too much in rehearsals and classrooms; modeling is an excellent means of avoiding verbosity. Knowledge about music and concepts about music can be clearly demonstrated in a modeling situation, consequently saving valuable time in the classroom.

A variation on modeling is *directed modeling*. This technique is similar to modeling except that students are asked to respond after the modeling or after each verbal direction. The teacher must carefully observe student reactions and assess their progress after each stop. When planning a lesson, the teacher must analyze each task to be performed in order to give directions in proper sequence. Of necessity, directed modeling can be accomplished only in small groups where the teacher can monitor each student and judge the student's demonstrated competency. An example of content applicable to directed modeling is the proper assembly of a clarinet. Faced with teaching this procedure to students, the instructor could simply talk about it, but the discussion would be complicated and time-consuming. The instructor could simply demonstrate the procedure and assume the student understood the task, but the teacher would have little notion whether the student actually could perform the task alone. Only through *directed modeling*, when the student holds the instrument and demonstrates following the directions, can the instructor be certain that there will be no bent bridge keys, no ungreased corks, and no shattered reeds.

Discussion

As can be seen in figure 7.1, teaching methods are not discrete entities but points along a continuum from the teacher-centered lecture to the student-centered discussion method. All discussion methods, however, require prior knowledge of the subject by the student. The size of the group must be limited to allow each student an opportunity to express

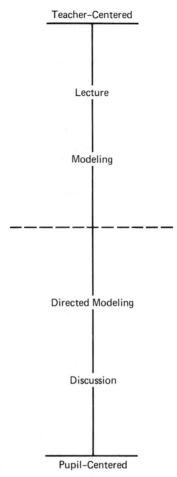

Figure 7.1 Teacher-Centered and Pupil-Centered Teaching Techniques.

himself or herself. The teacher can structure the discussion in one of three ways: directed discussion, reflective discussion, or inquiry discussion.

Directed discussion allows students to interact and discuss materials with the teacher leading the discussion to a predetermined conclusion by asking leading questions. The teacher commands the center of the verbal interaction and controls the direction the discussion takes. To do this properly, the teacher should respond positively to each student response, then rephrase the student response or question and provide additional information. This discussion method is very effective at the more sophisticated cognitive levels of analysis of information or application of knowledge.

Reflective discussion includes more student interaction with the teacher taking a lesser role in the interaction. This discussion method is appropriate when there may be more than one correct answer to the topic being discussed. The teacher guides the students by asking leading questions toward a suitable solution. Before any reflective discussion sessions, the teacher must prepare by planning the order of the questions to keep the topics fairly concise. The danger of reflective discussions is that student participants may ramble into peripheral discussions and lose the focus of the discussion.

The *inquiry discussion* is used less than the other two methods. This technique often explores or probes topics identified for further study. Students have a great degree of control over both content and process in this situation. The teacher's role is one of a referee, in that he or she assumes an authoritative stance only when necessary to prevent erroneous information from being accepted as true. The chief purpose of inquiry discussion is exploration. Based on asking questions, seeking answers, and asserting solutions, students control the outcome of the inquiry. An inquiry discussion may be used to begin a unit of study in a given cognitive area. Some prior student knowledge is certainly critical; however, the teacher does not control the interactions or the direction of the discussions. Inquiry is often used in social science instruction, especially history.

In reviewing these techniques, one can easily see how they *all* have been applied to music teaching in one situation or another. Many of us who teach tend to fall into using only lecture techniques, only modeling techniques, or only directed modeling. Performance ensemble directors tend toward teacher-centered classrooms and away from more time-consuming processes such as reflective discussion. Several techniques can be combined in one presentation rather effectively. The fact that a professor can lecture for twenty minutes while outlining an area of jazz history and then follow with twenty minutes of modeling in the form of playing recordings is a good example. As with teaching in general, we tend to meld teaching techniques into a plan for a day or a week. The experienced teacher will try several approaches in presenting the same material before settling on the best one for the particular students.

Educational Taxonomy: Cognitive Domain

Much of what we learn is cognitive information we collect and assimilate. Colwell states:

> The cognitive aspects of music learning are perhaps the easiest to teach, to discuss, and to evaluate . . . teaching for cognitive learning is appropriate at every age and every stage of development, from pre-school experiences

through post-doctoral studies, for it is the nature of facts that they can be extremely simple or vastly complicated.[4]

An important analysis of cognitive processes was presented in Benjamin Bloom's *Taxonomy of Educational Objectives*.[5] The concept of taxonomy was taken from the branch of biology that engages in the classification of plants and animals into genera, phylla, species, and so forth. This science is a study of the relationships between "taxa" and classification levels. The technique of structuring organisms by hierarchy and evolutionary relationships can be applied to educational objectives.

Bloom's taxonomy has received increased attention as educators have sought to improve schooling by analyzing the structure of each subject discipline and by evaluating more rigorously the results of their work. The National Survey of the Preservice Preparation of Teacher (NSPPT) gathered information about the use of Bloom's taxonomy. Comparing the usage of this approach to a similar survey in 1968, it was found that use of the taxonomy by educators had increased from 16 percent in 1968 to over 52 percent in 1975. The application of this classification system has proven useful both in curriculum development and in curriculum evaluation.

In considering the cognitive domain, Bloom established a hierarchy of categories that includes

1.00   Knowledge
2.00   Comprehension
3.00   Application
4.00   Analysis
5.00   Synthesis
6.00   Evaluation

Using this framework, teachers are able to establish sequentially ordered objectives to guide instruction and evaluation. This sequence can serve as a guide for the construction of curricula for the teacher and as a framework for learning for the student. Through sequencing the material to be taught, methods for evaluating the effects of instruction easily present themselves. Tests and other methods of evaluation become systematic rather than hit-or-miss affairs.

The advantage of evaluation plans that use a taxonomy is that they enable the evaluator to determine at what level of cognition students are

[4]Richard Colwell, *The Evaluation of Music Teaching and Learning* (Englewood Cliffs, N.J.: Prentice-Hall, 1970), p. 79.

[5]Benjamin Bloom, ed., *Taxonomy of Educational Objectives: The Classification of Education Goals, Handbook I: Cognitive Domain* (New York: Longman, 1956).

operating at any point in the instruction. Before this analytical tool was available to teachers, most testing operated at the level of knowledge of facts. Bloom's taxonomy pointed out to teachers the necessity for instruction and evaluation at higher, more abstract levels of thought. Research supports the idea that problems requiring knowledge of specific facts are generally answered correctly more frequently than problems requiring a knowledge of formulas, universal concepts, or abstractions in a given field, and yet most teachers seriously neglect instruction and testing at the higher levels.

The obvious question about this taxonomy for the prospective music educator is one of usage: What are the values of such a categorization in the teaching of *music*? What cognitive information is part of the *music* curriculum? To answer these questions, one need only review the objectives listed in any general music series teachers' guide or the syllabus of any course in music theory or music history at the college level. Knowledge about music—what it is, how it functions, its principles and its specialized languages—are all cognitive elements. Organizing this array so that learning is facilitated can result from the use of the taxonomy. A case in point: It is impossible to teach a child the aural analysis of a work for symphony orchestra unless the child can first name and identify the individual instruments. In this example, cognition involving learning names and the spellings of those names of the instruments is a lower-level cognition without which higher levels cannot be addressed.

A large body of information and learning, simple to complex, must be considered in the makeup of the "musically knowledgeable" person. Even within a division of the taxonomy, such as "knowledge of terminology," there is a continuum of difficulty. Terminology covers things as simple as *piano*, meaning "soft," and *piano*, meaning the musical instrument, to the term *sonata-allegro*. The latter term is obviously a more difficult one to know. To randomly assign these terms to children in the sixth grade, for instance, would be an error. To try your hand at this organizational task, sequence the following terms in an order that you would present them to a musically naive person. Keep in mind that age has little to do with naiveté. Whether the student is in sixth grade, is in the tenth grade, or is a college freshman, proper sequencing of the terms will facilitate comprehension.

Allegro
Syncopation
Tenor
Rondo
Secondary Dominant
Dominant Seventh
Quarter Note
Wind Section

While these terms have been pulled from many different areas of musical knowledge, one should be able to sequence them in an order that would allow students to identify terms as rather low-level bits of knowledge or information. "Tenor," for instance, holds no secrets to conceptual models other than the name of a voice quality and range. Musical terms should be considered more closely because some terms identify simple concepts while others label classifications of information and broad fields.

Knowledge, the first level of cognition, as defined by Bloom, includes behaviors such as remembering, recognizing, and recalling ideas, materials or phenomena. In progressing from the simple to the complex, Bloom lists twelve different levels of knowledge:

1.00   Knowledge of specifics
    1.11   Knowledge of terminology
    1.12   Knowledge of specific facts
1.20   Knowledge of ways and means of dealing with specifics
    1.21   Knowledge of conventions
    1.22   Knowledge of trends and sequences
    1.23   Knowledge of classifications and categories
    1.24   Knowledge of criteria
    1.25   Knowledge of methodology
1.30   Knowledge of universals and abstractions in a field
    1.31   Knowledge of principles and generalizations
    1.32   Knowledge of theories and structures

An examination of this section of the taxonomy reveals some assumptions about taxonomies in general. In order for a student to operate at the higher levels of cognition, mastery must be demonstrated over those classifications that are lower in number. A student cannot know principles and generalizations about music without first mastering terminology, specific facts, and the rest.

This level of the taxonomy, the *knowledge* level, does not address process. Cognition of this sort is "raw material" that may be used in some higher-level process; knowledge, in this sense, is not an end of education, but a means to higher-level skills. A particularly cogent example is level 1.21. Knowledge of conventions. Music of various periods is rife with conventions, which serve as the framework for style. If students are ever to "understand" music (which begins only at the second major level of the taxonomy, comprehension), they must first know that such and such is a convention and not some startling new invention of the composer. At this level, the student will not be able to apply this knowledge in solving a problem (e.g., "Which composer wrote this piece?"), but will only be aware that the convention exists. It is at the knowledge level that memorization and rote learning may be usefully employed.

Comprehension has been identified by Bloom as "probably the largest general classification of intellectual abilities and skills emphasized in schools and colleges."[6] When most of us think of comprehension, we immediately connect the concept with reading, but the use to which it is put in this taxonomy is broader, relating to a variety of communication. Three kinds of comprehension have been offered by Bloom:

2.00 Comprehension
    2.10 Translation
    2.20 Interpretation
    2.30 Extrapolation

Translation is the process of communicating information by translating or transforming the terminology into another form of communication. Translation requires factual information to be at hand before the process begins. Using a musical example, the translation of a musical line of notation into a performance assumes this ability. The translation here is from marks on a printed page to musical sounds; knowledge of facts, terms, principles, and so forth about music notation, plus beat groupings, keyboard fingerings, and the like, are prerequisites.

The second level of comprehension is *interpretation*. The ability to identify major elements or ideas through comprehension may require reordering the ideas into a new configuration. This process involves only the ability to locate elements or ideas and fit them together. The highest level of comprehension is *extrapolation*. This process or behavior includes making estimates or predictions based upon understanding trends or information described in the communication. The projection of information based on sequences is an excellent example. Another musical example would be expectations concerning a consequent phrase after hearing the antecedent phrase of music.

Great efforts are made in public school instruction to bridge the gap between students acquiring knowledge and their ability to comprehend and to communicate that knowledge to others. Establishing learning settings in which students have the opportunity to practice these levels of comprehension is critical to their cognitive development. Knowledge is not understanding; to assume that students who have memorized facts have mastery over understanding is a great miscalculation. Only at the levels of translation, interpretation, and extrapolation does understanding begin.

The next major step in the development of cognitive skills is *application*. Application skills begin to separate those who can function indepen-

---

[6]Ibid., p. 89.

dently from those who cannot. The delineation between comprehension and application is that in the former, a student can use the knowledge in a comprehensive way *when its use is specified beforehand*; whereas in application the student can correctly select information, knowledge, and process and apply them correctly when given a problem *with no suggested solution*. Bloom clearly defines the application level in figure 7.2.

This diagram may be used to draw a distinction between the comprehension and the application levels of the taxonomy. There are several states of completion, or stages in the development of a solution, at which a problem may be presented to a student. If most of the steps have been completed, the student may solve the problem by comprehension skills alone. Such would be the case if the teacher had already solved the problem down through step 5 on the diagram and had presented the problem and partial solution to the student. That is, the teacher would already have structured the problem and selected a method, theory, principle, or idea which, when used, would lead to the solution. This is the case when we present the normal arithmetic practice problem to a student in this form:

$$
\begin{array}{r}
15 \\
\times\ 6 \\
\hline
\end{array}
$$

The teacher has structured the problem, and through the arrangement of the numbers on the page and the insertion of the multiplication sign, has indicated the proper algorithm to apply to reach a solution. The solution can be derived by a student operating at the comprehension level.

At the application level, the problem might be presented this way: "There are three men on a road, travelling on a 50-day, 1500-mile journey. The leader of the group has selected a route that takes them through Florida for 15 of the 50 days. Each day they are in Florida they are able to steal a half-dozen oranges from farms along the road. By the time they get to Georgia, how many oranges will they have stolen?"

This, of course, is a different proposition from the first problem. The student must use the comprehension level to translate "half-dozen" to six. The student must structure the problem by removing all the extraneous information about miles and 50-day journeys, and must recognize that the problem solution will require multiplication. The student must derive:

$$
\begin{array}{r}
15 \\
\times\ 6 \\
\hline
\end{array}
$$

himself. This puts the problem at step 5, and the remainder of the solution can be derived by application.

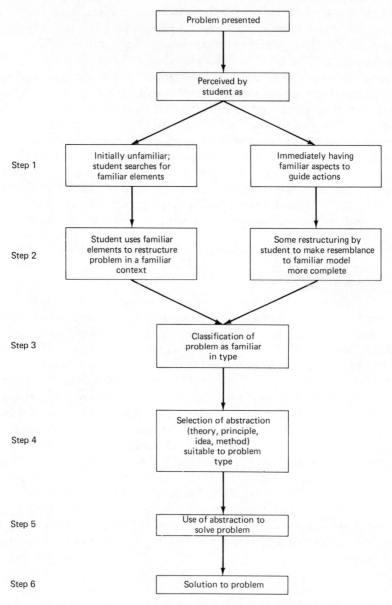

Figure 7.2 Application Stages of Problem Solving. *From Benjamin Bloom, ed.,* Taxonomy of Educational Objectives: The Classification of Educational
Goals, Handbook I: Cognitive Domain (*New York: Longman, 1956*).

The *analysis level* of the cognitive taxonomy subsumes three subcategories:

4.00   Analysis
    4.10   Analysis of elements
    4.20   Analysis of relationships
    4.30   Analysis of organizational principles

Analysis is, then, the level at which students divide cognitive information into elements, relationships, and organizational principles. Each subcategory is sequential; mastery over analysis of elements is prerequisite to analysis of the relationships among those elements, and so forth. A perfect example of proper sequencing of curriculum design at the analysis level is demonstrated by that portion of the CEMREL Aesthetic Education Program that deals with shape as an element of the visual arts. As with the remainder of the CEMREL curriculum, these materials are presented in the form of packaged units of instructions; in this case the units are *Shapes, Shape Relationships,* and *Shapes and Patterns.*[7]

In the first unit, students are taught to analyze the *elements* of shape. They are introduced to the infinite variety of shapes in the world around them and are taught to "break down" complex shapes into smaller, component shapes. They become aware that shape can be communicated through other component elements of the visual arts: texture, volume, color, size, and the illusion of depth.

The second unit, *Shape Relationships,* encourages students to perceive that shapes in art bear a relationship to shapes in the things represented by art. Students learn that many of the objects that make up the world are related by virtue of their shapes, and to understand the relationship between one major element, shape, and the remainder of a work of art —a clear example of analysis of relationships.

The third part of the instructional sequence is *Shapes and Patterns.* Madeja and Onuska describe the emphasis in this unit as follows:

> Color, texture, size, and shape are regarded from another point of view in the activities that investigate *Shapes and Patterns.* Students learn about order, repetition, and variation and how they apply to pattern formation. They find that a pattern is formed when one or more shapes are repeated or when elements such as color, texture, size, and volume are repeated.[8]

---

[7]*Shapes, Shape Relationships,* and *Shapes and Patterns* are part of the *Five Sense Store,* a curriculum in aesthetic education published by CEMREL, Inc., St. Louis, Mo.

[8]Stanley Madeja and Sheila Onuska, *Through the Arts to the Aesthetic: The CEMREL Aesthetic Education Curriculum* (St. Louis, Mo.: CEMREL, 1977), p. 36.

Higher-level thinking skills at the analysis level? Certainly. Difficult concepts? Not to you, but these instructional units emphasizing higher-order skills are in use in thousands of first-grade classes. This emphasizes an important point. While the higher levels of Bloom's taxonomy are more complex than the lower levels, education must provide opportunities for learning *at all levels* at each grade. Young children can do more than memorize facts. They can analyze, synthesize, and evaluate if the material and concepts considered are appropriate to their age.

In music schooling, many objectives can be classified as analysis. There is harmonic analysis, the analysis of musical form, aural analysis of melody, analysis of performance practice, and a host of others. Keep in mind that no matter what the subject of the analysis task, it will be facilitated by first analyzing the constituent elements, then the potential ways in which the elements may be related, and finally the organizational principles involved.

Bloom indicates several potential errors that students can make as they analyze, including gross errors, incomplete analysis, and overanalysis. Gross errors are those that misjudge the *nature* of the elements and the relationships among them. These errors often stem from misidentification of elements, failure to see the elements as part of the whole, or faulty knowledge and comprehension.

Incomplete analysis is the second error pointed out by Bloom. Here the student simply omits or overlooks some element in the analysis. Perhaps the most interesting error pointed out by Bloom is that of "overanalysis" in which students fragment the elements into such minute parts that their relationships become blurred. In analyzing a symphony by Mahler, for instance, the student analyst might easily be sidetracked with chord-by-chord analysis, neglecting to see the overall harmonic plan for the work as a whole.

If you are seeking a method for teaching at the analysis level, consider discussion to clarify analytical techniques. Certainly students should have the opportunity to continue problem solving learned at the application level, but extend their abilities to emphasize the breakdown of material into constituent parts and detection of relationships. These skills, like most skills, are heightened through practice. While a teacher may model an analysis of a measure or two in front of a class, the most traditional methods of teaching analysis involve some discussion, some tutoring, and at the college level, lecturing.

The process of analysis involves dividing the whole into its related parts; synthesis, on the other hand, implies the reverse: working with elements and combining them into a pattern that constitutes a whole. Bloom has divided this level into three sequential levels:

5.00 Synthesis
    5.10 Production of a unique communication
    5.20 Production of a plan or proposed set of operations
    5.30 Derivation of a set of abstract relations

If we look at synthesis from a composer's or an author's viewpoint, the unique synthesis results in an instrument for communication, whereas the intent of the communication may vary from simple information through entertainment to real art; the product is a unique communication of an idea.

The production of a plan is an act of synthesis as well. The outlining of operations to be carried out and the product that results represent a higher order of synthesis than does unique communication. This level of synthesis is faced by the teacher who is ready to develop a lesson plan or series of instructional units. In order to teach a specific set of musical skills, teachers must synthesize the knowledge the students must acquire and plan for the execution of instruction in the classroom.

The highest level of synthesis is represented by the drawing or inferring of abstract relationships. Bloom offers two kinds of tasks that students are often called upon to perform at this level. In the first, the student is presented with concrete data for which a previously nonexistent classification system must be derived. In the second example, the student is given a set of propositions from which he must deduce other relationships. An example of an educational task at this level is the formulation of a theory of learning applicable to classroom music. The creation of a theory from observation of the state of affairs of the world is well beyond the application of a theory in the formulation of lesson plans.

Students often make errors in synthesis. Faulty synthesis may result from a lack of understanding of the purpose of the problem presented or the omission of important elements as larger cognitive structures are built. Other errors are generated by students in applying irrelevant elements to a problem or in "overorganizing the synthesis" so that the results are artificial.

Having developed this discussion to the fifth level of the cognitive domain, one might consider synthesis to be a high-level endeavor reserved for students in graduate school. Bloom indicates that some goals are as appropriate at this level for the elementary school child as for graduate students. The only difference between goals for a school child and for a graduate student lies in the complexity or magnitude of the task. Children are certainly capable of synthesizing essays in English and melodies of their own composition.

Evaluation is the highest level of the taxonomy in the cognitive domain and is defined as the making of judgments about the value or purpose of ideas, works, solutions, methods or materials.[9] Bloom has placed the evaluation at the terminal point of the taxonomy because this process involves all the other mentations: knowledge, comprehension, application, analysis, and synthesis.

6.00   Evaluation
      6.10   Judgments in terms of internal evidence
      6.20   Judgments in terms of external criteria

The first kind of evaluation is based on internal standards of criticism. These standards are concerned with *accuracy* judged on consistency, logic, and the absence of internal flaws. This high-level task requires an understanding of the nature of thought. One example is the recognition that a philosophical argument has a logical flaw.

In evaluating a new musical work, the same kind of skill is employed. As the new work unfolds, it sets up its own logical framework. Say, for example, that the work begins firmly in major-minor traditional harmony, and suddenly a chord from out of the key appears. In evaluating the work, this internal inconsistency will color the eventual conclusion reached. Another example of a judgment at this level is made when one concludes that a musical work is too long, that it has too few "new ideas" in it to sustain interest.

The final level of the taxonomy supposes the ability to apply external criteria. Most performance criticism is rooted here. When the music critic concludes that a certain performance by a major symphony orchestra is the "best I have ever heard," he has arrived at that conclusion by the application of criteria external to the musical work: intonation, fluency, balance, and the rest. If the same critic were to conclude that a performance of the Oak Street Elementary School Band was the "best I have ever heard," the critic would doubtless add, "for an elementary school group." Although the critic applied the same criteria—intonation, fluency, balance, and so forth—the external nature of the criteria allowed for adjustments in the degree to which they had to be met to indicate high value. This is one difference between internal and external criteria: The former are rooted in the absolute, as they are in the nature of knowledge, while the latter are less absolute.

As one can see from this overview of the taxonomy of cognitive objectives, a systematic listing of objectives can be made from simple to complex and from factual information to abstract ideas and concepts. With a knowledge of this kind of instructional sequencing, the reader should be

[9]Bloom, *Taxonomy of Educational Objectives*, p. 85.

able to judge materials gathered in ensuing methods courses during the undergraduate curriculum. That schooling must be sequenced and structural cannot be overemphasized. A great deal of research in curriculum development and evaluation has added to our knowledge of the proper sequencing of cognitive information. The next chapter presents a taxonomy for the psychomotor domain. Although slightly different tech-

Taxonomic Level	Music Behavioral Objective
1.0 Knowledge	Presented with 15 pictures of instruments of the band and orchestra, all of them previously studied in class, the student will correctly name at least 13.
2.0 Comprehension	Given the scores for both familiar and unfamiliar compositions, the student will interpret each meter signature by demonstrating the appropriate conducting pattern to be used.
3.0 Application	Given an 8-measure figured bass line, the student will harmonize the upper three parts, following practices previously covered in class. Five mistakes or fewer will be considered satisfactory.
4.0 Analysis	Given the score for the first movement of Beethoven's *Sonata no. 11 for Piano*, Op. 31, no. 1, the student will identify in writing, with reference to specific measure numbers, the thematic material in the exposition, how this material is manipulated in the development, and how it is used in the recapitulation. Two or more references to the exposition, three or more to the development, and two or more to the recapitulation will be deemed satisfactory.
5.0 Synthesis	Given the basic chord progression for a 12-measure blues, as well as a set of words, the student will compose an original composition for voice, bass guitar, guitar, electric piano, and drums.
6.0 Evaluation	Given a score and a tape of his own singing, the student will judge his performance in terms of precise intonation, distinct pronunciation and enunciation, suitability of tone quality to enhance interpretation, and rhythmic and melodic accuracy.

Figure 7.3 Cognitive Behavioral Objectives. *Derived from Malcolm E. Besson, A. Tatarunis, S. Forcucci,* Teaching Music in Today's Secondary Schools— A Creative Approach to Contemporary Education, *2d Ed., (New York: Holt, Reinhart and Winston, 1980), p. 36.*

niques are used in training people to move muscles and react to external stimuli, the structuring of the instruction is of equal importance.

As an example of the usefulness of a taxonometric approach to objectives in the cognitive domain, examine figure 7.3. The logic of such a system is overwhelming.

Questions for Discussion

1. What teaching technique should be employed to teach your senior high school chorus proper breath control? If combinations of teaching techniques are to be used, in what order would you sequence the techniques?
2. In reviewing the taxonomy, at what level would you place instruction for seventh-grade band students learning about articulation markings?
3. Discuss the reasons for changing the curriculum and restructuring sequencing of the cognitive information in the 1960s and '70s.

Recommended Readings

Bloom, Benjamin, ed. *Taxonomy of Educational Objectives: The Classification of Educational Goals, Handbook I: Cognitive Domain*, New York: Longman, 1956.

Colwell, Richard. *The Evaluation of Music Teaching and Learning*. Engelwood Cliffs, N.J.: Prentice-Hall, 1970.

Bessom, Malcolm E., A. Tatarunis, S. Forcucci. *Teaching Music in Today's Secondary Schools—A Creative Approach to Contemporary Music Education*. 2nd ed. New York: Holt, Reinhart and Winston, 1980. Especially p. 36.

Dewey, John. *Logic: The Theory of Inquiry*. New York: Holt, Reinhart and Winston, 1938.

Engel, Martin. "An Informational Framework for Cognitive Research in Arts Education." In *The Arts, Cognition, and Basic Skills*, ed. Stanley S. Madeja, St. Louis, Mo.: CEMREL, 1978. Especially p. 24.

Madeja, Stanley, and Onuska, Sheila. *Through the Arts of the Aesthetic: The CEMREL Aesthetic Education Curriculum*. St. Louis, Mo.: CEMREL, 1977. Especially p. 36.

8/the psychomotor component

A great deal of the learning in music performance involves the acquisition of physical acuity skills. Prompted and guided by sensory perception, these skills are known variously as sensorimotor, perceptualmotor, or, most commonly, psychomotor skills. Psychomotor skills are defined as organized patterns of muscular activities controlled by changing stimuli from the environment. For the moment, let us consider this area of learning apart from the cognitive domain because guiding students in the acquisition of these skills requires a specific set of abilities on the part of the teacher.

We first address the seemingly simple task of a student's responding to the tempo of a composition with a foot tap. To perform this task a student must

1. Receive the musical stimulus (i.e., hear it)
2. Perceive the beat (isolating it from other rhythms, such as the rhythm of the melody)
3. Try out a physical response moving the foot
4. Receive and perceive the "correctness of the response" (a judgmental process governed by feedback from the internal neuromuscular system and the outside musical

stimuli mediated by the experience of the student)

5. Correct his or her actions and continue the response

The process happens so fast that its various elements are imperceptible to the person performing the task.

This is a simple example when we consider the complexities of other musical performance, such as perception of notes on a page and instant translation to action on the part of a woodwind player. With the task including feedback about attack, rhythm, tone quality, pitch, and intonation, one begins to see the enormity of the task and to appreciate the incredible efficiency of the well-trained human machine in coping with it. The speed with which a student acquires psychomotor skills is governed by many factors, which we discuss in this chapter.

Factors in Psychomotor Learning

For skills to benefit a student, they must be directly related to musical performance. Skills by themselves are not sufficient. There is a three-phase process that should be considered in making skills usable for the student. Acquisition of skills must be followed by a transfer of training and then by a retention of the learning. In some ways the process is similar to the acquisition of vocabulary. The pronunciation of a new word is learned with its common definition, then set in several contexts, and finally assimilated into the day-to-day language of the individual. A vocabulary of psychomotor skills is learned partly in isolation as part of exercises, etudes, and scales; is transferred to other musical contexts; and finally is absorbed as one of the working tools of the student musician.

Acquisition of Music Motor Skills

We use two examples throughout the discussion that follows to illustrate the psychomotor learning that takes place in the music classroom. Our first example is a beginning percussionist; his task is the mastery of certain *rudiments*.[1] The particular rudiment our young percussionist is attacking is the "single paradiddle." It is presented to the student as a succession of four taps—right-left-right-right—and then its corollary—left-right-left-left. Even the name of the rudiment, "par-a-did-dle," is an aid in

---

[1]"Rudiments" are isolated rhythm/sound patterns produced with a snare or field drum by specified use of stickings and accenting.

perception of the sound eventually to be produced by the student.

The student is instructed to begin slowly, playing the pattern as a series of slow eighth notes:

As he practices, attempting to make the execution of the pattern perfectly clean, rhythmic, and evenly accented, his progress is rapid. The tempo is increased slowly until the separate notes blend into one self-contained entity. Along the way, as he practices this isolated pattern, progress will be made at varying rates. This tendency to learn in spurts or surges, with the rapid acquisition of part of a skill and then a slowing down of progress, followed by another rapid increase in skill rate, has led to the conventional wisdom that people experience static periods in skill development known as *plateaus*. Teachers tend to accept these plateaus and to "stop pushing" when a student reaches them, backing off and allowing the student to coast for weeks or months until the next surge occurs. Psychologists have concluded that this is *not* an appropriate solution, for while progress is not always rapid, consistent practice almost always leads to some skills acquisition. The plateaus are not really flat spots in the learning curve but simply places of less rapid development. To get over these quickly, the teacher is admonished to reject the notion that lack of *perceptible* improvement is a sign of no improvement.

Our percussionist has developed a certain level of motor skill in executing a series of paradiddles. Is this a satisfying skill? Probably not, unless the student somehow is entranced by the sound of paradiddles, an unlikely occurrence. At this point we have a beginning-level psychomotor skill that is probably more "motor" than "psycho," acquired through the perceptual process. In music we have the perfect stimulus materials—the spots on the page, the musical notation. If our drummer has a wise teacher, he made certain that in learning the execution of the paradiddle, the student was presented with this stimulus material so that in the future the mere perception of the following notation pattern will cause the execution of the sound pattern by the student without conscious thought.

Our second example is of a young violinist. In most contemporary violin pedagogy a set of fingering patterns is used as a starting point, relying on transfer of these patterns to later use on the other strings, in other keys. The most common fingering pattern for beginning students when applied to the D and A strings results in a D-major scale:

This pattern is taught first in sequence as an ascending and descending pattern. Then the finger pattern is reinforced, leaving out various pitches, playing simple melodies, and moving from string to string. The notion is again one of execution of motor responses without conscious mental intervention. This unconscious execution is both a blessing (for its easy transfer) and a curse. If the pattern is not approached carefully and systematically, breaking the early bad habits is difficult, almost impossible, to do. The process through which the student learns involves *kinesthetics*, the subconscious awareness of the position and motion of the body through space and time. Just as a basketball superstar is somehow aware of his motion through the air above the court as he twists away from a defender while hurtling himself at the basket for a reverse layup, so the young violinist becomes aware of the position of the fingers, receiving feedback from the aural mechanism as to the tone quality and intonation of the pitches produced. The study of kinesthetic learning is a relatively new field, and the processes are not well understood, but rational analysis tells us that since music is an *aural* undertaking, the psychomotor processes are best reinforced by aural means. Although many string instructors see nothing wrong with marking the positions of the fingers on the fingerboard of the violin with tape, reliance on such visual devices detracts from and may slow the aural feedback mechanism on which the student must ultimately rely.

Transfer of Training

The term transfer of training is clouded in the psychological literature. It refers both to application of previously trained responses in new situations and to the facilitation of new psychomotor learning through previous related training. We will endeavor to sort out the application to music that exists in the literature, taking a middle-of-the-road position, one that concedes that transfer does take place but that warns against overreliance (which quickly can become wishful thinking) on skills transference in music motor skills.

To begin with the most easily comprehended case, consider our beginning percussionist again. With the paradiddle now firmly within his technical grasp, we must rely on his ability to receive, perceive, process, and act on the stimulus material when it is presented in new situations. Although it is painful to approach, we must address sight-reading of musical material. If the teacher has been assiduous in relying on both the notational and aural roots of the rudiment, the student should now be able to place the rudiment in context, able both to mimic a sequence dictated by the teacher (imitation) and read the rudiment in musical notation. To the extent that the student can do this, we can be assured that the desired transfer has taken place.

Unfortunately, in many music teaching situations, the notation-reading portion has been neglected in the original drill. The result is a sort of human tape recorder—a student who can mimic but who is musically illiterate. We venture to say that if English teachers did as poor a job of teaching children to respond to written English as music teachers do in teaching children to respond to written music, there would be a public clamor that would flatten school buildings across the country. Imagine a situation where a student is presented with a passage to "read aloud" (simple translation of the written material in sound, all comprehension aside. The student stumbles, the teacher "sings" the passage, the student stumbles again, the teacher "sings" it again, and so forth, until the student has painfully inched his way through the entire sentence. He is then sent off to practice "saying" the sentence. When he comes back, he performs the sentence by "reading" it aloud. Is this any evidence of literacy? Of course not. Yet in how many music classrooms does this scenario occur, and the teachers manage to get away with deluding the students, parents, and even themselves that "Johnny can read" music?

Music teachers must never forget that the physical act of performance may have absolutely nothing to do with a student's ability to handle the notation on the page. To accomplish the transference of training to new notational situations requires *drill* in as many situations as possible. Some students will be able to accomplish a great deal in a little time, others will take vastly longer; but until the student is well versed in the tremendous variety of contexts in which a notational unit can occur, there will be little evidence of real learning.

Taking our transferral one more step, we return to our violinist, who has learned a fingering pattern. If this pattern is shifted down one string, the student will be able to play melodies in the key of G; if it is shifted up a string, melodies in the key of A are possible—an easy transference. Another simple transference for most students is learning to finger the saxophone after having played the clarinet for a while, or the shift from trumpet to treble clef baritone. The degree and amount of transfer is contingent on the number of elements common to both tasks, the amount of and quality of drill on the original task, and the variety of situations to which the student has previously adapted. Perhaps the ultimate in deliberate transfer of training occurs in the brass bands of the Salvation Army. The music is all written in treble clef, with uniform fingerings. Even the tuba parts are transposed and written in this manner. Basic fundamental brass technique is taught, and the players find it easy to transfer from cornet to peck horn to valve trombone to tuba. A similar reliance on transfer can be found in the modern drum and bugle corps. One of the few professional corps, the United States Marine Drum and Bugle Corps, makes a regular practice of recruiting a well-trained trumpet player and then using him later on baritone bugle. Since all the fingerings are alike, bugles being all in the key of G, with the notation all in treble clef, the transfer is simple and direct.

We have used these rather simplistic transfer examples to raise an important point: This "common elements" transfer works. But beyond this, reliance on transfer can be inefficient at best. There are those who maintain that lots of general exercise builds the capacity for later specific activity. Thus you find basketball coaches running players through "shuttle drills" daily in the vain hope that it will somehow improve the "quickness" of the players, who will then react to a loose ball more quickly, preventing turnovers. Common sense shows that this is probably not the most efficient way to go about things. One thus finds some of the more savvy coaches training the players to go after loose balls by simply throwing the ball in their midst and having them fight for it. As we maintained earlier, "You learn to do what you do, and not something else." Application of this principle has brought about the great decline in teaching Latin. It was once widely held that training in Latin would somehow "exercise" the mind and make it more receptive to more useful pursuits, that the training would somehow magically transfer to the mastery of English and the like. We now realize that if such transference occurs, it probably does so in relatively small amounts. Unfortunately for Latin teachers, teaching Latin results in learning Latin, not in learning something else.

To use transfer to best advantage, teachers must first sort out those things that are logically transferable and teach them, ignoring other "exercise" schemes. Many generalizable skills can be taught involving basic principles of tone production, breath support, pitch discrimination, and so forth. Sight singing, for example, *can* transfer to better sight-reading abilities with an instrument if taught properly. The teacher must be careful in making assumptions about what will and will not transfer in the learning process. Practicing breath-support techniques used in singing has little transfer to those required to play oboe, which has a great deal of resistance.

Retention of Psychomotor Skills

Skill deterioration sets in as soon as a student has "learned" a new motor skill. Instantly, if reinforcement is not continued, the student begins to forget. The degree of this negative learning varies from almost imperceptible through slightly rusty to totally disastrous. Reversing this tendency is a constant battle for the music teacher.

Psychologists agree that one of the best preventatives to forgetting is "overlearning." For this reason, teachers must *not* stop "drill-and-practice" sessions simply because a student has seemingly "mastered" a particular fingering pattern, rudiment, or fundamental skill. Students must be instructed to continue for longer than they at first think necessary, then periodically review the skill sequence.

At first glance it would seem that the greatest enemy of maintenance of performance skills is time, but this is not totally the case. Although it is true that the longer the period of time between the original learning and the next application of the motor skill, the greater the skill loss, there is another and more influential factor—intervening but closely related motor skills acquisition. If a particular fingering pattern is learned at the keyboard, then the player does absolutely no playing for a week, the motor acuity lost will actually be less than if the player learned a different but closely related finger pattern without continuing review of the first. In the latter case, there would be a certain amount of *interference* from the newly acquired skill.

The review necessary to maintain skills need not be elaborate, but teachers must make their students cognizant of the necessity for constant brush-up work in motor-skill maintenance.

Systematic Motor-Skill Development

Teachers should take into account five influences on the development of motor skills in attempts at improving psychomotor development. These include

1. Physical preparation and warm-up
2. Practice allocation and scheduling
3. Feedback scheduling
4. Task analysis and sequencing
5. Learning environment

Physical Preparation. Although we have previously decried mindless warm-up exercises aimed at no particular musical goal, it is vital that teachers and students realize the importance of a proper, *purposeful* warm-up period prior to engaging in vigorous musical activity. For optimum development of motor skills, muscles must be operating at a functioning level. Just as no weight lifter or runner would dare begin vigorous energy expenditures without careful stretching and a mild exercise period, neither should a young musician be encouraged to attempt the rather violent muscle movements necessary in brass playing without a proper warm-up.

The warm-up period can be advantageous in optimizing coordination of mind and muscle prior to undertaking the new motor learning task. This time is excellent for concentrating on individual elements of performance: tone quality, intonation, and articulation.

The warm-up should progress from low, slow, and soft playing or singing through exercises that involve more articulation, louder playing, and higher tessiturae. Flexibility exercises should be employed as well, over the full range of muscle motion. Such preparation is important with all instruments and voice, but is perhaps most critical for brass players. The act of forcing an aperture that nature has designed for speaking, breathing, and receiving food to respond as a pair of vibrating flaps within a metal restraining device is an unnatural one at best. The physical forces, particularly in the higher registers, are immense. Younger players, especially, need to be told from the beginning that just as lifting a heavy weight with an unprepared muscle can be damaging, so can improper warm-up on the trumpet or trombone. The warm-up period should not be so long that concentration is destroyed and fatigue begins to cloud the learning picture, but it must be long enough for the player to reestablish connections with the instrument.

Practice Allocation and Scheduling.   One question that parents often ask school music teachers is, "How much should my child practice?" This is a legitimate inquiry, but like most questions concerning music education, one that has no easy answer. There simply is no optimum practice time. The usual response about a beginner is, "Oh, thirty minutes a day or so," but this response is mostly a conventional one with no real basis in reason. In advising students on practice, the old but true admonition should be invoked: "It's not how long you practice; it's how you practice." Consider the following general principles of musical practice:

1. *Complex continuous-action tasks, such as those used in musical performance, are best learned from distributed rather than concentrated practice.* If a student has a total of 140 minutes a week to practice, greater benefit will be gained by practicing 20 minutes daily rather than in two or three long-drawn-out sessions. This schedule would be best even if there were not the intervening variable of physical fatigue. We have found for beginning wind players that three 10-minute sessions a day are superior to one 30-

minute period. Young students, especially, are able to concentrate only for short periods. In addition, a lack of muscle development can quickly lead to poor embouchure formation. Ten minutes is about all a tender embouchure can withstand. A motivational problem can set in if, as a student tires, more and more errors are made because of fatigue. The practice session ends in defeat—clarinet 3, kid 2; hardly a good way to build positive attitude.

All other things being equal, the use of frequent short practice sessions is recommended. Perhaps the epitome of this approach is reached in the piano adaptation of the Suzuki violin method in which children aged three and four begin keyboard study. The method dictates that a child should be encouraged to play, even if only for a few seconds, every time he or she walks by the piano. The drop board is left open, and the child plays hundreds of short periods a week, even if the racket is annoying or inconvenient to the parents.

2. *Longer rest periods are superior to shorter rest periods in perfecting psychomotor tasks.* In scheduling the three practice periods for the beginner, one session before school, one after school, and one in the evening is better than three practice periods completed within a three-hour span.

As a student matures and the playing musculature and attention span are increased, the length of the practice sessions can be increased. But even for most professionals, the use of several shorter practice sessions rather than one long session is beneficial.

3. *Scheduled practice is essential in perfecting psychomotor skills.* Perhaps the most important thing that can be told to parents is that the child must be encouraged to keep a practice schedule, even at the expense of a popular morning television show or some family activity. Parents typically invest a great deal of money in instruments and music lessons. Most want to cooperate in making the endeavor pay off for the child, but at times they need to be reminded to help the student practice by providing a time when other household activities and distractions stop.

Feedback Schedule.   A vital part of effective practice involves the learner's receiving information concerning the physical act he or she is attempting to execute. Without proper and frequent feedback, the student's practice time is almost a total waste. For the experienced musician, practice is effective because the player has the ability to provide his own feedback; he plays, hears, and adjusts. This process is not possible for the beginning musician.

Several tools are available to fill this feedback vacuum for the student. The best and most often used solution is the private lesson. The teacher-observer can see and hear the results of the student's attempts and provide instant feedback. When giving individual instruction, teachers must remember that the amount of retention students will exhibit is directly proportional to the amount of feedback they receive. Most teachers are quick to give feedback concerning errors but negligent in providing feedback concerning actions performed correctly. An intelligent approach to the problem of feedback for every action is demonstrated in the fixed-distance rifle training in the U.S. military. After each shot is fired, the target is lowered, and a marker clearly visible to the firer is inserted in the bullet hole. The firer knows in a matter of a few seconds exactly where the bullet struck the target.

Studies have shown that increased feedback to the student not only facilitates retention but also increases learning of psychomotor skills. Ideally, the feedback is immediate; less perfect, but better than nothing, is feedback that occurs later. The widespread use of tape recorders in music education can benefit the learning process. Simply playing a tape of a student's performance is good, and the aural feedback is made even more positive if the teacher reviews and critiques the tape with the student.

Many skills useful in musical performance can be checked visually as well as aurally. No practice room should be without a large mirror: beginning wind students should be encouraged to carry a small pocket mirror with which they can check their embouchure formation periodically. With a simple list of positive and negative embouchure points as reference, students can be equipped to provide themselves with visual feedback.

The University of Illinois String Project[2] relied heavily on the systematic use of videotape for aural and visual feedback for young beginning string players. Similar work with piano students has shown that video feedback is an effective tool for both learning and long-term retention. Again, emphasis must be placed on teacher input in the feedback process. Simply playing a videotape of a student's performance is of little value if the student is unable to discriminate between error-free and error-laden performances.

The admonition to teachers to "use your eyes as well as your ears" in evaluating psychomotor tasks such as instrumental performance is an important one. We spoke to a well-known high school orchestra director who was trained as a euphonium player and came to string teaching rather late in life. When questioned about his great success, he noted that string teaching is particularly easy when measured against other instrumental teaching because all the students' actions are clearly visible. His point is valid: "If it looks right, it probably is." Visual feedback is less possible with wind players, and most difficult with singers; but even in these cases, a great deal of information can be gleaned by both teacher

---

[2]Paul Rolland, *Development and Trial of a Two Year Program in String Instruction* (Urbana, Ill.: University of Illinois, U.S. Office of Education Grant 5–1182, April 1971).

and student from visual cues. Embouchure, posture, and hand and finger position can be evaluated effectively for the wind player; for the vocalist, posture, the action-breathing mechanism, and assignment of facial tension are three visual cues that come to mind that can be of value in the teacher's evaluation and feedback process.

The serious problem in providing feedback occurs when the student is practicing in the absence of the teacher. Knowing that practice, lacking in feedback, is insufficient, teachers should encourage students to tape practice sessions for later spot-check review by both teacher and student. In addition, beginners can be given a taped presentation of the material to be practiced before each practice session to provide a basis for student judgment. Although overuse of this technique might cause an overreliance on rote methods, teachers must remember that unless a student has some basis for providing his or her own feedback, the practice session may be fruitless.

Another feedback device that can be successfully employed is peer teaching. Advanced students can make excellent teachers for less experienced students *if* they have been given specific instructions on peer teaching. Simply sending a student out to work with a beginner is not as effective as instructing the young teacher what to listen for and what to monitor. For instance, if a beginning clarinetist is having embouchure difficulties, a quick review or checklist, provided to the peer teacher before instruction begins, can give direction and structure to the practice session. The peer teacher will never be a substitute for the master teacher, but still can be a great help in extending teacher effectiveness.

Task Analysis and Sequencing. Before proper sequencing of instruction can take place in psychomotor skill development, the "series" of tasks that comprise the skill must be analyzed. Task analysis, the breaking down of a motor task into constituent parts and the ordering of their presentation by complexity level, is a logical concern of the music teacher. While no teacher would assign a Rose etude to a clarinet student with two weeks' experience, we have seen flute teachers introduce vibrato before breath-support concepts are firmly established, brass teachers introduce double tonguing before single-tonguing habits are established, and other violence done to music instruction logic.

As an example of ordering tasks into logically manageable fragments, consider the hierarchy of complexity extant in the fingering of the clarinet.

1. *Single finger movements, one hand.*

   The simplest fingerings to master are those that involve motion of only one digit, such as E to F in the middle register, which involves motion of one finger of the left hand only:

Next, the motion of one of the less dextrous fingers (the ring finger of the left hand playing C to D) should be mastered.

2. *Sequenced single finger movements, one hand.*

Movements that involve the motion of only one finger at a time but continue in sequence are more difficult:

3. *Sequenced single finger movements, two hands.*

These motions, which involve coordination of both hands should be attempted after the single finger movements for each hand are mastered.

4. *Combined finger movements, one hand.*

The motion of *two digits at once,* with the fingers using similar motion, comes next in the hierarchy:

5. *Complex motion involving more than one digit on one hand.*

These tasks include complex finger movements such as the example C to B-flat in which the student must raise three fingers while rolling the thumb to the register key.

Obviously, this list could go on and on through an established set of complex movements involving all the digits at once; we place it here to indicate that while task analysis is not a particularly difficult task for a class in which all students are learning the same instrument, the situation becomes much more complicated for heterogeneous classes. Our first example, the simple movement of one finger from written D to E for the clarinet, involves a much more complicated movement for the cornet player, who must simultaneously lift the third finger while pressing down the second valve. Yet in heterogeneous class instruction, these two movements are presented at the same time.

More complicated is the motion involved in the simple stepwise progression from B-flat to C for the trombonist, who must move a slide precisely 27.5 inches, no more and no less, to accomplish what is done on clarinet by the motion of a single digit, playing C to D.

This sequencing, or lack of it, is the greatest weakness in heterogeneous beginning class instruction. The impossibility of exercising proper sequencing through logical task analysis greatly complicates the music teacher's job. Additional time must be spent in individual instruction to facilitate sequencing for beginners.

Learning Environment.   A proper learning environment not only facilitates mastery of a task but also can aid in retention. Great care should be taken, when teaching motor skills, to provide practice areas that enable the student to execute the tasks properly. If, for instance, teachers do not encourage parents to provide a proper music stand, students will often practice with the method book propped on an open case or lying flat on the bed. The improper posture and instrument position thus learned is difficult to correct. Although it is common to have mirrors in school practice rooms, most students do not have access to this feedback device at home. Parents should be encouraged to provide a mirror in the practice area.

For any concentrated work, such as musical practice, it is essential that the environment be comfortable, well-lighted, and quiet. The notion of a scheduled practice period can aid in getting the parent's cooperation in turning off television and eliminating other noise.

Teachers, too, must often conduct protracted battles with elementary school principals to provide quiet and properly equipped teaching facilities. Observation of school music programs reveals that a great many elementary school instrumental programs are conducted in storage rooms or cafeterias or gyms, which carry heavy traffic. We venture to say that if English or mathematics instruction were carried out in such environments, there would be a public outcry.

Educational Taxonomy: Psychomotor Domain

Once the teacher has some knowledge of the five factors that influence the development of psychomotor skills, a more systematic look at structuring learning experiences may be undertaken. These factors—*physical preparation and warm-up, practice allocation and scheduling, feedback scheduling, task analysis and sequencing,* and *learning environment*—are a continuing concern to teachers involved in teaching motor skills. To order the learning experiences properly while considering these factors, educational objectives must be established on a broad scale. To accomplish this, we utilize the findings of ongoing research in the development of psychomotor taxonomies.

Early work in the psychomotor domain of educational taxonomies was conducted by Simpson[3] and follows a model in the cognitive domain developed by Bloom[4] and others. Simpson's work outlined a psychomotor taxonomy that, though "considered tentative, flexible, and incomplete,"[5] provides an excellent framework for our discussion.

The reason for having such a classification system is to order knowledge and the development of "intellectual abilities" for the purposes of developing curriculum and curriculum evaluation devices. The psychomotor domain is important in various fields in education including music and art, which entail motor abilities. Physical education and vocational education are other fields in which motor skills are requisite parts of learning.

The proper ordering of the psychomotor taxonomy can be applied to performance skills required of musicians, students and professionals alike. Simpson's taxonomy involves cognition *and* motor activities because the interaction between the two was not resolved by Simpson when the taxonomy was first outlined.

The taxonomy, as used in our application, contains five major classes:

1.00   Perception
2.00   Set
3.00   Guided response
4.00   Mechanism
5.00   Complex overt response

Each classification has many subdivisions to aid the teacher in consider-

[3]Elizabeth Jane Simpson, *The Classification of Educational Objectives, Psychomotor Domain,* Office of Education Project No. 5–85–104 (Urbana: University of Illinois, May 1966).

[4]Benjamin S. Bloom, *The Taxonomy of Educational Objectives, A Classification of Educational Goals. Handbook I: Cognitive Domain* (New York: Longman, 1956).

[5]Simpson, *Educational Objectives,* p. 1.

ing the sequence of development of motor skills, and each classification must be mastered in sequence. Skill in classification 3.00, guided response, is not possible unless all classifications lower in the hierarchy have been learned previously. Each of these major divisions is further broken down into a number of categories and subcategories. Simpson's work was general in nature, designed to account for all possible psychomotor responses. Keep in mind that some subdivisions to be presented here may have no bearing on that part of the psychomotor domain used in musical performance.

The first level, *perception*, is "the process of becoming aware of objects, qualities, or relations by way of the sense organs."[6] Perception is an awareness, an observation, or a sensing of a stimulus. Levels of perception have been divided into.

1.1 Sensory stimulation
1.2 Stimulus selection
1.3 Stimulus mediation

These are also sequential.

Sensory stimulation involves the receiving of a stimulus by one or more of the senses. The six sensory stimuli outlined by Simpson are:

1.11 Auditory
1.12 Visual
1.13 Tactile
1.14 Taste
1.15 Smell
1.16 Kinesthetic

In considering the stimuli musicians receive in preparing for motor responses, all categories except taste and smell seem applicable. Although taste and smell may be present during performance, they have no bearing on the motor skills related to performing music. The reception of auditory stimuli (hearing) is of obvious importance.

Visual stimuli, those concerned with images and movement, are received by the brain through the eyes. Examples of visual stimuli that are critical to the musician include seeing a conductor and seeing music notation. Teachers make many assumptions about student perception. The question of note-reading abilities can stem from this very low level in the taxonomy, that of the initial stimulus. Students unable to see music notation cannot respond to it with the proper motor response.

Tactile stimuli are received through the sense of touch. In music, the

[6]Ibid., p. 25.

impact of sound is often felt as much as it is heard. The volume, stress, or impact of music can be received through the sense of touch. Also received through this sense are stimuli produced by the physical properties of percussion mallets, trumpet valves, or piano keys, which induce sensitivity to texture, pressure, and weight. The marimba player receives a stimulus from the weight of a mallet as he takes it in hand. This stimulus will later be translated into the amount of effort applied to that particular mallet in striking the bars.

Kinesthetic stimuli are received from the activation of nerve centers (proprioceptors) in muscles, tendons, and ligaments; they allow us to make judgments about motion and the position of the body in space. The kinesthetic stimulus of feeling the position and motion of a bouncing drumstick aids the drummer in continuing a measured roll. The initial stimuli may have been visual (music notation) and tactile (texture, shape, and weight of the stick), but sensing kinesthetic stimuli (through activation of receptors in the muscles) is required to continue the action.

Stimuli in the perception classification are not presented in any particular order. Simpson notes that "the visual cues are said to have dominance in western cultures whereas in some cultures, the auditory and tactile 'cues may preempt the high position given to the visual."[7] Despite this, visual stimuli should be considered no more important (or less important) than auditory stimuli in playing music. At some point, the cues that guide psychomotor movements may be exchanged as learning progresses. An example of this occurrence is the memorization of music. Eventually, remembered auditory stimuli replace earlier reliance on visual stimuli (music notation).

The second category, *stimulus selection*, is a matter of filtering information or selecting stimuli that relate to the performance of a motor-skill task from those that are not informational (e.g., noise). An example of selecting a stimulus in music would be your concentration on visual stimuli from a choral conductor even as your peripheral vison senses the pianist standing up and the rehearsal room door being opened. In order to sing with the ensemble, the selection process is critical. If auditory stimulation were heightened in this situation by the piercing noise of a fire alarm, even though the conductor continued to conduct, the selection of the stimulus required to continue to sing would become more difficult as a new relevant stimulus was discerned. Stimuli relevant to singing are selected as a guide to action. Other cues are ignored or discarded.

The third category of the perception classification is *stimulus mediation*. At this level the selected stimulus is translated into meaning, which serves to mediate or guide the motor response. This process involves a continual refreshing or updating of the sensory information.

---

[7]Ibid., p. 26.

Consider a clarinetist during a band performance. From the mass of auditory stimulation she receives, she selects a portion of it, say her own sound and that of the rest of the clarinet section. She further filters this stimulus to that portion that concerns the frequency of vibrating air serving as stimulus. The mediation process now is applied and provides the meanings "pitch" and "flat," upon which she can base muscular responses to correct her intonation. These processes are continually repeated, providing feedback to govern further changes.

Set

The next level in the psychomotor taxonomy is *set*, which includes preliminary modifications in the organism as preparation for the motor response. The three categories of set, as numbered by Simpson, do not presuppose any particular order.[8]

2.1   Mental set
2.2   Physical set
2.3   Emotional set

Mental set is not a necessary precondition to physical set and emotional set. "Set" is used in the same sense as in the phrase, "Take your marks. Get *set*. Go." A set implies a disposition of the organism toward further action. While these categories draw on information and processes in both the cognitive and affective domains, their inclusion in a psychomotor taxonomy is nevertheless necessary.

Mental set includes those conceptions and knowledge from the cognitive domain that are prerequisites for physical action. In the performance of the G-major scale, a singer must, perforce, *know* what such a scale sounds like. The singer must *know* the starting pitch and the relationships of the notes within the scale. If the scale is to be read from notation, a part of the mental set would include the knowledge of the notational system.

Physical set is another obvious precondition to motor activity. Just as a tennis player cannot move to the ball easily if he is standing flat-footed with straight-locked knees, neither can a musician hope to achieve motor acuity if such elements as correct posture, hand position, and embouchure are not present beforehand. The teaching of physical set is easiest when visual cues can be used, as in string or keyboard performance. If the requisite physical set involves kinesthetic perception, the task

[8]Ibid., p. 27.

is more complicated. This is the case in teaching tonguing on a wind instrument or open, relaxed throat in singing.

Emotional set concerns attitude, or the emotional disposition to complete the motor act. Fine musicians are noted for their ability to maintain a high level of emotional set, striving for perfection throughout a strenuous performance. The presence or absence of proper emotional set can be the difference between success or failure in an effort to execute a complicated and difficult passage. A failure of will, a "giving up," can destroy all chances, even though perfect mental and physical set are achieved. Remember, too, that attentiveness and concentration are large components of emotional set.

Guided Response

The first level at which the motor act is physically demonstrated is guided response. Its inclusion in the taxonomy indicates that guided response is a stage or level through which persons must progress. Defined as "the overt behavioral act of an individual under the guidance of the instructor,"[9] this level is one of dependence rather than independence in musical performance. The two categories of this classification are familiar in musical settings:

3.1 Imitation
3.2 Trial and error

Imitation is the "execution of an act as a direct response to the perception of another person performing the act."[10] We noted earlier that imitation is one of the principal modes of learning in education, not just in the psychomotor domain. The performance of a musical phrase by the instructor, with its repetition by the student, is an example of guided response through imitation. Imitative teaching, or rote learning, is used by all music teachers, and it is used frequently because it is applicable to so many situations and is efficient if properly applied.

Trial and error is an approach to learning that is repetitive in nature. Through a process of playing, hearing, and judging the similarity to a model, the student eventually approximates the model more closely. This process often takes the form of learning to reproduce a melody provided in a recorded model. Trial and error is usually distinguished from direct imitation in that the task to be performed is generally so complex that the

[9]Ibid., p. 28.
[10]Ibid.

first attempt is insufficient for performance. Depending on the application, trial and error may be an efficient or a wasteful use of instructional time. The latter is the case when the performance might be accomplished through independent music reading by the student but because of a lack of reading proficiency it must be done by successive approximation to a model. The higher-level nature of the reading performance indicates the usefulness of the taxonomic approach to education. It is doubtful that a student could ever achieve music reading if he could not first demonstrate the ability to learn by trial and error or imitation. A delicate balance must be struck in the education of a performer; if reading is overly stressed without some early reliance placed on imitation of sounds and the musical judgment making involved in trial and error, progress will be greatly slowed. If, however, students are not forced to read, their progress toward musical independence will be retarded.

Mechanism

This level of the taxonomy (level 4.0) is the point at which motor actions and responses have become automatic or habitual. Guidance and modeling by the instructor are no longer required as a sort of mastery over physical action takes place. Musical performance involves a battery of mastered skills that the student must be able to call upon without conscious effort. Such skills as various scale fingering patterns, habits of breathing, bowing, and embouchure adjustment must reach the *mechanism* level for performance to proceed.

A great problem faces teachers when the mechanism level of response to a stimulus is achieved so quickly that bad habits become ingrained. This is often the case with improper breathing on wind instruments. An example that will show the dependence of the mechanism level on perception, set, and guided response is demonstrated in attempts at correcting bad breathing habits in wind players. Take the instrument away from the student, and the teaching of proper inhalation is greatly facilitated; the student quickly can be taught to inhale using the diaphragm rather than the chest muscles Return the instrument to the student, however, and the bad habit nearly always returns immediately, despite all efforts by the student. The stimulation provided through both visual and tactile senses causes cuing of the improper response. To block this cuing, take the instrument away, have the student inhale, return the instrument to the student's hands, and have him play. Many repetitions of this process can cause the stimuli to trigger new responses; eventually the guided response of proper breathing becomes mechanism when triggered by the visual and tactile stimuli of the instrument.

Responses at the mechanism level are simple, for example, breathing alone, the ability to double-tongue isolated from a musical context, arpeggio performance, and so forth. These simple tasks are assumed to be a repertoire of individual components that are combined at the next higher level of the taxonomy.

Complex Overt Response

With the repertoire of potential responses practiced, habituated, and soundly available at the mechanism level, students proceed to level 5.0, at which they use these responses in the execution of complex combinations of skills. This level of skill requires that the responses be made virtually without thought and with a minimum expenditure of time and energy. This is the level at which the complex actions of real musical performance skill must be demonstrated, for musical performance includes motor responses governing articulation, embouchure, breath support, posture, tone quality, intonation, phrasing, and so on down the list in an almost infinite number of combinations, for which the stimuli are presented rapidly. Simpson identifies two categories within this classification:

5.1 Resolution of uncertainty
5.2 Automatic performance

Resolution of Uncertainty. This is related to emotional set, but is at a much higher level. Emotional set involves willingness and attentiveness to execute the task, whereas resolution of uncertainty is at the level of confidence. The accomplished performer not only possesses a repertoire of responses but the sure feeling that even the complex task before him is within his grasp. In a sight-singing audition, for instance, lack of totally integrated confidence may result in an awkward and halting performance. Without this confidence, the player must reason out "chunks" of the passage over which he has mechanism mastery and perform these one at a time. The resolution of uncertainty depends on the ability to get a mental picture of the task sequence in its entirety. It is with this purpose that golf instructors often tell duffers to strive for a mental image of both the complete swing of the club and the resultant flight of the ball before they attempt a shot, rather than have them concentrate on a number of disjunct rules ("swing keys"), such as "keep the head down" and "keep the left arm straight."

Automatic Performance. This is the level at which an individual may perform any combination of finely coordinated motor skills with ease and sophisticated muscular control. Truly the level of musical performance, only at this level is the conscious mind of the performer freed to concentrate on the aesthetic elements of the performance. Musical performance is such a fine example of this level that Simpson, even though she developed this taxonomy for vocational-technical education, used "performing on the violin"[11] as her example for this level.

Self-Initiated Response

The first five levels of this taxonomy form the functional core necessary for music teaching in most instances. There is, however, a sixth level, labeled "tentative"[12] in Simpson's work, that teachers may from time to time experience in their students. At the level of self-initiated response a certain amount of intuition or insight is provided by the student as he succeeds at novel reactions to stimuli. This may include a completely new motor response to a rather mundane stimulus or may involve a completely foreign and new stimulus set. Colwell agrees that these levels "seem to be valid for the development of musical skills" but indicates that they are not directly teachable; they should be guided and fostered if and when they are attained.[13] The two levels of self-initiated response include

6.1   Adaptive performance
6.2   Original performance

Adaptive Performance. This consists of the restructuring of parts of past mechanisms into a newly integrated whole to attack a new skill problem. A prime example of this was displayed by the snare drummer who first executed the "triplet roll." In the normal measured roll, the sequence is a tap and one rebound per hand, alternated thus: rr-11-rr-11. In the triplet roll, many of the motor patterns from this and other rudiments are combined into a new whole consisting of a string of tap-bounce-bounce: Rrr-Lll-Rrr-Lll. A new rudiment skill has been adapted from existing ones in a unique manner.

Original Performance. This is the creation of a new psychomotor pattern in response to an entirely new stimulus. To be original rather than adaptive, the new response relies on a completely different set of motor

[11]Ibid., p. 18.

[12]Ibid., p. 30.

[13]Richard J. Colwell, *The Evaluation of Music Teaching and Learning* (Englewood Cliffs, N.J.: Prentice-Hall, 1970), p. 172.

patterns. An example might be the flute player who first attempted multiphonics or microtone slides.

While it may be argued with some validity that practically all such behaviors are to some degree adaptive, some, such as the examples given, are sufficiently different from previous skills as to be virtually unique. In learning ever more complex motor skills, some adaptation undoubtedly occurs at lower levels as well, but these are most often *guided* adaptations, initiated by instruction rather than by individual insight into problem solving.

Application of the Psychomotor Taxonomy to Music Teaching

The psychomotor taxonomy can be a useful tool in music teaching, both in initiating structured learning sequences for students and in diagnosing psychomotor learning difficulties. Before it can be applied, however, some important points must be made.

Although a strength of the taxonomy is its sequential organization for a given, single motor task, musical performance is a highly complex mixture of motor responses. Until the fourth or fifth stage, where this complexity is properly reflected, keep in mind that the taxonomy is addressing one task at a time. A student may have fully attained the level of *mechanism* concerning the trilling of C to D and still be at the level of *set* with other trills. Further, a student may have fully attained the level of muscle movements necessary to play in the key of D major on the violin and may even be able to integrate this skill with others to be able to perform at level 5.0 (complex overt response) if the cues from the visual stimuli remain in D major; but he may be back at level 2.1 (mental set) in his lack of ability in flat keys. In a diagnosis of playing problems the taxonomy serves as a tool for organizing thought, not as a substitute for thought.

An important way in which the taxonomy can be used is in the guidance of student learning by giving structure to the learning sequence. Checking back with the taxonomy often reminds us that we are neglecting to teach students to perceive kinesthetic sensory stimulation for example, or that we are overemphasizing mental set (cognitive process) at the expense of emotional set.

As a diagnostic tool, the taxonomy is a great aid. Some examples will illustrate ways in which it can be used. Consider the trombone student who can perfectly execute the motor requirements of a Blazevitch study in bass clef, but when presented with precisely the same etude in alto clef, fails. Analysis tells us that level 4.0 of the taxonomy is possible; after all, he just did it. Level 3.0 (guided response) has already been accomplished as you took him through every step of moving the slide to proper position. When you get to an examination of level 2.0 (set), you find that he has the *desire* to perform the passage correctly (he really doesn't hate you) and is physically prepared. The problem is not at level 2.1 (mental set). He has an understanding of the cognitive demands of the alto clef, knowing the names of the notes on the various lines and spaces. At level 1— perception—we quickly find the problem. Although the student receives and selects the proper visual cues, he fails to translate them into meaning. No mediation (level 1.3) is taking place. We have uncovered a reading problem. We have discovered a blockage. We stated that if a student has one missing link in the sequence, further performance at higher levels is impossible. Our ears now reaffirm this: the student cannot play the passage. The route the teacher must now take is clear. He goes straight to the mediation or translation problem, prescribing simple reading exercises to correct it. Once it is mastered, the student's progress through the subsequent levels is rapid. Although this example is rather obvious, others are less so.

Looking in another teaching studio, we see a teacher working with a young cornetist. The student is sometimes able to play above fourth space "e" correctly, but often misses pitches completely. She exhibits good embouchure and breath support. The teacher is demonstrating over and over again, in a vain effort to make progress. Is this a logical approach? No. The imitation phase has already taken place. The student, by performing correctly sometimes, shows that she *can* imitate. Her misses are most likely the result of a lack of sufficient trial-and-error practice (level 3.2). If she is ever to get to the level of mechanism, the teacher must provide time for the trial and error to take place. We chose this particular example advisedly because we have observed that lack of trial-and-error time is a serious failing in music teaching, especially in group teaching. Even though it produces a din, a few moments given to the students so that they can "noodle around," using trial and error on a difficult passage, is often far more effective than more explanation (level 2.1) or singing to them in hopes that they will imitate.

Students and professional musicians must learn and maintain psychomotor skills through a systematic process. The psychomotor taxonomy offers a framework for instruction in such skill development in music performance. The taxonomy is also useful in analyzing problems that music performers encounter as they work to achieve these skills. This analysis can also be applied to materials used in "teaching" skill development in music. Poorly sequenced materials encumber psychomotor development, as discussed earlier in task analysis.

Although skills develop at different rates of speed, research has indicated that this taxonomic organization is applicable in all cases. Using the psychomotor taxonomy as a guide, the next chapter turns to affective information organized in a similar hierarchy. This chapter does not suggest that the development of psychomotor skills is isolated within the organism. Information in the cognitive and affective domains interact as a stream of information, much as we have indicated that information, knowledge, and feedback operate in the psychomotor area.

Questions for Discussion

1. How does psychomotor skill development relate to the general music curriculum? What skills are required as part of this area of instruction?
2. If feedback is delayed or not given to a student, what will be the effect on the performance level? Think of examples where this delayed feedback would have the greatest effect.
3. Define task analysis as it applies to psychomotor development in voice performance.
4. Based on information supplied in this chapter, what is the effect of consistent long-term practice as opposed to intensive short-term practice? Why?
5. Why are learning plateaus considered valid in the educational curriculum? Think of situations that support the plateau idea in skill development.

Recommended Readings

Bloom, Benjamin. *The Taxonomy of Educational Objectives, A Classification of Educational Goals, Handbook I: Cognitive Domain*, New York: Longman, 1956.

Colwell, Richard. *The Evaluation of Music Teaching and Learning*, Engelwood Cliffs, N.J.: Prentice-Hall, 1970.

Gordon, Edwin. *Learning Sequences and Patterns in Music*. Rev. ed. Chicago: G.I.A. Publications, 1977.

Rolland, Paul, et al. *Development and Trial of a Two Year Program of String Instruction*. U.S. Office of Education Project No. 5–1182, Urbana: University of Illinois, April 1971.

Simpson, Elizabeth J. *The Classification of Educational Objectives, Psychomotor Domain*. U.S. Office of Education Project No. 5–85–104 Urbana: University of Illinois, May 1966.

9/*the affective component*

Recalling the discussion of the meaning of music in chapter 5, the reader should be able to conceive a greater purpose for music than the utilitarian purposes society often allocátes to it. Before that greater purpose can be achieved in an individual, that person must have a system of values in place, an "affective" parallel to cognitive structure. It is in the affective component that we place a value on the music that we hear; we discriminate among "good" music, "great" music, and music of "poor" quality. Holding values is the purview of the affective domain.

Can we teach students to value music? If we can, what values should we teach to children? For that matter, *should* we teach students to value music? Many music educators are hesitant to accept obligations such as teaching attitudes and values, believing that a value system is something that should be provided by a part of education that is distinct from schooling—perhaps the home, the community, or the church.

The Arguments

Those of you who feel some reticence in talking about the value and quality of music are not alone. Some who argue against including affective domain components in education list reasons of poor evaluation techniques in this domain, difficult grading procedures, or, more seriously, philosophical disagreement with the whole concept.

Perhaps the most serious hesitation listed by Krathwohl as he developed a taxonomy in the affective domain[1] was based on cultural and philosophical values. Achievement, competence, and productivity are regarded as public matters. Honors are awarded for high achievement in them and honors lists may be published by the dean or school principal, or even in the news media. In contrast, one's beliefs, attitudes, values, and personality characteristics are more private matters. Each person's interests, values, beliefs and personality may not be scrutinized unless he or she voluntarily gives permission to have them revealed. This public-private status of cognitive versus affective behavior is deeply rooted in the Judaeo-Christian tradition and is a value highly cherished by democratic traditions in the Western world.

Those who argue against structured learning in the affective domain draw analogies between free education and indoctrination in a democratic society. *Education* offers possibilities of free choice and individual decisions. Education helps individuals explore many aspects of the world and even their own feelings and emotions, but choice and decision are left to the individual. *Indoctrination*, on the other hand, reduces the possibilities for choice and decision by attempting to persuade or coerce the individual to accept a particular viewpoint or belief, to act in a particular manner, and ultimately to profess a particular value or way of life.

By avoiding education in the affective domain, we may have gradually relinquished the schools to control by cognition, without regard for feeling and intuition.

As Krathwohl observed,

> Gradually education has come to mean an almost solely cognitive examination of issues. Indoctrination has come to mean the teaching of affective as well as cognitive behavior. Perhaps a reopening of the entire question would help us to see more clearly the boundaries between education and indoctrination, and the simple dichotomy expressed above between cognitive and affective behavior would no longer seem as real as the rather glib separation of the two suggests.[2]

[1]David Krathwohl, Benjamin Bloom, and Bertram Masia, *Taxonomy of Educational Objectives, Handbook II: Affective Domain* (New York: Longman, 1956), p. 17.

[2]Ibid., p. 18.

The question of imposing one's own value system (values surrounding music, in our case) on students is one not to be taken lightly. Many beginning teachers and student teachers are hesitant to inculcate values and attitudes in young children. The personal nature of an individual's values gives them a kind of sanctity.

The most concise argument against teaching and learning in the affective domain concerns evaluation. While it is simple to grade children on the ability to name the notes in the D-major scale, assessing the attitudes and interests students hold about music is much more difficult. If objectives in the affective domain are clearly stated, however, the evaluation of students is much easier.

Examine the difference between a cognitive educational objective and an affective educational objective:

Cognitive objective: To develop the ability to notate all major scales in half notes, ascending and descending, one octave.

Affective objective: To develop a positive attitude and love for a broad scope of music.

One can quickly see how a teacher could teach the first objective because the task is defined clearly by learning music notations, key signatures, clef signs, limited range (one octave), and stem direction. All these components are cognitive and can be taught systematically; more important, they can be evaluated in concrete terms.

Now consider the affective domain objective. The terms used in the objective are ambiguous; they do not hold the same meaning for all teachers or students. What is a love for music? How broad should student interest be? How do we evaluate students' interest level? As you look at this affective objective, you should see major problems in its formulation. The problems are not with its intent but with its statement as an educational objective. First, we cannot determine the scope of what to teach. Second, we cannot evaluate, even peripherally, whether students have fulfilled the objective or not.

To state an affective objective more clearly, consider something that is teachable and that can be measured or evaluated:

Affective objective: To develop the ability to become sensitive to and perceptive of different aspects of a musical work.[3]

To evaluate a student before a semester class in music appreciation (pretest), we might present a selected musical work and test for the student's ability to determine which musical elements were perceived and which were not. To assess the affects of the music appreciation class, a

[3]Ibid.

test should be given at the end of the semester (posttest) to determine any difference in the student's ability. With the second objective, teachers should be more willing to rank students based upon the developed perception skills. The first objective is not a clear statement, making it nearly impossible to structure instruction, as well as impossible to evaluate. The second affective objective comes closer to the concrete statements we find in the cognitive area.

Learning how to structure educational objectives through a taxonomy should result in the teacher's being less hesitant to evaluate students in this area of music teaching. At this point, we should clarify the evaluation process and the grading process used in schools. Colwell suggests that "the solution to the dilemma seems to be to keep evaluation of the affective domain separate from the giving of grades. The grade is the reward or penalty for the student's effort in school. This may be unsatisfactory but it is a fact. If the development of attitudes and values is to be free from authoritarianism, it must never be mixed with decisions concerning academic grades."[4]

What happens if there is no difference in the pretest and posttest results? This is a constant fear, familiar to all teachers. What if Mr. Johnson employs every trick learned, every teaching skill at his disposal, only to find in an evaluation that the children fail to meet the educational objectives? The teacher's conclusion is that (1) he failed as a teacher, or (2) the students did not apply themselves. These conclusions might be drawn rather rapidly in the cognitive domain. Small, well-sequenced units of information are easily evaluated. Such is not always the case in the affective domain. The development of attitudes, and eventually values, requires longer periods of time. To assume that a third-grade student can develop a positive attitude toward a twelve-tone Schoenberg composition in a six-week grading period is folly. Although this example is radical, the plight is really not so different when we consider a positive attitude toward an art song, or toward string quartets.

The process of developing a complete system of values takes years. While we tend to jump to higher categories when discussing educational objectives, there are levels in this affective domain that can be achieved rapidly. An awareness of music, for instance, can be developed quickly. As one reviews the affective taxonomy, the speed of attainment of objectives should be placed in perspective. The development of a value system is a complex endeavor for an individual, and such a system will not be shaped by one music teacher. This realization may come as a relief to some apprehensive teachers concerned about warping the perspectives of their students to their own musical tastes.

[4]Richard Colwell, *The Evaluation of Music Teaching and Learning* (Englewood Cliffs, N.J.: Prentice-Hall, 1970), p. 127.

There is interplay between the cognitive information discussed in previous chapters and the affective domain. Students rely on cognitive information as they make judgments in the affective domain. The student who states that she likes to hear waltzes must have cognitive information about waltzes, for example, a definition of three-four time and the form of the music. The awareness of the music and the decision of liking or disliking the music are elements of the affective domain.

Teaching a Value

"I don't like that classical music." The student has made the decision and confronted the teacher with a fact. Or is it a challenge? The student points out that music performed by a symphony orchestra does not have a solid beat, and he only likes music that features vocalists singing meaningful lyrics. It is tempting for teachers to accept these attitudes and use popular music as the basis for their lessons, but such a maneuver is unwise. Students already "know" popular music. They have built a value system for it and use it in their daily lives. Pop music is for them a "commonsense" thing, and education in commonsense things is not the proper role of schooling. If the goals of a music teacher include helping students build a value system, use of music about which values are already strongly established gives little room for improvement.

What can be done about students' attitudes toward music? One of the things that can be done is to provide well-structured cognitive instruction. Although common wisdom has it that "familiarity breeds contempt," research has shown that this is not always the case with art objects and music. Students *reject* that which they do not understand. There is a certain truth here to the phrase "fear of the unknown."

What does *not* work is a verbal attack on rock and pop music by the teacher. Even well-reasoned arguments are to little avail. Direct attack on a person's value system is psychologically difficult to differentiate from direct attack on a person. When such an attack is made, the value system hardens for defense. It is probably best to acknowledge that pop and rock are of value to students by resisting an urge for confrontation. The receptivity students have toward music, as a result of their attitudes, has a direct effect on their ability to experience music. The student who hates classical music will be difficult to teach unless his attitudes about classical music can be changed. Since attitudes are learned, they can also be altered. Although a willingness to learn is not the only condition required for successful teaching, a great deal is achieved in a positive atmosphere in which all students have positive attitudes toward the subject being studied.

Leonhard states that musical attitudes are acquired through four major means:

1. Long exposure to cumulative experiences which influence the individual.
2. Vivid or traumatic single experiences in music.
3. Emulation of a person or an organization.
4. Association of positive or negative factors in a situation.[5]

The first means of acquiring musical attitudes is more or less environmental. If a student's exposure to "serious" music has been pleasant, with a favorable attitude toward music presented by his peers and his parents, the resultant attitude toward music will be positive. Consider, however, the student who comes from a home in which all such music has been decried as "long hair" and irrelevant. A negative attitude toward orchestral music, chamber music, or solo recital music is easily transmitted to the offspring. The positive or negative environment or, as Leonhard suggests, the *cumulative experiences*, are brought to the classroom by the student. This set of attitudes has been beyond the teacher's control before the student's first appearance in the classroom.

Sometimes affective structures can change rapidly. Here we suggest the possibility of a *vivid experience* that radically alters the student's attitude toward music. For example, the student who has maintained a negative attitude toward orchestras until seeing one moving performance. Or the child who has never liked violins attends a concert by Itzhak Perlman.

Do not assume for a moment that all single experiences will have a positive effect. Many students "swear off music" for life based on one or two embarrassing moments in music. If a self-conscious, unskilled student is required to perform before a class, that one incident may be so upsetting that the student will refuse to participate in music in the future.

The power of the single experience to alter attitude is the logic behind having large groups of students attend "youth concerts" by major symphony orchestras. The hope of the concert producers is that of providing the vivid experience. In having students attend concerts by the New York Philharmonic, Chicago Symphony Orchestra, or the great number of community orchestras in this country, it is hoped that inspiration will occur. Through the student's own experiences, vivid or traumatic, musical attitudes can be directly acquired.

Attitudes are also acquired by *association*. The association of music with positive, successful experiences will yield positive attitudes about music in general. Associations that affect musical attitudes can be direct

[5]Charles Leonhard and Robert House, *Foundations and Principles of Music Education* (New York: McGraw-Hill, 1974), pp. 122–23.

in yielding positive or negative results. The requirement to practice long tones for thirty minutes a day might adversely affect a trumpet student's desire to perform music, or continue study of the trumpet at all.

In examining attitude acquisition by association, the teacher must consider the classroom environment. Although we are not suggesting that you can please all of your students all of the time, teachers should be sensitive to the association between classroom content, atmosphere, and the attitudes that develop toward music.

Association with the musical attitudes of a particular music teacher is commonplace. Often, students will take an unusual interest in, and a positive attitude toward, a subject because of strong positive feelings toward a teacher. Some of the readers currently majoring in music education are doing so based upon initial positive attitudes toward a music teacher that resulted in positive attitudes toward music and, later, positive attitudes toward teaching. These *emulations* are important to the learning process. While teachers cannot control the associations students make in all cases, this means of acquiring attitudes is another reason for maintaining a positive classroom atmosphere.

The acquisition of attitudes through emulation reaches much further than a student choosing one person or teacher as a model. *Esprit de corps* shapes the attitudes of participants in music ensembles. The quality of performance and the attitude toward the music performed is directly affected by the group's attitude and approach to music and the performance of music. If students join a music ensemble with "a tradition of excellence," their attitudes are affected positively toward maximizing their efforts in performance. One of the teacher's most difficult jobs can be to develop this feeling of musical worth and performance excellence in a newly organized musical ensemble.

In considering approaches to teaching in the affective domain, the following steps can be taken to modify attitudes that students may have developed before enrolling in a music class:

1. *Assess current student attitudes toward music.* Before launching a campaign to alter student attitudes about music, teachers should assess the attitude students bring with them to the classroom. To gain this information, various tests can be used as a pretest of attitudes toward music.

2. *Use group discussions to affect attitude changes.* Students normally are more receptive to the values and attitudes of the "peer group" than to those of the teacher. Since attitudes are linked to a student's self-concept, the attitudes may be more easily changed by group discussion than by teacher lecture.

3. *Utilize firsthand experiences (and modeling) for more effective results in modifying attitudes.* One extraordinary experience can rapidly shift an attitude in the affective domain. Firsthand experiences in music might include performing, listening to, and creating music. The New York Philharmonic Young People's Concerts provide this kind of firsthand experience. This listening experience has much more impact on the listener than a phonograph recording does, but even a phonograph has more impact than a teacher talking about a performance she experienced two weeks ago.

4. *Assess influences on student attitudes and develop student critical abilities.* Students are all too often barraged with negative information by peer statements, such as, "You don't like *that* kind of music, do you?" The teacher can modify these attitudes only by becoming expert in anticipating the source and scope of the negative information. By developing students' critical abilities, the teacher can aid them in forming and defending their judgments. This ability to judge music can then be used by the student to make independent decisions and counter some of the negative influences.

5. *Assess student attitudes toward music periodically.* After an initial pretest of student attitudes, the teacher should assess the "progress" that has been made in the affective domain by the students. Do the students hold different attitudes after a year of instruction? When given the chance to choose what to listen to, do they make different choices than before? This information is important to the evaluation of the *total* effect of a music program, for a program can produce students who score high on cognitive tests but actually hold a more negative view of music after a year of instruction. They may "do well" but hate it.

These five approaches have been used and tested by many successful teachers. Either knowingly or unknowingly, teachers nurture attitudes toward music in the students with whom they come in contact. The challenge is to develop a systematic approach to establishing positive attitudes toward music and to develop the listener's ability to evaluate music.

The Exemplar Approach

In developing a means for the building and modification of student attitudes, music teachers should examine the "exemplar" approach. This approach is drawn from realist philosophy, and as the name indicates, relies heavily on the use of musical examples predetermined as "exemplars" or landmarks in musical tradition.

The basis for the approach, developed under a grant from the U.S. Office of Education, is the writings of Harry Broudy, an educational philosopher concerned with the quality of American educational systems. Broudy, whose interests are specifically in the content areas in the arts, as well as education in general, indicates that the direction that education must take is toward the goal of "self-cultivation."[6]

Broudy views today's world as much different from the community of the last century. Mass communication, large societal groups, rapid social change, and increased social mobility have lessened our society's dependence on *shared beliefs*, which are the basis of our value systems.

In defining the exemplar approach, Broudy describes the process as one directed to the consumer or the connoisseur of the arts. In music, this population would be the audience, the listener, or the consumer of music. Broudy, in discussing general education, does not consider the music specialist—the select, participating student. A student in "music performance" has selected (or has been selected) to participate in a program apart from the general curriculum. The exemplar approach is shown as one way to present aesthetic value education to the nonselect, nonparticipating student. In transmitting shared societal beliefs and values, aesthetic education can be considered a specific area of value education. The term that Broudy has attached to this system of value education, "enlightened cherishing," then becomes the primary goal of aesthetic education. Broudy states that "cherishing is enlightened whenever judgments are justified by reasons which show objects to be worthy of claim."[7]

The preferred approach to teaching a value system in aesthetics is through perception. Broudy discusses "imaginative perception which enables the student to apprehend sensory content, thus forming an image that expresses some feeling quality."[8] In using this definition and approach, the teacher can avoid discussion of different values held by various segments of society.

The exemplar approach, then, is a combination of the third and fourth steps listed to the approaches in teaching the affective domain. Utilizing firsthand experiences, or modeling, can establish or modify attitudes students hold about music. Through establishing examples, or models, the teacher can influence student attitudes by developing the students' perceptive and critical abilities toward music.

When attaching feelings or images of feelings to art objects (music), the approach is indirect because students must broaden the "repertoire of feelings," as Broudy puts it: "The quality of life is measured by the repertory of feelings which pervades it."[9] Few music teachers work to develop a base of feelings or a perception of feelings that a music composition

[6]Richard Colwell, *An Approach to Aesthetic Education* (Urbana: University of Illinois, U.S. Office of Education Grant No. 3-6-06279-1609, September 1970), p. V–1.

[7]Harry Broudy, *Enlightened Cherishing: An Essay on Aesthetic Education* (Urbana: University of Illinois Press, 1972), p. 53.

[8]Ibid., p. 57.

[9]Ibid., p. 58.

presents. The task, throughout the performance rehearsal, is one of correcting mistakes perceived by the teachers, not by the students. Music
"appreciation" class is often trapped in discussions about musical content
or the "elements of music," and often neglects discussion of expression
or feelings. In considering approaches to aesthetic education, Broudy con-
centrates on aiding the student to perceive the work of art in a way that
artists in that art generally perceive them. Using this approach, he rejects
two common forms of art education: the performance approach and the
appreciation approach as we know it in the traditional music appreciation
classroom. Though the performance approach is rejected, it is not dis-
missed as an ineffective means to relate the arts to students through the
acquisition of skills. Rather, it is rejected because of the small percentage
of students that can be accommodated by performance programs.

The traditional approach to music appreciation does not satisfy aesthetic
education or values education because the student is learning only about
music. The traditional approach allows students to gain knowledge about
music history, composers, and musical form. Learning about the childhood of a composer does not aid the perception of music nor the perception of feelings attached to music. For this reason, many music history
courses are dull affairs.

The music information is not all bad; in fact, this information can be
helpful in setting the stage for the perceptions that are so valuable. Here
again, we note the close tie between cognitive information and affective
perceptions. To learn more about a composer's life or the situation in
which he wrote a particular composition is interesting, but it should not
replace the major purpose of the music. The question is, What effect will
such knowledge have on the student's perception of music in the future?
Knowledge of a composer's lifestyle does not change the listener's
musical perceptions; hence it cannot replace them. Parallel problems exist
in teaching the other arts. Enormous amounts of time can be devoted to
transmitting knowledge about music or visual arts, dance or drama, but
the perceptions required for valuing can be deficient and remain so.

The key to the perceptive model is *experiencing*. One cannot offer a
valid comment or judgment about a music composition unless one has
"experienced it." For some music this could simply mean hearing a music
composition in a live performance or even hearing a recording of the performance. Consider, however, that the experiencing of some music requires more than a phonograph recording to complete the experience.
Examples include new music that entails theatrical movements in proximi-
ty to the audience, and opera, which includes staging, movement,
orchestral scores, and dramatic projection by the cast. To listen to a recording of an opera is not to experience the musical work of art as it was
intended. The television screen, although somewhat better in relaying
this medium, is limited in its ability to project the experience perceived by

the audience in an opera house. Here again, we emphasize the value of firsthand experiences of music performance.

The perceptions that are important in the process of experiencing extend beyond liking a composition or disliking it. The enlightened cherishing of a composition extends to the ability to discriminate through perceptions those features of the music that "deserve to be liked." The right to make such judgments presupposes the ability to defend them by virtue of the experience of, and serious reflection on, an experience.[10] This does not mean that you must like a thing universally. In order to make judgments about music or the other arts, however, the judge (student or teacher) should have the ability to perceive the art object. The formal properties of music seem conceptualized in such a way that they are "teachable" and can be transmitted through schooling. The ability to perceive the sensory differences in music is also something that most would agree can be taught.

The weakest part of the existing music curriculum lies in developing or fostering sensitivity to the expressiveness of music. The question whether students can perceive the expressive nature of music is amplified because the teacher hesitates at some point to discuss expressiveness as he (she) has discussed the concrete, formal qualities of music such as form, style, or melody. The perception of the formal qualities of music can be clarified if one element at a time is varied for observation purposes. Varying the rhythms in a melody while retaining the sequences of pitches is a simple example. At what point does the melody, a combination of pitches and rhythms, lose its identity or become unidentifiable?

The manipulation of the elements of a melody gives the listener insight into the perceptual approach to the arts. The situation is changed when the expressive qualities of the perceptual experience are considered. The same approach can be used in the presentation of expression, but the concrete examples and clear definitions are not evident. The difficulty arises when one tries to define the expressive nature of a work of art using the concept that the contents equal the "sum of the parts." Broudy asks, "To what in the aesthetic object do we direct the attention of the observers as evidence for our characterization? In other words, what can you point to as an ingredient in a music example which makes the work a 'happy, bubbly piece'"? The answer cannot be one ingredient because the expressive qualities of the music cannot be pinpointed as a characteristic of the melody or the rhythm or the tempo. People tend to agree about the expressiveness *in* a music composition, judging the total work on a holistic basis.

This issue of music's expressive qualities is further clouded from empirical treatment by the view that the idea of an "international lan-

---

[10]Ibid., p. 65.

guage of music" is not accepted by those in aesthetic education. Music plays such an important role in our lives in part because we can express things musically that we cannot express in words. The obvious difficulty is in trying to verbalize feelings (those feelings expressed in music) using the English language or the French language or the Arabic language. It is difficult, if not impossible, to assign meaning to any single part of music that is combined to compose the whole.

The question of instruction must be addressed at this point. If we cannot discuss musical expression, how do we approach the subject in the elementary school classroom? How should you as potential teachers be taught to approach this area of the arts with your students? A simplistic solution is *not* to discuss the expressive aspects of music. As this is a negative solution, consider that any discussion of a music composition should require that a person be able to point to something in the music that can be perceived when discussing aesthetic perception and expression. A curriculum in which students learn to assess music, interact with it, and perceive music as a fundamental underpinning is missing in many music programs.

To answer questions of classroom implementation of approaching the affective qualities of the arts, a research study was conducted that involved selecting examples of the arts for classroom instruction. The teaching method used in the exemplar approach to the arts followed rather common steps associated with teaching methods. It included

1. Preparation for instruction
2. Motivation
3. Presentation of learning task
4. Inducement of trial response
5. Correction of trial response
6. Fixation of response
7. Test response and evaluation

More time was spent in the inducement and correction of trial responses than in the other steps. Steps 3, 4, and 5 became the critical part of the exemplar approach as it was tested and developed. The *level* of presentation (step 3) was kept rather simple because major concerns focused on the inducement and correction of trial responses to the arts. Learning tasks consisted of having pupils learn such concepts as subject, formal relations, and mood as aspects of works of art, and practice in *attending to* these aspects in a variety of objects.[11] During the course of inducing a trial response and clarifying or correcting the responses, students developed some critical capacities for looking at works of art. This

[11]Colwell, *An Approach to Aesthetic Education*, p. V–37.

attention to the expressive qualities of art was exhibited by students who participated in the project.

The advantage of the exemplar approach has been demonstrated in the "regular" classroom. The playing of "good" music has been discussed in terms of the value of the music and the mood of the music. This kind of inquiry formerly occurred all too frequently in the school music rehearsal room. If the music curriculum is set so that "music students," those enrolled in band, orchestra, and choir, do not become involved in music appreciation, this values discussion seems one way to allow music participants to evaluate the music they play and its "artistic" value.

It is possible to organize a curriculum in which music students have less information with which to evaluate music than do students enrolled in quality survey courses. The reader should consider the number of discussions in a music rehearsal that were centered on musical quality, mood, or music expressiveness. The implied values of the teacher-director normally result from the prior selection of music. The aim of the exemplar approach is to lead students to a trial response to the expressiveness of music, which should be followed by the teacher's correction of that trial response.

At this point, consider the value of having the performing music student play materials that have varied worth. Too often, music performance programs are based on methods materials that are unmusical. The drill on these methods materials may be followed by student performances on solo and ensemble music of marginal quality. In this situation the music student receives less information about the value of music than does the interested music listener enrolled in a music appreciation class. The music teacher obviously should work to avoid this weakness. The gap between student performance ability and student ability to respond to music in the exemplar manner is large during the beginning phases of instrumental music, for instance. Some clear differentiation between the function and purpose of training materials and "real" music should be made by the teacher. A discussion of the expressiveness of piano fingering exercises is an example of this futility.

To summarize: In the exemplar approach to music performance instruction, students should work in a modeling environment to imitate performance style, expression, and nuance. This training should give way to an establishment of values *about* music: what music is "great," what music should be performed, and how music should be performed. Students learn to develop psychomotor skills through visual and oral imitation. This imitation process can be used effectively to establish values about performance style. A question may be asked: "Was that performance appropriate?" In other words, two questions are related: (1) Was the performance acceptable, and (2) was the composition acceptable? While a music composition can be "great" by any evaluation standard, the quality of the performance of the piece may vary. This is yet another area that the listener must be capable of evaluating. At the base level of this value structure must be a set of exemplars—good music examples and good performances of these compositions. The teacher's guidance in formulating, inducing, and correcting responses to these musical examples is a critical part of music instruction in the affective domain.

The Taxonomy: Affective Domain

To this point we have discussed attitudes and values rather indiscriminately, using the terms in a commonsense way, as they are used in everyday language. To discuss the taxonomy meaningfully, we must be more precise, deferring to terms defined by Krathwohl for the development of educational objectives in the affective domain:

1.0 Receiving (attending)
2.0 Responding
3.0 Valuing
4.0 Organization
5.0 Characterization of a value or value system[12]

Our purpose for presenting this taxonomy is different from Krathwohl's intent of its use as a basis for evaluation. We present it as a means of organization of *what* to teach and *when* to teach it. As with the cognitive domain taxonomy, the structure offered should aid the teacher in sequencing instruction, a major concern of the schooling process.

The portion of the affective domain that can be applied to schooling is limited. First, readers should note that valuing (level 3.0) is at a fairly high level in the affective domain and that several lower levels must be attained before the student is able to "value" music. The second observation, one offered by Colwell, is that characterization (level 5.0) in the affective taxonomy is at the operational level of the "dedicated artist, scientist, statesman, teacher, or whatever, whose life and decisions all revolve around a single focus."[13] This level of endeavor is far beyond what is appropriate for the public schools.

For a discussion of sequencing in the affective domain, let us consider only the first four levels outlined by Krathwohl. As with the cognitive taxonomy, these four levels are sequenced, each depending on the attainment of those levels below it in the taxonomy.

[12]Krathwohl et al, *Taxonomy of Educational Objectives*, p. 95.
[13]Colwell, *The Evaluation of Music Teaching and Learning*, p. 177.

Receiving

The first level is *receiving*, which is concerned with the learner being sensitized to the existence of certain phenomena and stimuli; that he or she be willing to receive or attend to them.[14] By this definition, receiving is an essential first step to responding to music. This level of the taxonomy is divided into three levels:

1.1 Awareness
1.2 Willingness to receive
1.3 Controlled or selected attention

The *awareness* classification is in many respects analogous to "knowledge" in the cognitive taxonomy. The awareness level is not concerned with facts, however, but merely with a consciousness of stimuli such as objects or sounds. The concept of awareness in the taxonomy is not of earth-shattering educational significance. Still, its inclusion is necessary to the logical completeness of the sequence. Considerations of awareness in the music classroom lead to questions such as these: Can the students hear a musical example? Is Billy aware that this example is being played, or is he absorbed in reading a book? Is the general din in the classroom so loud that it masks the music I want the students to hear? More specific objectives are difficult to specify at this level because once a student has *processed* the aural information in any way, a higher level of the taxonomy has been achieved.

Objectives at the awareness level are so simplistic that they are rarely stated. An example of one such objective might be: *Students will become aware that there is music being played in the room.*

The second category, *willingness to receive*, moves student from the passive role of being aware (knowing that music is there) to being willing to tolerate the stimulus. This is still a neutral ground, for no judgments are made. The only thing new in the situation is that the student will now sit and listen to the music without leaving the room. Responses at the willingness level range from the lowest level, at which the student tolerates the music (stimulus) without trying to avoid it by reading a book or changing the radio station, to a higher level, at which the student is willing to attend to the music (stimulus).

An example of an educational objective at this level would be that the student "develops a tolerance for a variety of types of music."[15] One can see that it would be easier to test for achievement of objectives in the second category than the first level. Attending to music is a rather com-

[14]Krathwohl, et al., *Taxonomy of Educational Objecteries*, p. 98.
[15]Ibid., p. 108.

mon concern of the general music teacher and forms a low-level objective for the listening activities that are part of general music instruction.

The willingness to listen should not be confused with any valuing of music, for this level does *not* include judgments of musical worth, nor a preference for one kind of music over any other. All that is present at this level is the willingness to listen to different stimuli. Questions for evaluation at this level tend to be phrased in a "would you be interested" or "would you like to" manner. Consider specific examples for an evaluation of this objective.

The student is willing to take part in a musical activity:

I would be interested in listening to jazz
records with the high school music club   ____ yes ____ maybe ____ no

I would like to be able to play the music
that I hear on radio   ____ yes ____ maybe ____ no

This is the kind of pretesting (although at a very low level we have suggested as important to the teacher in assessing students' attitudes towards music.

Even this second subcategory is lower than most teachers' initial aims or objectives for a class in general music. The real attention of the listening component in general music or music appreciation courses begins with the third level, that of *controlled* or *selected attention*. After assessing the students' willingness to receive music stimuli, the next step is obviously one of focusing the students' ability to receive. This is the first level at which the learner is in some control of the situation, for the student selects and pays attention to the preferred stimulus. Stimuli are competitive; the learner can now decide on which stimulus to focus attention. Even this focusing should not be deemed a true value judgment; the emphasis here is not so much on the selection process but on the ability to control the attention to one stimulus, given several. Students who cannot control their attention to perceived stimuli will have great difficulty proceeding further in the taxonomy of objectives.

Many cognitive objectives in general music presuppose attainment of the awareness level in the affective domain. For example, general music teachers often present lessons designed to teach students to label one sound "clarinet" and another sound "trumpet." This cognitive task is impossible if students cannot hear the sounds (1.1 awareness), will not attend to them (1.2 willingness to receive), and will not "filter" the desired portions of the sound stimuli from traffic noise or the conversation of their classmates (1.3 controlled or selected attention).

Responding

The second category of the affective domain *responding*. This category of the taxonomy is also divided into three levels:

2.0 Responding
  2.1 Acquiescence in responding
  2.2 Willingness to respond
  2.3 Satisfaction in response

In this category of the taxonomy, the student is motivated beyond mere willingness to attend; there is also a willingness to *process* the information receive. As the first stage in the "learn by doing" process, the student is willing to commit himself or herself in some small way to the stimulus. This remains a low-level commitment, still below the level as which we can identify positive and negative student attitudes or the value of the stimulus.

The first subcategory, *acquiescence in responding,* is the level as which the first active response to the stimulus by the learner is displayed. The student at this level makes a response but does not feel any personal necessity for doing so. Krathwohl suggests, "Should the conditions be such that other alternatives of response are open, and there were no pressures to conform with the teacher-held standard or social norm, the student might well choose an alternative response."[16] Two conditions are suggested here, one being an absence of hostility and the second being little evidence of active pleasure in responding. Objectives are difficult to state at this level and are usually in terms of passive compliance, for example: *The student will sing when told to do so.*

This example of an objective gives a clear view of the compliant nature at this level of response. In evaluating behaviors at this level, one should establish whether the student was asked to respond or initiated the response. A student who initiates a response in a free-responding manner is probably acting at a higher level of the affective domain taxonomy. All that can be assessed is the student's acquiescence or compliance.

The second level of responding, *willingness to respond,* is the beginning of voluntary activity. Cooperation is a term applicable at this level, which extends beyond acquiecence. The subtle difference between levels 2.1 and 2.2 of responding is that at the first, the student participates if asked or told to participate, whereas at the second level, the student participates without being told. An example of a music objective at this level would be: *A student displays an interest in voluntarily participating in choirs.*

[16]Ibid., p. 119.

Most students who participate in music performance groups are at the willingness to respond level. That these students elect to participate in music places them beyond the acquiecence level demanded of students in the general music classroom. This level is a starting point for performance ensembles with the hope that these students will quickly move to the next level in the affective domain.

The third level of responding, *satisfaction in response*, is the salient component of the category, for here the student receives some apparent enjoyment or satisfaction from his or her actions. Note that satisfaction is closely associated with reinforcement or reward, which we know increases the likelihood of a particular behavior or response. Satisfaction in responding is close to the first level of true valuing; for the first time, the student receives positive feedback in the form of satisfaction or pleasure. That the responding delivers some satisfaction will help the student build a value for it later. There is a relationship between responding in order to derive satisfaction and the next level, which is the acceptance of a value or the establishment of a value. Educational objectives at this level might be stated as: *The student derives satisfaction from singing with others. The student derives satisfaction from listening to good music.*

Terms such as "thrilling," receiving an "emotional kick," and "excitement" might be attached to this level of the taxonomy. Teachers should be aware that students can be satisfied with some parts of the music program while only willing to respond in others, or even at an acquiescence stage with still other parts of a program. An evaluation of student progress in the affective domain should account for the aspects of a program that the student finds satisfactory, exciting, dull, boring, or uninteresting. All these reactions come together to make up the base for student feelings, attitudes, and finally values as they apply to music or any other subject matter.

Valuing

Valuing, the third major level of the taxonomy, implies that the stimuli or phenomena valued have the abstract quality of personal worth. The concept of worth is in part the result of an individual's self-reinforcement from level 2.3, but it is also a product of socialization that has been slowly internalized or accepted and has come to be used by the student as his or her own criterion of worth.[17] This category of the taxonomy has been divided into three levels:

[17]Ibid., p. 139.

3.0 Valuing
    3.1 Acceptance of a value
    3.2 Preference for a value
    3.3 Commitment to a value

At the first level of this category, *acceptance of a value*, students accept the set of values from society, from their peers, or from their parents. The term *belief* is often associated with this cognitive acceptance of value. Beliefs have varying degrees of acceptance, and at the acceptance level, a value is not firmly a part of an individual's own beliefs or attitudes. At this lowest level of valuing, it is implied that the value is internalized deeply enough "to be a consistently controlling force on behavior."[18]

Acceptance of a value can be exemplified in an educational objective, as follows: *The student understands the values that may accrue from performing in a musical organization.*

In testing for this acceptance level of the taxonomy, evidence must be sought that the student wishes to perform music because it has worth (holds value) and is important as an entity. If a student wishes to perform music only to receive rewards of money, fame, and glory, the acceptance of a value level has not been reached. In this case, the student still remains at level 2.3 (satisfaction in response). Value has been placed on receiving reward, not on performing music. The reward in this case is external and not intrinsic to the actual performance. Although a student's initial reason for playing music may be to gain parental approval, if the valuing level is to be obtained, these external satisfactions must be replaced by internal ones.

Preference for a value is the next level of affective response. A student may hold many values simultaneously, but when these values are used to decide the allocation of scarce resources, preferences for one or another of the values become observable. At this level the value has become internalized and begins to become part of a operant value set. The value of musical experience, for example, has become greater than, say, the value of free time. This is the level at which a student can be expected to practice just for the sake of making music, rather than to fulfill some requirement. It is here that a student begins to "give up" certain things to receive musical value in return.

Assessment and evaluation at this level often involve the use of preference scales to ascertain the student's values ranking. Such questions might include, "Which would you rather do, go to a concert or go to a basketball game?" Or, at a more sophisticated level of response, "Would you rather attend an all-Baroque or an all-Classical concert?"

[18]Ibid., p. 141.

The final stage in the value category is *commitment to a value*. Remember our discussion of levels of teacher concerns when we pointed out that a high-level activity involved the "collaboration" stage, at which teachers became actively involved in telling others about their teaching and trying to convince them that theirs was the right way to do things? That is related to this commitment level of value. At this level a person attempts to "further the cause" of the thing valued. The difference between this level and the values below it is a matter of degree. Whereas in the lower orders of values learners derive pleasure from a particular activity or area of study, at this level of commitment there is a sense of urgency that was not present before. Krathwohl goes so far as to say that at this level, the exercise of the value has become an aroused need or drive.

Ministers, especially evangelicals, operate at this level of valuing. So do students who organize themselves into small ensembles or hold part-time jobs to pay for lessons or new instruments. A person does not have to hold only *one* value at this level; there can be many coexistent values.

Organization

The fourth major category for the affective domain is *organization*. Organization implies a reasoned structure of values, more complex than mere judgments of dominance or preference. There are only two levels to this category of the taxonomy:

    4.0 Organization
         4.1 Conceptualization of a value
         4.2 Organization of a value system

Conceptualization of a value is a process in which a student is able to form abstractions and conceptualizations about a value, which allows that value to be related to those already held or to new values he or she may come to hold in the future. Instead of merely displaying positive behaviors in the presence of a Debussy piece, which, if consistent, would characterize the valuing level, a student is able to provide reasoned argument concerning which parts of the compositions he or she values, and why.

The conceptualization displayed about a musical work will be abstract rather than concrete, and as Krathwohl points out, "In this sense, it will be symbolic. But the symbols need not be verbal symbols."[19] An appropriate educational objective at this level would be:

[19]Ibid., p. 183.

The student can explain the relationship between some feelingful situation in his own life and its musical analogue.

Organization of a value system occurs when a student has conceptualized a value system or complex and has brought those values together into an internally consistent system that can serve to guide his or her actions. It is at the level of organization of a value system that personal philosophies arise, and it is at this level that you as music education students are now formulating a set of closely held beliefs and personal principles to give direction to your future endeavors.

It is important to realize that the complexity of values in the system may change through time. Some persons constantly reassess their values; others are willing to internalize dogma. An example of an objective at this level might be:

The student begins to form judgments about the major directions in which music education should move.

Characterization by a Value or a Value Complex

Krathwohl's fifth category in the affective domain is usually held to be beyond the responsibility of schools. At this level

> the values have a place in the individual's value hierarchy, are organized into some kind of internally consistent system, have controlled the behavior of the individual for a sufficient time that he has adapted to behaving in this way; and an evocation of the behavior no longer arouses emotion or affect except when the individual is threatened or challenged.[20]

The value system is now so strong that it is impossible to separate the system from the person holding it. Indeed, at this level the value system is the best characterization of the person. For instance, it is impossible to conceive of Joan of Arc without conceiving of the strongly held value system that led to her martyrdom. Her philosophy was totally integrated into her view of the world.

The great teachers, those rare academics whose very being is their teaching, have achieved this level. People like George Wythe, the father of America legal education, or Nadia Boulanger, the great composition teacher of the twentieth century, come to mind. There are probably a few great teachers on your campus as well. Seek them out. They are the best role models that can be found.

[20]Ibid., p. 165.

Questions for Discussion

1. Select a music performance area and write one educational objective for each category and subcategory from the "awareness" level through the "commitment" level. Using your series of objectives, what age would be the earliest at which you could start training for your first objective at the awareness level?
2. Which of your attitudes toward music have been affected since your entrance into university life? What caused you to change your attitudes either positively or negatively?
3. What is the relationship between attitudes, values, and beliefs? Relate your discussion to the study of music.
4. Describe the interaction between the cognitive domain and the affective domain. Why must we rely on cognitive information to develop expertise in the affective domain?

Recommended Readings

Broudy, Harry. "Arts Education as Artistic Perception." Address to the Conference on the Foundation of Education, Lehigh University, 1974.

———. *Enlightened Cherishing: An Essay on Aesthetic Education*, Urbana: University of Illinois Press, 1972.

———. "Tacit Knowing and Aesthetic Education." In *Aesthetic Concepts and Education*, Urbana: University of Illinois Press, 1970.

Colwell, Richard. *An Approach to Aesthetic Education*. Urbana: University of Illinois, U.S. Office of Education No. 3-6-06279-1609, September 1970.

———. *The Evaluation of Music Teaching and Learning*. Engelwood Cliffs, N.J.: Prentice-Hall, 1970.

Krathwohl, David; Bloom, Benjamin; and Masia, Bertram. *Taxonomy of Educational Objectives, Handbook II: Affective Domain*. New York: Longman, 1956. Especially p. 17.

Leonhard, Charles, and House, Robert. *Foundation and Principles of Music Education*. New York: McGraw-Hill, 1974.

part
five

10/*assessment: personal and professional*

After completing this text, the prospective music teacher may still be left with basic questions. For the most part, these questions will center on a general evaluation and assessment of the professional. This assessment will have an impact on the manner in which you develop as a teacher. Of immediate concern will be situations you observe during your early undergraduate methods courses. These situations include four assessment areas: teacher competence, teaching environment, student achievement, and the school curriculum.

Universities spend much time and energy selecting suitable teaching centers for student observers and student teachers, but you should consider methods of reviewing each component of the total learning environment. Some criteria for observation will undoubtedly be given by your professors to aid you in determining the positive and negative aspects of the teaching and learning you observe. These observation criteria will include many points discussed in this text concerning various applications of teaching technique to the domains of educational objectives. Another major decision point each teacher must pass is the determination of his or her own qualifications as a teacher. In chapter 3, we defined a large number of prerequisites for becoming a music teacher. They include academic and musical preparation plus a genuine commitment to teaching as a profession. The personal assessment process should be a continuing one as you complete your courses in methods and educational theory at the undergraduate level.

In this personal assessment of commitment to teaching, the teacher-to-be should consider the world of teaching *as it will be in a few years*, not as it is now or was five years ago. The teaching profession is changing as societal pressure places new demands and expectations on schools and consequently on teachers. These areas of consideration discussed in this chapter can serve as a summary for the text as well as a framework for personal assessment as the reader continues to pursue the coursework, the practice, and the observations of the educational system that will lead to a professional life as a teacher of music.

Assessment of the Profession

Several observation trips to review specific teachers and their performance in the classroom are scheduled during undergraduate studies in education. At times, specific assignments include observation of how closely the teacher follows a lesson plan, how well the music teacher conducts, or how well the music rehearsal is organized. Other observations relate to the teacher's use of time in the classroom and classroom management. For example, how many minutes does the music teacher consume in verbal discussions?

Since most undergraduate students are critical of everything they observe (including their university professors), we are not asking you to become a hypercritical henchman in the back of the classroom. We *do* ask that you apply a realistic evaluation tool to your observation assignments. Time spent in observing teachers can be profitable if you have a list of items to check during your visits. You will surely be assigned a checklist. If you have some notion of what you are looking for in a teacher, your observations will have a focus for later discussions with the teacher you observe and with your methods teachers at the university.

Figure 10.1 indicates nine areas that most teacher rating forms include for evaluation. Rating scales can vary greatly, employing checks or minuses, various point systems, or weighted scales. This sample rating form employs a five-point scale with one (1) being the highest rating.

The following items have been selected for teacher rating through observation of teachers in the classroom. Factors other than those listed herein enter into an evaluation of the teaching staff; nevertheless, observation techniques should be sufficient to rate staff members on the items listed. Ratings are to be made on a five-point scale; a rating of (1) is the highest score; and a rating of (5) the lowest.

	Rating				
Personality	1	2	3	4	5
1. Appearance and manner					
2. Reliability and punctuality					
3. Poise and emotional stability					
4. Resourcefulness (originality)					
5. Leadership					
Professionality					
1. Teaching efficiency					
2. Pupil interaction					
3. Student discipline					
4. Classroom management					
TOTAL					

Comments:

Figure 10.1 Teacher Observation Chart.

Woodruff devised a checklist for self-evaluation that includes procedures a competent teacher should follow. His six-point checklist (figure 10.2), is stated in behavioral terms. Woodruff indicates that the checklist is a simple one; you will note the topics overlap with the teacher rating form. Some of the topics cannot be observed in a single visit to a teacher's classroom, and it is important to remember that observation trips tend to be isolated glimpses of what teachers are doing in their classes. To condemn a teacher for poor classroom management after only one visit would be unfair.

A number of checklists might be cited that are more complex than those offered here, but the basic components would be much the same. For your purposes as students of education, it is sufficient to watch the teacher in action and discuss his or her techniques, successes, and fail-

A competent teacher is one who performs the following acts skillfully and thereby brings about effective learning of the content of the curriculum by the students:

1. The teacher clearly distinguishes among concepts, skills, and habits in his subject matter.
2. In teaching conceptual material, the teacher:
   a. Plans a lesson around a clearly stated concept.
   b. Presents the referent of the concept vividly to the class.
   c. Sees the students perceive the referent adequately for understanding the stated concept.
   d. Clarifies the concept adequately through exchanges of ideas among class members.
   e. Clearly identifies new vocabulary terms required for discussing the referent, and provides for memorization of them.
   f. Clearly identifies the details of the concept which should be remembered, and provides for their memorization.
   g. Coaches the students in altering their behavior to harmonize with the newly formed concepts.
   h. Determines the clarity of each student's concept by means of an appropriate testing procedure.
3. In teaching skills, the teacher:
   a. Helps the student identify the parts of the skill and the sequence of the parts.
   b. Helps the student develop good form in the skill.
   c. Helps the student know when progress is made.
   d. Assists the student in correcting poor form and errors.
   e. Controls practice and rest periods to the best advantage for learning.
4. In affecting habits of students:
   a. Distinguishes clearly between true habits and behavior which is conceptually directed.
   b. Helps students recognize proper and desirable forms of habit-type actions related to the objectives of education.
   c. Is effective in preventing the recurrence of undesirable habit reactions by students in his classes in oral language, written language, observance of standards of prepared work, and social actions, and is effective in helping them establish desirable habits.
5. The teacher maintains a workable relationship with his students, i.e., the teacher and the students communicate effectively, free from disturbing clashes.
6. The teacher runs a business-like classroom in which students work seriously and honor the rules and standards of the school.

Figure 10.2 Checklist for Self-Evaluation. *From Asahel D. Woodruff,* Basic Concepts of Teaching *(San Francisco: Chandler, 1961), pp. 230–31.*

ures. You can learn from a simple observation of both excellent and mediocre teachers; it is important to see techniques that work when masterfully employed, but it is equally important to realize that the teacher is the single element that can make a teaching technique successful or unsuccessful.

In reviewing the teacher's success or failure, the student observer should also consider the "Stages of Concern" section in chapter 3. At what level was the teacher operating as you viewed the class? If your professors can arrange it, your early observations will be of "master teachers" who have achieved a "collaboration" or "refocusing" level. You will undoubtedly see teachers struggling at the lower levels of concern also. Your ability to identify, or attempt to identify, this development in teachers should answer some questions concerning their actions in the classrooms.

A master teacher is fascinating to see working with students. Elements of training and years of experience have combined to allow a free interaction with students. The emotional stability that confidence lends a master teacher can be sensed not only by an observer but also by the students. This person usually possesses a quality we call *magnetism, enthusiasm,* or *charisma,* which draws students to the teacher and also to the subject being taught.

The Teaching Environment

The school environment is the second area of assessment for the observer of instruction. What elements interfere with instruction? What distractions are great enough to divert the student and even the teacher from the task at hand? The school environment is something one senses almost on entering a school building. Some schools are warm centers of activity; others are noisy, unorganized, and cluttered. Students adapt to their surroundings as best they can. The "presence" one feels on entering a school is a composite of teacher attitudes, administrative policy, physical conditions, student attitudes, and community support.

The attitude teachers take toward students, the administration, and the teaching profession reflects the support they receive from the administration, the school board, and the community. If teachers feel trapped and helpless in trying to teach, if they get no support—whether that support be for student discipline or teaching materials—their attitude has to be affected adversely. A sense of helplessness can quickly surface in discussions with teachers in these situations. Conversely, teachers who have the advantage of community and administrative support, who have the equipment and materials needed for their teaching task, and who enjoy their position approach their work enthusiastically; and this has a direct, positive effect on the school environment.

The administrative policies established by principals, school boards, and district-level administrations are reflected in the school environment. The most obvious result of these policies is seen in school discipline and student conduct. Administrative policies go much further than establishing rules for conduct, however. The tone of the schooling environment is established with these rules and the enforcement of them. Students can learn in schooling environments that are strict and arbitrary or in schooling environments that are relaxed and casual. As we noted in chapter 6, the *consistency* of policy may be the single most important influence on the learning environment.

Physical conditions vary greatly from school to school. Although bright, well-lighted classrooms encourage learning, the observer will find a great disparity in the physical surroundings in classrooms. In music education, the physical conditions outlined in chapter 6 must be carefully considered because of the added requirements of physical space for music performance and sound transfer. That classrooms should be well lit and heated almost goes without saying. Your observations should include the unique classroom needs we have outlined for music instruction.

Student attitudes vary from day to day in any school. Nevertheless, one can sense the level of pride, or *esprit de corps*, that a student body has. Many believe that this "school spirit" is confined to the high school level, but equal pride is felt by students in elementary, middle, and junior high schools. Student attitudes toward learning are as much a product of peer interaction as they are a result of teacher attitudes or administrative policy. Having a group of students interested in academic excellence is part of a positive school environment.

Something that is difficult to observe directly in the classroom is community support. Schools that enjoy a high level of community support seem prosperous, industrious, and pleasant to attend; but the observer cannot be certain of the level of support by sitting in one classroom. When teachers feel they are underpaid and overworked, their attitude suffers not only toward the community and administration but also toward their student charges. Usually, when school fulfills the responsibilities outlined by the community, a high level of support is forthcoming. Only when school administration or teacher unions resist the aims and objectives of the community do difficulties arise. Visiting a classroom immediately before or after a teachers' strike will reveal some of the frictions that can result from a perceived lack of community support.

A checklist is not needed to assess the schooling environment. A brief discussion with the music staff will give you a clear perception of the attitudes and expectations teachers hold. Some teachers feel overworked and resentful about their situations; others feel that their programs are successful and are fully supported by the administration, their colleagues, and the community.

Student Assessment

Your assessment of the students you observe can take several forms. Some observation trips can focus simply on performance abilities including musicianship, technical fluency, intonation, tone quality, balance, blend, and diction. Most of your work in assessing students will be related to student achievement. How well have students performed on nationally standardized tests? What is the level of student achievement in music performance? What is the level of student achievement in understanding musical concepts? Achievement can be examined in the cognitive domain, the affective domain, and the psychomotor domain. The task in student assessment is to determine what level students have achieved as a general student body and then what their achievement levels are on an individual basis.

As you observe in classrooms, the level of student achievement is most obvious in music ensemble rehearsals. Teachers talk about a class being slow to learn one year, and faster to learn the next. Such assessments by classroom teachers are made against their general levels of expectation for an average classroom. If you observe enough classes, you can develop criteria you feel are appropriate for students after two months of instruction, after three years of instruction, or after other instructional periods.

In observing student achievement, two other factors should bear on your judgments. The first is the student's attitude or concern for achievement. To what degree do the students care whether they sing well, perform well, or can listen discriminately to music in the general music classroom? We are looking for seriousness of purpose or interest in subject matter. As noted in chapter 6, this interest in learning directly affects student achievement.

We are concerned not only about the students' level of interest in music instruction but also their ability to assess their performance. The teacher can help students place their level of achievement into a musical context. Students value knowing how well they are doing for their age, in their class, and in their school district. Whether the students receive a score on a standardized test or through casual comments from the teacher, they should develop the ability to determine how well they are doing in a specific subject area. For most students, true self-assessment is no problem. For a few students, objective self-assessment is a major problem. Some students *overestimate* their level of achievement, their abilities, and their skills. These students often sense that they are markedly better performers than their immediate classmates, but are oblivious to the possibility that they may not stack up well against students in other local schools, or other school districts. Such students often do not work terribly hard, feeling they are well ahead of the game. For them in particular, we recommend attendance at concerts presented by other students of their ages and self-assessment against greater than local norms.

As the general music classroom teacher works with children on singing skills, another group of students may emerge. These students *underestimate* their vocal or musical performance skills and become unwilling participants in music. It is critical to identify these students and pay particular attention to them. As you observe music classrooms, you will note students sitting in the back of the classroom, trying to avoid any participation in music. For the most part, these students have adequate musical skills but at some point have been made to feel that their level of achievement is inferior to the norm. A masterful teacher can draw these people into musical situations in which they can be successful and consequently will reassess their level of achievement.

As a classroom observer, you will rarely be allowed to review student achievement records such as grades, rating sheets, or other standardized test information. You may wish to ask the cooperating teacher about specific children you have observed and about whom you have particular concerns. In an observer's role, you should take notes of the general level of achievement and the manner in which students master the task presented the day you observed. As with the evaluation of a teacher, it is unfair to make gross judgments of student achievement with only one visit to a classroom. Several visits spread across several weeks will give a much clearer picture of student achievement and will allow you to assess abilities more precisely.

School Curriculum Assessment

The school curriculum is difficult to review. If you have prior knowledge of the curriculum plan, you will have a resource to assess how well a teacher is meeting the goals and objectives of the curriculum. It becomes very difficult to determine what the curriculum might be simply by observing several isolated classes. Many teachers will hand you a lesson plan for a specific day of observation as you enter their classrooms. You can then measure the classroom results with the expected outcomes of the lesson plan. The same is true with the curriculum plan. Often a copy of the school's curriculum guide will be made available to you. If so, you can evaluate the curriculum plan as an educational document or can evaluate the school's implementation of the plan and its ability to accomplish the goals and objectives outlined.

Evaluating the curriculum as an educational document—its expectations, goals, and objectives—should be done by *domain* as outlined in chapters 7, 8, and 9. The curriculum need not be set up as a taxonomy, but it is important that the various components of learning be included in the music program. Often school music curricula embrace the psychomotor domain through embodied musical performance to the neglect of the cognitive and affective development of students. If you have the opportunity to review a clearly stated music curriculum guide, consider the components carefully for balance and expectations of achievement levels.

Much time and energy is spent in trying to assess teacher effectiveness and student achievement in relationship to a stated music curriculum. If the curriculum is well written and acceptable to the teaching staff, how well do the music teachers accomplish the goals and objectives stated therein? This is the other side of the coin. It is not a task for the undergraduate observer, however, since such evaluations take professional educators months of research and testing. On an introductory level, you should be able to relate the classroom activities you observe to the stated curriculum. If, for instance, the teacher you observe is initiating a unit on Balinese folk music, the curriculum should have stated goals for students to learn the music of other cultures, or ethnomusicology. If no such goal is stated in the curriculum, the teacher is not following the guidelines established for the school music program.

Your questions to the teacher should be limited to the things that you observe, asking how they apply to the general curriculum plan. Such questions might include, "How many hours of instruction are planned for Balinese music?" "What other cultures will students study at this grade level?" "What is the value of Balinese music as it relates to the curriculum goals for a fifth-grade general music student?"

Your assessment of a school music curriculum should be accomplished by comparing stated goals and objectives to those goals and objectives that are currently in practice in the classroom. Certainly at the university you have enrolled in at least one course with a given title and course description, only to find that the professor has redefined the course. Your choice may have been to drop the course or select another section of the course, if one exists. Teachers must take care to fulfill the objectives and goals of a specific curriculum without too much deviation. Academic freedom and personal differences in teaching style give considerable latitude in defining how we attend to goals and objectives, as long as we do not deviate from the ultimate aims and objectives of a course of study.

As you start a teaching position, you should consider the stated curriculum for the music department. If your personal goals as a music teacher diverge too much from the stated goals of the school's music program, your life will be difficult and your successes will be few.

Professional Self-Assessment

In chapter 3 we outlined numerous qualifications for the music teacher that you should consider as you assess your abilities and skills as a developing teacher. You will need help from your professors in assessing the skills that are important to your success as a teacher. There are five areas you should address:

Writing skills
Verbal skills
Musicianship skills
Teaching skills
Personal interaction skills

The ability to express yourself well *in writing* will be essential to writing student assessment statements, drafting proposals for educational change, and defining curriculum requirements. In addition, we feel that a teacher who cannot write logically and correctly is a poor role model for students in any academic discipline—even music. Often college music faculty are derelict in their duty to encourage good writing from their students. After the required freshman course in English composition, few music students receive careful criticism of their written work. If you have any doubts about your writing ability, consult with a member of the English faculty. Many colleges maintain "writing centers" to help with student writing problems. See if one is available to you.

The first critical test of your writing ability will come when you must write application letters for a teaching position. Many teachers are never afforded the opportunity to interview for a position because of the bad impression fostered by their written application. The ability to present yourself well in writing will affect the entire course of your teaching career. One learns writing by practice—you learn to do what you do, not something else. If your college or university does not have a rigorous enough writing program, you owe it to yourself—and your future students—to seek one out.

Like writing skills, *verbal skills* do not fall under the purview of the music curriculum. Some states require one or two courses in speech communication for teacher certification. Again, these courses tend to be at the freshman or sophomore level, with little careful criticism of student verbal skills after that. The assumption that your ability to perform music in front of an audience will carry you through verbal presentations is false. Many veteran performers stumble in embarrassment when they are asked to make a statement about their music.

Verbal skills can be developed and practiced through early field experiences and student teaching. Classroom skills are essential, but not the entire requirement. A teacher also must be able to stand up in a faculty meeting or before the school board and lucidly present a definition of a program or justify a budget item that is under review. That the setting is different, that you are not talking to students, can make a critical difference in this verbal interaction. Presentations in your methods classes to your peers and teachers can aid you in polishing your verbal skills. Other available avenues for polishing these skills include lecture recitals, student conducting with commentary, and the use of videotape. Whether you should enlist the aid of the speech communication faculty is a matter between you and your academic adviser. Successful teachers must be able to speak well in the classroom and in public.

In another sense of the term, "verbal skills" refers to the capacity to reason in verbal symbols and to understand the logic of verbal thought and communication. These skills (many of which were measured by the verbal portion of the SAT or ACT test you took prior to college entrance) have been identified as the most powerful factor differentiating teachers whose students learn from those whose students do not. Persons with high verbal skills possess large vocabularies and are fluent in using them. They seem to be able to structure arguments effectively and to compose clear, insightful, well-reasoned dialogue. How does one learn these skills? Even a great university cannot make a Kant out of most of us, but a rigorous, broad-based general education can do wonders.

Musicianship skills are easily assessed as you complete your undergraduate degree. You receive much feedback as to your abilities in your major applied field and in other areas of musical endeavor. Since most music education programs are housed in the department of music, care and attention are directed toward skills in music theory, music history, and performance. As stated in chapter 3, these skills are essential to your success as a teacher. Your ability to conduct and perform musically is necessary for the musical development of your students. If you have any reservations about your musicianship, you should discuss them with your academic adviser or your applied music teacher. One thing to keep in mind: Grades are only a broad indication of your success in a given field. Whether you received an *A* or a *B* in a conducting course might have been based on a written final examination and not on the degree of psychomotor skill and perceptual acuity you actually displayed while conducting.

Teaching skills are, for the most part, untested during your undergraduate studies. Much of the time spent in education and methods courses is consumed with taking notes and listening to lectures. Being told how to teach is a far cry from actually doing it. Numerous programs are being developed to allow undergraduate students to develop teaching skills early in their undergraduate degree programs. This early field experience concept allows freshmen, sophomores, and juniors to teach in controlled situations. We strongly urge you to participate in these programs to develop your teaching skills and assess your teaching style.

Student teaching at the senior level is the "acid test" of your teaching skills. Your ability to teach is assessed by a university supervisor and a cooperating teacher. The student teaching experience can allow you a final chance to test your skills, try new techniques, and experiment with your approaches to conveying information to children. If you come to this experience honestly, and assess your development at each stage, you should have a clear picture of your ability to teach. The use of videotape in student teaching is of great value in self-assessment. Having others tell you what you did correctly and incorrectly is more abstract than seeing a tape of yourself groping for the right word to explain a concept to a slow student or smoothly conducting your first overture.

Personal interaction skills constitute a subjective area that must be considered even though it usually falls outside of university grading systems and evaluation procedures used in student teaching. Whether you like to teach or not is a personal decision. Whether you like interacting with children, or students of any age, is a critical question you must ask yourself before entering the teaching profession. We can relate the experiences of many A students who had the requisite musicianship, verbal and writing ability, and even the teaching skills to become fine professionals and yet performed poorly in real teaching situations. The reasons for these failures are usually personal in nature.

The poorest prospective teacher is the person who would rather be doing something else. In music, this is often the person who aspired to perform in a large jazz band, on the operatic stage, or in a symphony orchestra and didn't have the talent to "make it." Teaching is a second choice, and often the lower-caste attitude attached to music teaching is reflected in bitterness and in a lack of attention to the learning that must take place if one is to become an excellent teacher.

The ability to relate to students and colleagues is critical to success as a teacher. If you have difficulty relating to people, have a short temper, or are annoyed by having to deal with people, perhaps you should consider a profession that does not involve so many personal interactions. These skills cannot be evaluated in any formal schooling situation. You can discuss your concerns about interaction skills with professors and with friends. If you feel hesitant about dealing with thirty to one hundred students a day on a personal level, seek some advice before continuing in the program.

Assessing Your Future

Many new teachers are amazed to find that teaching is not what they anticipated. Somehow, the state of affairs in the schools has changed since they were students. Society has placed new pressures and responsibilities on teachers, or there has been a change in economic conditions that has affected school funding levels, or the federal government has instituted a completely new set of regulations that force teachers to do unexpected things. The music education student should attempt to keep up with the changes in education while he or she is still in school.

Added to a misperception caused by changes in the school is the sudden role reversal from student to teacher. Most college music education students formed their role model of a music teacher when they were students in a high school band, orchestra, or chorus. As students they saw the best parts of the job: conducting beautiful music, interacting with students, and receiving the approbation of audiences at concerts. What they did not see were the mountains of paperwork, the reports, the committee assignments, or the many problems teachers face daily.

In assessing the future, we must define and delineate the difference between fads and trends. In chapter 4 we projected several trends and shifts in conditions in education. We must separate long-term changes and shifts from the fads that last only a few months to a year or so. The veteran teacher seems able to sense the shallowness and short life of fads as they come and go. Your ability to develop this sensitivity will aid you in developing materials and methods of teaching.

The trends we cited in chapter 4 are real phenomena in our society. The population of school-age children is diminishing and will continue to diminish during the next few years. Population projections show that there will be 4 million fewer students of school age in 1995 than we have in the schools now. As this scenario evolves, the general population will age. In 1980, there were 25 million people aged 35 to 44 and 22 million people aged 45 to 54. Consider the radical change projected in these population groups for the year 2000. At that time, 40 million people will be in the first age group (35–44) and 35 million people will be in the second (45–54).

We must develop better programs for adult education in music. The idea of "lifelong learning" is taking hold as the society grays. The push for a "youth society" is slowly giving way to a more traditional attitude toward aging. This decade and the next will see more money and more interest directed at the older person.

Concerns that surfaced in the mid-1970s for those with learning disabilities and handicaps have materialized into viable programs in the schools. No longer experimental in nature, these programs, mandated by federal and state laws throughout the nation, have become integrated into the regularity of the school day. The music teacher who feels that his or her program is immune from involvement in these programs is sadly mistaken.

As society develops programs for special learning and for lifelong learning, the use of currently available technology will become commonplace. Microcomputers, videodiscs, and other technical devices will be widely available to the schools and to members of the society at large. As the cost of these technological products drops, their use will become more widespread. Already the cost of computer assisted instruction has dropped from approximately $7 an hour in 1960 to less than $1 an hour today. These costs will continue to diminish. The teacher who plans a curriculum for the 1980s without considering assistance from videotape, electronic devices, and other technological devices may be limiting the music program badly. Orchestras will still play the music of Beethoven under the baton of a conductor; nevertheless, our teaching techniques must be reviewed for efficiency and individualized instruction.

We found in the 1970s that the individualization of instruction made teaching and learning much more efficient. With the aid of new technologies, this mode of instruction will also be financially feasible. There are still music teachers who are unwilling to use cassette tape recorders, but the acceptance of technical teaching and learning aids will be important for every teacher in the 1980s and '90s.

The coursework to consider in your elective hours at the university should include some work in technology to allow you to master taping techniques, music synthesis, computer applications in education, and video taping. Although it is not essential to sign up for full semester courses in these areas, some knowledge of the advantages and limitations of these teaching tools is important.

Teaching is a great endeavor. And it will always be essential to society. The notion that schools will disappear and their function be taken over by cable television, computer terminals, and programmed instruction is absurd. The real strength of schooling in our society lies in the role the teacher takes in interacting with students. Your ability to interact well and to adapt to new societal demands, new curriculum requirements, and new teaching techniques will determine how well you will fare in your profession.

Questions for Discussion

1. Review a music curriculum guide from a local school system and evaluate the components included. Are the levels of objectives realistic in terms of cognitive, affective, and psychomotor educational goals?

2. After a discussion of self-assessment, list what you feel are your strengths and weaknesses in your chosen profession in teaching. What weaknesses do you feel you can bolster with the help of your teachers?

3. Check with a school system and review the shift in student population. What trends do school officials see within the next ten years? What plans have been made to account for the shift in school populations, if any? Based on this factual information, what recommendations would you make for the schooling situation?

Recommended Readings

White, Howard. "The Professional Role and Status of the School Music Teacher in American Society." Ed.D. University of Kansas, 1964. University Microfilms #65–4968.

Woodruff, Asahel. *Basic Concepts of Teaching*. San Francisco: Chandler, 1961.

references in music and education

Music Texts

Abramson, Robert M. *Rhythm Games*. New York: Music and Movement Press, 1973.

Andrew, Frances and Cockerile, Clara. *Your School Music Program*. Englewood Cliffs, N.J.: Prentice-Hall, 1958.

Andrews, Jay A., and Wardian, Jeanne F. *Introduction to Music Fundamentals: A Program Text for Elementary Education*. 3rd ed. New York: Appleton-Century-Crofts, 1972.

Aronoff, Fran. *Music for Young Children*. New York: Holt, Rinehart and Winston, 1969.

Austin, Virginia. *Learning Fundamental Concepts of Music: An Activities Approach*. Dubuque, Iowa: William C. Brown, 1970.

Bacon, Ernst. *Words of Music*. Syracuse, N.Y.: Syracuse University Press, 1960.

Batcheller, John M., and Monsour, Sally. *Music in Recreation and Leisure*. Dubuque, Iowa: William C. Brown, 1972.

Beer, Alice S., and Hoffman, Mary E. *Teaching Music: What, How, Why*. Morristown, N.J.: General Learning Press, 1973.

Bergethon, Bjornar, and Boardman, Eunice. *Musical Growth in the Elementary School*. 3rd ed. New York: Holt, Rinehart and Winston, 1975.

Berning, Alice B. *Keyboard Experiences for Classroom Teachers*. Dubuque, Iowa: William C. Brown, 1976.

Birge, Edward B. *History of Public School Music in the United States*. New York: Oliver Ditson, 1938.

Brian, Dennis. *Experimental Music in Schools: Towards a New World of Sound.* London: Oxford University Press, 1970.

Brooks, B. Marion. *Music Education in the Elementary School.* New York: American Book, 1946.

Cheyette, Irving, and Cheyette, Herbert. *Teaching Music Creatively in the Elementary School.* New York: McGraw-Hill, 1969.

Children and Music. Washington, D.C.: Association for Childhood Education (International), 1948.

Clough, John. *Scales, Intervals, Keys, and Triads: A Self-Instruction Program.* New York: W.W. Norton, 1964.

Colwell, Richard. *The Evaluation of Music Teaching and Learning.* Englewood Cliffs, N.J.: Prentice-Hall, 1970.

————. *The Teaching of Instrumental Music.* New York: Meredith, 1969.

Cope, David. *New Directions in Music.* Dubuque, Iowa: William C. Brown, 1971.

Darazs, Arpad, and Jay, Stephen. *Sight and Sound.* Oceanside, N.Y.: Boosey and Hawkes, 1965.

Dobbs, Jack P. *The Slow Learner and Music: A Handbook for Teachers.* New York: Oxford University Press, 1966.

Elliott, Raymond. *Learning and Teaching Music.* Columbus, Ohio: Charles E. Merrill, 1966.

Ellison, Alfred. *Music with Children.* New York: McGraw-Hill, 1959.

Ernst, Karl D., and Gary, Charles L., eds. *Music in General Education.* Washington, D.C.: Music Educators National Conference, 1965.

Farnsworth, Paul R. *The Social Psychology of Music.* New York: Dryden Press, 1958.

Fleming, William. *Art, Music and Ideas.* New York: Holt, Rinehart and Winston, 1970.

Garretson, Robert. *Music in Childhood Education.* 2nd ed. New York: Appleton-Century-Crofts, 1976.

Gary, Charles L. *The Study of Music in the Elementary School: A Conceptual Approach.* Washington, D.C.: MENC, 1967.

Gelineau, Phyllis R. *Experiences in Music.* 2nd ed. Hightstown, N.J.: McGraw-Hill, 1976.

Gordon, Edwin. *Psychology of Music Teaching.* Englewood Cliffs, N.J.: Prentice-Hall, 1971.

————. *Learning Sequences and Patterns in Music.* Rev. ed. Chicago: G.I.A. Publishing, 1977.

Grant, Parks. *Music for Elementary Teachers.* 2nd ed. New York: Appleton-Century-Crofts, 1960.

Green, Elizabeth. *Teaching Stringed Instruments in Classes.* Englewood Cliffs, N.J.: Prentice-Hall, 1966.

Greenberg, Marvin, and MacGregor, Beatrix. *Music Handbook for the Elementary School.* New York: Parker, 1972.

Hall, Doreen, and Walter, Arnold. *Music for Children.* Vols. 1–4. New York: Associated Music Publishers, 1969.

Hargiss, Genevieve. *Music for Elementary Teachers: A Programmed Course in Basic Theory and Keyboard Chording.* New York: Appleton-Century-Crofts, 1968.

Henry, Nelson, ed. *Basic Concepts in Music Education.* Chicago: National Society for the Study of Education, Fifty-Seventh Yearbook, 1958.

Hermann, Edward J. *Supervising Music in the Elementary School.* Englewood Cliffs, N.J.: Prentice-Hall, 1965.

Hickok, Dorothy, and Smith, James A. *Creative Teaching of Music in the Elementary School.* Boston: Allyn and Bacon, 1974.

Hood, Marguerite V. *Teaching Rhythm and Classroom Instruments.* Englewood Cliffs, N.J.: Prentice-Hall, 1966.

Hughes, William O. *A Concise Introduction to Teaching Elementary School Music.* Belmont, Calif.: Wadsworth, 1973.

Humphreys, M. Lois, and Ross, J. *Interpreting Music Through Movement.* Englewood Cliffs, N.J.: Prentice-Hall, 1964.

Jacobs, Norman. *Foundations and Frontiers in Music Education.* New York: Holt, Rinehart and Winston, 1966.

Janson, H.W., and Kerman, Joseph. *A History of Art and Music.* Englewood Cliffs, N.J.: Prentice-Hall, 1969.

Jones, Archie L., ed. *Music Education in Action.* Boston: Allyn and Bacon, 1964.

Kaplan, Max. *Foundations and Frontiers of Music Education.* New York: Holt, Rinehart and Winston, 1966.

———— and Steiner, Frances J. *Musicianship for the Classroom Teacher.* Chicago: Rand McNally, 1966.

Kinscella, Haze, and Tierney, Elizabeth M. *The Child and His Music.* Lincoln, Neb.: University Publishing, 1952.

Knuth, Alice, and Knuth, William. *Basic Resources for Learning Music.* Belmont, Calif.: Wadsworth, 1966.

Kohut, D.L. *Instrumental Music Pedagogy.* Englewood Cliffs, N.J.: Prentice-Hall, 1973.

Kowall, Bonnie C., ed. *Perspective in Music Education: Source Book III.* Washington, D.C.: Music Educators National Conference, 1966.

Krone, Beatrice, and Krone, Max. *Music Participation in the Elementary School.* Chicago: Neil A. Kjos Music, 1952.

Lament, Marylee McMurray. *Music in Elementary Education.* Riverside, N.J.: Macmillan, 1976.

Land, Lois Rhea, and Vaughn, Mary Ann. *Music in Today's Classroom: Creating, Listening, Performing.* New York: Harcourt Brace Jovanovich, 1973.

Landon, Joseph W. *Leadership for Learning in Music Education.* Costa Mesa, Calif.: Educational Media Press, 1976.

Landeck, Beatrice. *Children and Music: An Informal Guide for Parents and Teachers.* New York: Sicane, 1952.

Landis, Beth, and Carder, Polly. *The Eclectic Curriculum in American Music Education: Contributions of Dalcroze, Kodaly, and Orff.* Washington D.C.: Music Educators National Conference, 1972.

Langer, Susanne K. *Feeling and Form: A Theory of Art.* New York: Scribner's, 1953.

————. *Philosophy in a New Key.* 3rd ed. New York: New American Library of Word Literature, 1957.

Lehman, P.R. *Tests and Measurements in Music.* Englewood Cliffs, N.J.: Prentice-Hall, 1968.

Leonhard, Charles, and House, Robert W. *Foundations and Principles of Music Education*. Rev. ed. New York: McGraw-Hill, 1972.

Lundin, Robert W. *An Objective Psychology of Music*. 2nd ed. New York: Ronald Press. 1967.

Meyer, Leonard B. *Emotion and Meaning in Music*. Chicago: University of Chicago Press, 1956.

Monsour, Sally; Cohan, Marilyn; and Lindell, Patricia. *Rhythm in Music and Dance for Children*. Belmont, Calif.: Wadsworth, 1966.

Mursell, James. *Music and the Classroom Teacher*. New York: Silver Burdett, 1951.

———. *Music Education: Principles and Programs*. New York: Silver Burdett, 1956.

———. *The Psychology of Music*. New York: W.W. Norton, 1937.

Myers, Louise K. *Teaching Children Music in the Elementary School*. Englewood Cliffs, N.J.: Prentice-Hall, 1961.

Nash, Grace. *Creative Approaches to Child Development with Music, Language and Movement*. New York: Alfred Publishing, 1974.

National Education Association. *Music and Art in the Public Schools*. Research Monograph 1963–M3. Washington, D.C.: National Education Association, 1963.

Nettl, Bruno. *Music in Primitive Culture*, Cambridge, Mass.: Harvard University Press, 1956.

Nielsen, Floraine, and Folstrom, Roger J. *Music Fundamentals: A Creative Activities Approach*. Reading, Mass.: Addison-Wesley, 1969.

Nordholm, Harriet. *Singing in the Elementary Schools*. Englewood Cliffs, N.J.: Prentice-Hall, 1966.

Nordoff, Paul, and Robbins, Clive. *Therapy in Music for Handicapped Children*. New York: St. Martin's Press, 1972.

Nye, R.; Aubin, N.; and Kyme, G. *Singing with Children*. Belmont, Calif.: Wadsworth, 1962.

——— and Bergethon, Bjornar. *Basic Music, An Activities Approach to Functional Muscianship*. Englewood Cliffs, N.J.: Prentice-Hall, 1968.

———. *Basic Music for Classroom Teachers*. Englewood Cliffs, N.J.: Prentice-Hall, 1962.

——— and Nye, Vernice T. *Exploring Music with Children*. Belmont, Calif.: Wadsworth, 1966.

———. *Music in the Elementary School*. 4th ed. Englewood Cliffs, N.J.: Prentice-Hall, 1977.

——— and Nye, Virginia H. *Toward World Understanding with Song*. Belmont, Calif.: Wadsworth, 1967.

Nye, Vernice. *Music for Young Children*. Dubuque, Iowa: William C. Brown, 1975.

Raebeck, Lois, and Wheeler, Lawrence. *New Approaches to Music in the Elementary School*. 3rd ed. Dubuque, Iowa: William C. Brown, 1974.

Reimer, Bennett. *A Philosophy of Music Education*. Englewood Cliffs, N.J.: Prentice-Hall, 1970.

Rinderer, Leo. *Music Education, A Handbook for Music Teaching in the Elementary Grades*. Park Ridge, Ill.: N. A. Kjos Music, 1961.

Rolland, P., and Mutschler, M. *The Teaching of Action in String Playing*. Urbana, Ill.: Illinois String Research Associates, 1974.

Runkle, Aleta, and Eriksen, Mary. *Music for Today*. 3rd ed. Boston: Allyn and Bacon, 1976.

Sacher, Jack, and Eversole, James. *The Art of Sound: An Introduction to Music*. Englewood Cliffs, N.J.: Prentice-Hall, 1971.

Saffran, Rosanna B. *First Book of Creative Rhythms*. New York: Holt, Rinehart and Winston, 1963.

Schafer, R. Murray. *Creative Music Education*. New York: Schirmer Books, 1976.

———. *The Composer in the Classroom*. Toronto, Canada: BMI Canada, 1965.

———. *Ear Cleaning*. Toronto, Canada: BMI Canada, 1965.

———. *The New Soundscope*. Con Miles, Canada: BMI Canada, 1969.

Schubert, Inez. *The Craft of Music Teaching in the Elementary School*. Morristown, N.J.: Silver Burdett, 1978.

Schwadron, Abraham A. *Aesthetics: Dimensions for Music Education*. Washington, D.C.: Music Educators National Conference, 1967.

Smith, Robert B. *Music in the Child's Education*. New York: Ronald Press, 1970.

Swift, Frederic F. *Together We Sing and Play*. New York: Marks Music, 1964.

Swanson, Bessie R. *Music in the Education of Children*. Belmont, Calif.: Wadsworth, 1969.

———. *Planning Music in the Education of Children: A Personal Handbook*. Belmont, Calif.: Wadsworth, 1965.

Timmerman, Maurine. *Let's Teach Music in the Elementary School*. Evanston, Ill.: Summy-Birchard, 1958.

———, and Griffith, Celeste. *Guitar in the Classroom*. Dubuque, Iowa: William C. Brown, 1976.

Ulrich, Homer. *Music, A Design for Listening*. 3rd ed. New York: Harcourt Brace Jovanovich, 1970.

Van Ess, Donald H. *A Listener's Guide to the Heritage of Musical Style*. New York: Holt, Rinehart and Winston, 1970.

Wagner, Willis J., and McGrath, Earl J. *Liberal Education and Music*. New York: Bureau of Publications, Teachers College, Columbia University, 1963.

Educational Texts

Adams, Don, ed. *Education In National Development*. New York: Longman, 1971.

——— and Reagan, Gerald. *Schooling and Social Change in Modern America*. New York: Longman, 1972.

Berg, Ivar. *Education and Jobs: The Great Training Robbery*. New York: Praeger, 1970.

Bandura, Albert. *Principles of Behavior Modification*. New York: Holt, Rinehart and Winston, 1969.

Becker, Wesley C. *An Empirical Basis for Change in Education*. Chicago: SRA, Inc., 1971.

———. *Parents Are Teachers*. Champaign, Ill.: Research Press, 1971.

———, and Engleman, Sigfried. *Teaching: An Applied Course in Psychology*. Chicago: SRA, Inc., 1972.

Bijou, S.W., and Baer, D.M., ed. *Child Development: Readings in Experimental Analysis*. New York: Appleton-Century-Crofts, 1967.

Blackman, G., and Silberman, A. *Modification of Child Behavior: Principles and Procedures*. Belmont, Cal.: Wadsworth, 1970.

Bloom, Benjamin, ed. *Taxonomy of Educational Objectives: The Classification of Educational Goals, Handbook I: Cognitive Domain*. New York: Longman, 1956.

Brookover, Wilbur B., and Erickson, Edsel L. *Society, Schools, and Learning*. Boston: Allyn and Bacon, 1969.

Broudy, Harry S. *Democracy and Excellence in American Secondary Education*. Chicago: Rand McNally, 1964.

Brown, Claude. *Manchild in the Promised Land*. New York: Macmillan, 1965.

Bruner, Jerome S. *On Knowing: Essays for the Left Hand*. New York: Atheneum, 1965.

———. *The Process of Education*. New York: Vintage Books, 1960.

———. *Toward a Theory of Instruction*. Cambridge, Mass.: Belknap Press, 1966.

Buckley, Nancy K., and Walker, Hill M. *Modifying Classroom Behavior: A Manual of Procedure for Classroom Teachers*. Champaign, Ill.: Research Press, 1971.

Carnoy, Martin, ed. *Schooling in a Corporate Society*. New York: Longman, 1972.

Dennsion, George. *The Lives of Children*. New York: Random House, 1969.

Dewey, John. *Art as Experience*. New York: Minton, Balch, 1934.

Dinkmeyer, Don, and Driekurs, Rudolf. *Encouraging Children to Learn*. Englewood Cliffs, N.J.: Prentice Hall, 1963.

Dreikurs, Rudolf. *Children: The Challenge*. New York: Hawthorn Books, 1964.

———. *Psychology in the Classroom*. New York: Harper & Row, 1968.

Drews, Elizabeth Monroe. *Learning Together*. Englewood Cliffs, N.J.: Prentice-Hall, 1972.

Drucker, Peter F. *Age of Discontinuity: Guidelines to our Changing Society*. New York: Harper & Row, 1969.

Elkins, David, and Flavell, John, eds. *Studies in Cognitive Development*. New York: Oxford University Press, 1969.

Featherstone, Joseph. *Schools Where Children Learn*. New York: Liveright, 1971.

Furth, H.G. *Piaget and Knowledge*. Englewood Cliffs, N.J.: Prentice-Hall, 1969.

Gagne, Robert M. *The Conditions of Learning*. New York: Holt, Rinehart and Winston, 1966.

Gallagher, James. *Teaching the Gifted Child*. Boston: Allyn and Bacon, 1964.

Gardner, John W. *Excellence*. New York: Harper & Row, 1961.

———. *Self-Renewal*. New York: Harper & Row, 1964.

Ginott, Haim. *Between Parent and Child*. New York: Macmillan, 1965.

———. *Between Parent and Teenager*. New York: Macmillan, 1969.

———. *Teacher and Child*. New York: Macmillan, 1978.

Ginsberg, H., and Opper, S. *Piaget's Theory of Intellectual Development*. Englewood Cliffs, N.J.: Prentice-Hall, 1969.

Glasser, William. *Schools Without Failure*. New York; Harper & Row, 1969.

———. *Reality Therapy*. New York: Harper & Row, 1965.

Goodman, Paul. *Compulsory Mis-education and the Community of Scholars*. New York: Vintage Books, 1964.

Gosciewski, F. William. *Effective Child Rearing: The Behaviorally Aware Parent*. New

York: Human Sciences Press, 1976.

Gross, Beatrice, and Gross, Ronald. *Radical School Reform*. New York: Simon and Schuster, 1969.

Hall, R. Vance. *Managing Behavior, Parts I, II, and III*. Merriam, Kans.: H & H Enterprise, 1970.

Hamblin, Robert L.; Buckholdt, David; et al. *The Humanization Process*. New York: John Wiley, 1971.

Hertzberg, Alvin, and Stone, Edward F. *Schools Are for Children: An American Approach to the Open Classroom*. New York: Schocken Books, 1971.

Holt, John. *How Children Fail*. New York: Pitman, 1964.

———. *How Children Learn*. New York: Pitman, 1967.

———. *The Underachieving School*. New York: Pitman, 1969.

———. *What Do I Do on Monday?* New York : E.P. Dutton, 1970.

Homme, Lloyd. *How to Use Contingency Contracting in the Classroom*. Champaign, Ill.: Research Press, 1969.

Howes, Virgil. *Individualization of Instruction*. New York: Macmillan, 1970.

Illich, Ivan. *Deschooling Society*. New York: Harper & Row, 1971.

Inhelder, B., and Piaget, J. *The Growth of Logical Thinking from Childhood to Adolescence*. New York: Basic Books, 1958.

Jones, Richard. *Fantasy and Feeling in Education*. New York: University Press, 1968.

Kagan, Jerome, ed. *Creativity and Learning*. Boston: Houghton Mifflin, 1967.

Kohl, Herbert. *The Open Classroom*. New York: Random House, 1969.

Krathwohl, David, ed. *Taxonomy of Educational Objectives: The Classification of Educational Goals, Handbook II: Affective Domain*. New York: Longman, 1964.

Long, Nicholas; Morse, William; and Newman, Ruth. *Conflict in the Classroom*. Belmont, Calif.: Wadsworth, 1965.

Madsen, C.K., and Madsen, C.H. *Parents/Children/Discipline: Behavioral Principles Toward a Positive Approach*. Boston: Allyn and Bacon, 1972.

———. *Teaching/Discipline: A Positive Approach for Educational Development*. Boston: Allyn and Bacon, 1974.

Mager, Robert. *Developing Attitudes Toward Learning*. Belmont, Calif.: Fearon, 1966.

———. *Preparing Instructional Objectives*. Belmont, Calif.: Fearon, 1962.

Meachan, M.L., and Wiesen, A.E. *Changing Classroom Behavior: A Manual for Precision Techniques*. Scranton, Pa.: International Textbook, 1969.

Mink, O.G. *The Behavior Change Process*. New York: Harper & Row, 1968.

Muenzinger, Karl F. *Contemporary Approaches to Creative Thinking*. New York: Atherton Press, 1967.

Neill, Alexander S. *Summerhill*. New York: Hart, 1960.

Osborn, A. *Applied Imagination*. New York: Scribner's, 1957.

Parnes, I.J. *Creative Behavior Workbook*. New York: Scribner's, 1967.

Patrick, Catherine. *What Is Creativity Thinking?* New York: Philosophical Library, 1955.

Raths, Harmin, and Simson. *Values and Teaching*. Columbus, Ohio: Charles E. Merrill, 1966.

Rogers, Carl. *Freedom to Learn*. Columbus, Ohio: Charles E. Merrill, 1969.

———. *On Becoming a Person*. Boston: Houghton Mifflin, 1961.

Rosenthal, R., and Jacobson, L. *Pygmalion in the Classroom: Teacher Expectations and*

Pupils' Intellectual Development. New York: Holt, Rinehart and Winston, 1968.

Russell, Bertrand. *Education and the Good Life.* New York: Avon Books, 1926.

Shumsky, Abraham. *Creative Teaching in the Elementary School.* New York: Appleton-Century-Crofts, 1965.

Skinner, B.F. *The Technology of Teaching.* New York: Appleton-Century-Crofts, 1969.

Silberman, Charles E. *Crises in the Classroom.* New York: Random House, 1970.

Silberman, Melvin L., ed. *The Experience of Schooling.* New York: Holt, Rinehart and Winston, 1971.

Simpson, Ray. *Teacher Self-Evaluation.* New York: Macmillan, 1966.

Simpson, Elizabeth. *The Classification of Educational Objectives, Psychomotor Domain.* Washington, D.C.: USOE Final Report OE 5-85-104.

Singer, Robert. *Motor Learning and Human Performance: An Application to Physical Education Skills,* New York: Macmillan, 1971.

Woodruff, Asahel. *Basic Concepts of Teaching,* San Francisco: Chandler, 1961.

index